Adopting new and much more comprehensive concepts of both *power* and *politics, The Retreat of the State* develops a theoretical framework to show who really governs the world economy. It goes on to explore some of the non-state authorities, from mafias to the Big Six accounting firms and international bureaucrats, whose power over who gets what in the world encroaches on that of national governments. The book is a signpost, revealing fresh ideas and pointing to some promising new directions for research and teaching in international political economy.

CAMBRIDGE STUDIES IN INTERNATIONAL RELATIONS: 49

The retreat of the state

Editorial Board

STEVE SMITH (*Managing editor*)
CHRISTOPHER BROWN   ROBERT W. COX
ANNE DEIGHTON   ROSEMARY FOOT   JOSEPH GRIECO
FRED HALLIDAY   ANDREW LINKLATER
MARGOT LIGHT   RICHARD LITTLE   R. B. J. WALKER

International Political Economy
ROGER TOOZE   CRAIG N. MURPHY

Cambridge Studies in International Relations is a joint initiative of Cambridge University Press and the British International Studies Association (BISA). The series will include a wide range of material, from undergraduate textbooks and surveys to research-based monographs and collaborative volumes. The aim of the series is to publish the best new scholarship in International Studies from Europe, North America and the rest of the world.

CAMBRIDGE STUDIES IN INTERNATIONAL RELATIONS

Series list continues after index

The retreat of the state

The diffusion of power in the world economy

Susan Strange

University of Warwick

Published by the Press Syndicate of the University of Cambridge
The Pitt Building, Trumpington Street, Cambridge CB2 1RP
40 West 20th Street, New York, NY 10011–4211, USA
10 Stamford Road, Oakleigh, Melbourne 3166, Australia

© Cambridge University Press 1996

First published 1996

Printed in Great Britain at the University Press, Cambridge

A catalogue record for this book is available from the British Library

Library of Congress cataloguing in publication data

Strange, Susan, 1923–
    Power diffused: state and non-state authority in the world
economy / Susan Strange.
        p.   cm. – (Cambridge studies in international relations; 49)
    ISBN 0 521 56429 8 (hc). – ISBN 0 521 56440 9 (pb)
    1. International economic relations – Political aspects.
    2. Economic policy.   3. Power (Social sciences)   4. World
politics – 1989–   I. Title.   II. Series.
    HF1359.S769   1996
    337 – dc20   96–375   CIP

ISBN 0 521 56429 8 hardback
ISBN 0 521 56440 9 paperback

VN

Contents

Preface

There is no great originality in the underlying assumption of this book – which is that the territorial boundaries of states no longer coincide with the extent or the limits of political authority over economy and society. In an earlier antitextbook for students of international political economy, *States and Markets*, I laid out a simple framework for analysing the who-gets-what of world society based on four basic structures. In these, power over others, and over the mix of values in the system, is exercised within and across frontiers by those who are in a position to offer security, or to threaten it; by those who are in a position to offer, or to withhold, credit; by those who control access to knowledge and information and who are in a position to define the nature of knowledge. Last but not least, there is the production structure, in which power is exercised over what is to be produced, where, and by whom on what terms and conditions. All of these power structures spill over those often arbitrary lines that are drawn on maps to indicate the territorial limits of the authority of one state from that of another. While *some* structural power over your security is still exercised within these territorial lines by the political authority of that state, not all of it is provided, nor all of it threatened, only by that state authority. This is even more true of the financial structure of the international political economy. A young wheeler-dealer trader for a British bank is able by his insufficiently supervised arbitraging in Singapore to bring about the downfall of Barings. His Japanese counterpart working for Daiwa in New York was able to run up losses of over $1 billion, leading to the closure of the bank's US operations. Between the cracks in the regulatory structure agreed among the world's major central banks since the mid-1970s, it seems that private operators can function somewhat beyond the control of any of them.

ix

As for the knowledge structure and the production structure, it is a long time since territorial states lost such control as they may once have had over the production of goods and services within their borders, and over the creation, storage and communication of knowledge and information.

This simple framework essentially challenged all those approaches to teaching and research in international relations and political economy which continued to focus on the bargaining between governments over international trade in goods and services, over exchange rates and bank supervision, and over foreign investment. For them, the adjective 'political' in political economy related merely to the policies of states, and not to the activities and policies of non-state actors in the world system. The structural approach came more easily to sociologists and was also developed by Anthony Giddens who had earlier coined the rather clumsy term, 'structuration' (Giddens, 1979, 1985). It was also implicit in the work of Robert Cox (Cox, 1987). What the notion of structural power in world politics, society and economy did was to liberate the study of international political economy from the so-called realist tradition in the study of international relations. What was wrong with *States and Markets* was the title. It obscured the point, made clear enough in the text, that out of the four kinds of structural power described and analysed, states took the lead role in only one – in security – and even there often needed the support of other states. In all the other structures, non-state authorities played a large part in determining the who-gets-what. *Markets and Authorities* would have been a more accurate title.

Thus, the present study is really an extension, or elaboration, of the same ideas about power and transnational relations that characterise the contemporary world scene. These ideas actually had roots even further back than *States and Markets*. They had emerged in the course of a research project I directed at Chatham House in the mid-1970s. It was on transnational relations, and was funded by the Ford Foundation for three years. My colleagues were Marcello de Cecco and Louis Turner. Marcello developed some new ideas on international money and finance which, with characteristic verbal economy, he put into a seminal article in *International Affairs*;[1] Louis worked on the world oil business – hot stuff in those days – and produced a book.[2] I produced two articles,

---

[1] M. De Cecco, 'International Financial Markets and U.S. Domestic Policy since 1945', *International Affairs*, July 1976.

[2] L. Turner, *Oil Companies in the International System*, Allen and Unwin for RIIA, 1978.

one general and vaguely theoretical, the other specific and empirical.[3] I now see the latter as the forerunner of the present volume. For it identified a series of non-state authorities as exercising structural power by determining the arrangements according to which sea trade was conducted, regulated and paid for. It showed how the risks and opportunities, the costs and benefits were shared among those engaged in the transnational business of sea-trade, whether as shippers or shipping enterprises, as workers or regulators. Not least among these – then as now – was the international insurance business, together with the cartel of shipping firms organised as a shipping conference. (For an updated analysis of both, see chapters 9 and 10 in the present volume.)

Over the two decades that have gone by since that Chatham House project on transnational relations, it seems to me that the powers of most states have declined still further, so that their authority over the people and their activities inside their territorial boundaries has weakened. Non-state authorities, meanwhile, have impinged more and more on those people and their activities. The present book is an attempt to explain, with examples, *how* this has happened, and to explain by theoretical analysis *why* it has happened.

Not everybody, of course, will agree with the premise that the authority of the state – with the notable exception of the United States of America – has declined in recent years. The intrusion of governments into our daily lives in the 1990s, as compared, say, with the 1890s, is palpably greater. Statutory or administrative law now rules on the hours of work, the conditions of safety in the work-place and in the home, on the behaviour of citizens on the roads. Schools and universities are subject to more and more decisions taken in ministries of education. Planning officials have to be consulted before the smallest building is started or a tree is cut down. The government inspector – once a rare (and sometimes comical) visitor – has become a familiar and even fearful figure. None of this government interference comes without a cost. The growing intrusiveness of government is reflected in the surplus value extracted by the state from the economy, from a man or woman's day's work in farming, in manufacturing, in trade or in service enterprises. This shows in the share of Gross Domestic Product pre-empted by government. The revenues of government now appropriate up to 60 per cent of national income where once the maximum figure was barely half that. 'Reform', these days, is apt to mean cutting

[3] S. Strange, 'Transnational Relations and "Who Runs World Shipping?"' *International Affairs*, July 1976.

back on the activities of government, shrinking the bureaucracy and imposing husbandry and economy on government offices. It used, within living memory, to mean the exact opposite: using the authority of government to impose more humane and regulated behaviour on business and the private sector generally.

How then is it possible to proclaim a retreat by government, a decline in the authority of the state within its territorial frontiers? The answer, developed in some more detail in chapter 5, relates not to the quantity of authority exercised by the governments of most territorial states, but to the quality of that authority. It rests on the failure of most governments to discharge those very basic functions for which the state as an institution was created – the maintenance of civil law and order, the defence of the territory from the depredations of foreign invaders, the guarantee of sound money to the economy, and the assurance of clear, judicially interpreted rules regarding the basic exchanges of property between buyers and sellers, lenders and borrowers, landlords and tenants.

The necessity of the state as a public good, in short, arose with the emergence of a developed market economy. Modern nationalism – as often imagined as real – was in large part the creation of modern capitalism. The market economy could not function properly without the political framework provided by the state. National sentiments of identity and loyalty provided the glue that gave social cohesion to the political framework. Where territorial states had existed before the birth of a capitalist economy, they had done so not so much as a public good but as a private perquisite of the powerful.[4] The very idea of a social contract could not have been conceived without the economic necessity of civic cooperation between state and society.

The other implicit assumption I have made in writing the book at all is that change in the international political economy has so far been inadequately described and diagnosed for what it is by most of my colleagues in the academic community of social scientists. The evidence for that statement is to be found in a string of vague and woolly words, freely bandied about in the literature, but whose precise meaning is seldom if ever clearly defined.

---

[4] The idea of the territory of the state as private property persisted into the twentieth century. The Belgian Congo before gaining independence was claimed as the personal property of the King of the Belgians. The Sultan of Brunei and the Ruler of Kuwait similarly claimed the territory of their respective states as belonging to them personally, and in the latter case that the revenues accumulated as national monetary reserves were private assets and therefore need not be reported to the International Monetary Fund (Strange, 1971).

The worst of them all is 'globalisation' – a term which can refer to anything from the Internet to a hamburger. All too often, it is a polite euphemism for the continuing Americanisation of consumer tastes and cultural practices.

The much older term 'interdependence' similarly hides the truth behind a persuasive euphemism for asymmetric dependence. It is true that many writers who have used the term since the economist Dick Cooper first used it in the title of a book in the late 1960s (Cooper, 1968), have explicitly admitted that the prefix 'inter' does not sufficiently convey the inequality of dependence between the parties. Nevertheless, its everyday use often serves to dull or even conceal the reality of relationships, the crude facts of structural power over other governments and over other societies. 'Interdependence' is much like the word 'multinational'. That term was allegedly coined by the PR division of International Business Machines in the early 1960s to conceal – or at least divert attention from – the fact that IBM was an American enterprise, even though it was seeking market access to many countries throughout the world. The firm was in no sense 'multinational', although its operations were. I do not suggest that Cooper also deliberately used the word interdependence in order to conceal the fact that the intergovernmental cooperation he argued was necessary for the continued prosperity of all the advanced industrialised economies was more in the American than, say, the Swiss or the Swedish interest. But that was the truth of the matter since the Americans, as guardians of nuclear weapons and thus of the security of all the members of the affluent alliance, reserved to themselves the right to decide, with or without consultation, when to use military power or the threat of it.

The latest of these semantic euphemisms that have crept into common parlance – even when we recognise them for what they are – is the phrase 'global governance'. There are now innumerable centres for the study of global governance. There are books using the phrase in their sub-titles; there is even a journal so called. What it is usually taken to mean is cooperation and harmonisation or standardisation of practice between the governments of territorial states, most often effected through an international bureaucracy. The implicit assumption conveyed by the two words, 'global' and 'governance', is that government is being achieved on a world scale by a world authority. Yet the truth, as any student of inter-governmental organisations is well aware, is that the limits and the nature of any intergovernmental bureaucracy's decision-making power are set by the most powerful of its member governments. The international organisation is above all a tool of national government, an instrument for the pursuit of national interest by other means. This elementary perception of old-fashioned realists is obscured – probably unconsciously – by most of the rather extensive literature on international regimes. Too often, a regime is represented as merely the consequence of a harmonising process, through which governments have coordinated their common interests. The power element is underplayed. Yet in reality, many international regimes have not so much been the result of a coming-together of equals, but the end-result of a strategy developed by a dominant state, or sometimes by a small group of dominant states. Sometimes, it has been necessary to conduct some bargaining with the representatives of less powerful member governments. But the *blocco storico* so formed by such bargaining between the hegemon and its dependents is really – as the neo-gramscian critical theorists have rightly pointed out – no more than a subtle exercise in political hegemony. Even the secretariats of the international institutions concerned are subliminally socialised into administering an international 'order' that is by no means neutral either in its intentions nor its consequences (see below, chapter 11).

Against this orthodoxy, I must protest that politics is larger than what politicians do, and that power can be exercised – and is every day being exercised – by non-state authorities as well as by governments. This also draws heavily on earlier work. It follows the conclusions laid out as a result of close collaboration with John Stopford in *Rival States, Rival Firms*. This book argued that the outcomes in the political economy of the countries we wrote about had been determined by the triangular diplomacy between states, between states and firms, and between firms and other firms. Some of these diplomatic bargains were struck within the countries, and therefore looked like 'domestic politics'. Others had been struck between government representatives and looked like international politics. And yet others where firms alone were engaged could be categorised as 'transnational politics'. Although by drawing on empirical evidence from three developing countries – Brazil, Malaysia and Kenya – it had seemed to be a study in comparative economic development, the book had actually grown out of a shared conviction that international politics could not be fully understood or analysed without paying attention to international business, and conversely, that international business and management could not be fully understood without paying attention to international and domestic politics.

Such ideas, however, were fundamentally subversive of the exclusivity of the 'disciplines' and sub-disciplines of social science. They denied that there could be a basic distinction between domestic politics within the state, and international politics between one state and others, or that national economies could be analysed in isolation from the world economy. They seriously undermined the pretensions to particularity propounded by professors of international relations from the 1930s to the present day. I firmly believe that the new realism of the Stopford–Strange analysis of corporate strategies and state development policies makes it imperative to look seriously at the power exercised by authorities other than states. Not only have such collectivities brought about structural changes in world production, in technology and in the mobility of capital, but they also continue to constrain the options open to states and to individuals in the international political economy.

This new realism, a term also used by the veteran analyst of international business, Peter Drucker, to describe fundamental technological and managerial changes of recent years (Drucker, 1991), is a realism quite different from the neo-realism developed by writers in international relations. That merely added new issues to the agenda of inter-state diplomacy and new bit-players to the cast of actors in international politics. It left the state and its concerns still always at the centre of the stage.

It is the *always* that I now find unacceptable, and which leads me to feel that perhaps I have at last reached the final parting of the ways from the discipline of international relations. I have been involved with it now, as student, foreign correspondent and teacher over more than half a century. But I can no longer profess a special concern with international politics if that is defined as a study different from other kinds of politics and which takes the state as the unit of analysis, and the international society of states as the main problematic.

This is not to deny the importance for students of a grounding in international political history. But it must be combined with an equal grounding in world economic history, just as familiarity with great writers on political theory is incomplete without an equal familiarity with great writers on economic theory. And for the foreseeable future, I would add to these a grasp of the fundamentals of the domestic politics of the United States, as well as perhaps of Japan and Germany.

In short, there is no escaping the imperative of multidisciplinarity in the understanding of change and outcomes in the international political economy. Geography, demography, sociology, law, anthropology all have valuable insights to contribute. On many issues an understanding of scientific principles behind technological innovation is not only valuable but indispensable. In saying good-bye to international relations, I am only suggesting that our times no longer allow us the comfort of separatist specialisation in the social sciences, and that however difficult, the attempt has to be made at synthesis and blending, imperfect as we know the results are bound to be.

The other message which I hope is implicit in this study is the inseparable nature of theory and empirical research. Behind the selection of 'facts' from empirical material, there is always a theory, whether it is explicit or not. And theory, whether consciously or not, is not produced from abstractions, by a kind of intellectual hydroponics in which theories, like plants, grow without soil, with their roots in water with a few minerals added. Like plants in nature, theories and explanations grow out of the dirt of observations of reality. The observations may not be 'scientific' in the sense that an experiment in chemistry can be objective. But they are not invented either. Getting your hands dirty with the nitty-gritty details of a technology, or with the decision-making processes of corporate strategies, or of ministerial policymaking, is a good way to test the abstractions of theory, and perhaps to develop alternate theory, or modifications of theories. Moreover, if you can illustrate a theory or a hypothesis with reference to a concrete situation, it often serves to explain more clearly the thrust of the ideas.

That is part of the point of my rather scrappy descriptions of non-state authorities and how they affect power structures to be found in part II of the book. They may have been chosen somewhat at random, out of personal interest. But they are supposed to illustrate the theoretical propositions laid out in the earlier chapters. It is my sincere hope that these examples will serve to stimulate younger scholars to more innovative work, theoretical and empirical, on non-state authority in the international political economy. They are by way of being a signpost, pointing not along an open well-trodden track but rather into a mysterious forest of the unknown. Just where the path will lead, I am not at all sure. That is the nature of exploration – and its appeal to the mentally adventurous.

In writing this book, I have had valuable support from the Research Council of the European University Institute in Florence. I spent four years there, from the end of 1988 to the end of 1992. My stay there allowed me more time to read than I would have ever got in a British university. And I was generously given funds to invite a bunch of kindred spirits to the Institute to comment on my first trial balloon. Their comments and those of other colleagues and of students too numerous to mention have been invaluable. If I do not mention them by name it is because doing so would risk leaving out someone whose chance remark has been unconsciously incorporated in the pages that follow.

For one of the chapters, on mafias, I had the expert collaboration of Letizia Paoli without which I would never have dared to write it. For another, on Telecoms, Michael Hepburn fed me useful material. He and Sheetal Mehta also gave cheerful and willing help with bibliographical references. And always from Judy Weedon at LSE and Maureen Lechleitner in Florence, I have had the kind of secretarial back-up that is better, more efficient and more unstinted than anyone could possibly deserve.

Part 1
Theoretical foundations

1   The declining authority of states

Today it seems that the heads of governments may be the last to recognise that they and their ministers have lost the authority over national societies and economies that they used to have. Their command over outcomes is not what it used to be. Politicians everywhere talk as though they have the answers to economic and social problems, as if they really are in charge of their country's destiny. People no longer believe them. Disillusion with national leaders brought down the leaders of the Soviet Union and the states of central Europe. But the disillusion is by no means confined to socialist systems. Popular contempt for ministers and for the head of state has grown in most of the capitalist countries – Italy, Britain, France and the United States are leading examples. Nor is the lack of confidence confined to those in office; opposition parties and their leaders are often no better thought of than those they wish to replace. In the last few years, the cartoonists and the tabloid press have been more bitter, less restrained critics of those in authority in government than at any other time this century. Although there are exceptions – mostly small countries – this seems to be a worldwide phenomenon of the closing years of the twentieth century, more evident in some places than others, but palpable enough to suggest that some common causes lie behind it.

This book is written in the firm belief that the perceptions of ordinary citizens are more to be trusted than the pretensions of national leaders and of the bureaucracies who serve them; that the commonsense of common people is a better guide to understanding than most of the academic theories being taught in universities. The social scientists, in politics and economics especially, cling to obsolete concepts and inappropriate theories. These theories belong to a more stable and orderly world than the one we live in. It was one in which the territorial

3

borders of states really meant something. But it has been swept away by a pace of change more rapid than human society had ever before experienced.

For this reason I believe the time has come to reconsider a few of the entrenched ideas of some academic colleagues in economics, politics, sociology and international relations. The study of international political economy has convinced me that we have to rethink some of the assumptions of conventional social science, and especially of the study *i* of international relations. These concern: firstly, the limits of politics as a *7*social activity; secondly, the nature and sources of power in society; *3*thirdly, the necessity and also the indivisibility of authority in a market *4*economy; and fourthly, the anarchic nature of international society and the rational conduct of states as the unitary actors within that society. The first and second are assumptions commonly taken for granted in political science. The third is an assumption of much liberal, or neo-classical economic science. And the last is an assumption of much so-called realist or neo-realist thinking in international relations. Each of these assumptions will be examined more closely later in the book.

But first it may help to outline briefly the argument of the book as a whole. That will show the context in which these more fundamental questions about politics and power arise and have to be reconsidered. The argument put forward is that the impersonal forces of world markets, integrated over the postwar period more by private enterprise in finance, industry and trade than by the cooperative decisions of governments, are now more powerful than the states to whom ultimate political authority over society and economy is supposed to belong.

Where states were once the masters of markets, now it is the markets which, on many crucial issues, are the masters over the governments of states. And the declining authority of states is reflected in a growing diffusion of authority to other institutions and associations, and to local and regional bodies, and in a growing asymmetry between the larger states with structural power and weaker ones without it.

There are, to be sure, some striking paradoxes about this reversal of the state-market balance of power. One, which disguises from many people the overall decline of state power, is that the *intervention* of state authority and of the agencies of the state in the daily lives of the citizen appears to be growing. Where once it was left to the individual to look for work, to buy goods or services with caution in case they were unsafe or not what they seemed to be, to build or to pull down houses, to manage family relationships and so on, now governments pass laws, set

4

up inspectorates and planning authorities, provide employment services, enforce customer protection against unclean water, unsafe food,
faulty buildings or transport systems. The impression is conveyed that
less and less of daily life is immune from the activities and decisions of
government bureaucracies.

That is not necessarily inconsistent with my contention that state
power is declining. It is less effective on those basic matters that the
market, left to itself, has never been able to provide – security against
violence, stable money for trade and investment, a clear system of law
and the means to enforce it, and a sufficiency of public goods like drains,
water supplies, infrastructures for transport and communications. Little
wonder that it is less respected and lacks its erstwhile legitimacy. The
need for a political authority of some kind, legitimated either by
coercive force or by popular consent, or more often by a combination of
the two, is the fundamental reason for the state's existence. But many
states are coming to be deficient in these fundamentals. Their deficiency
is not made good by greater activity in marginal matters, matters that
are optional for society, and which are not absolutely necessary for the
functioning of the market and the maintenance of social order. Trivialis-
ing government does not make its authority more respected; often, the
contrary is true.

The second paradox is that while the governments of established
states, most notably in North America and western Europe, are
suffering this progressive loss of real authority, the queue of societies
that want to have their own state is lengthening. This is true not only of
ethnic groups that were forcibly suppressed by the single-party government of the former Soviet Union. It is true of literally hundreds of
minorities and aboriginal peoples in every part of the world – in Canada
and Australia, in India and Africa, even in the old so-called nation-states
of Europe. Many – perhaps the majority – are suppressed by force, like
the Kurds or the Basques. Others – like the Scots or the Corsicans – are
just not strong enough or angry enough to offer a serious challenge to
the existing state. Still others such as the native Americans, the
Aboriginals, the Samis or the Flemish are pacified by resource transfers
or by half-measures that go some way to meet their perceived need for
an independent identity. Only a few, such as the Greenlanders, the
Slovaks or Slovenes or the unwanted, unviable Pacific island-states,
have succeeded in getting what they wanted – statehood. But once
achieved, it does not seem to give them any real control over the kind of
society or the nature of their economy that they might have preferred. In

short, the desire for ethnic or cultural autonomy is universal; the political means to satisfy that desire within an integrated world market economy is not. Many, perhaps most, societies have to be content with the mere appearance of autonomy, with a facade of statehood. The struggle for independence has often proved a pyrrhic victory.

The final paradox which can be brought as evidence against my basic contention about the hollowness of state authority at the end of this century is that this is a western, or even an Anglo-Saxon phenomenon, and is refuted by the Asian experience of the state. The Asian state, it is argued, has in fact been the means to achieve economic growth, industrialisation, a modernised infrastructure and rising living standards for the people. Singapore might be the prime example of a strong state achieving economic success. But Japan, Korea, Taiwan are all states which have had strong governments, governments which have successfully used the means to restrict and control foreign trade and foreign investment, and to allocate credit and to guide corporate development in the private sector. Is it not premature – just another instance of Eurocentrism therefore – to assume the declining authority of the state?

There are two answers to this third paradox. One is that all these Asian states were exceptionally fortunate. They profited in three ways from their geographical position on the western frontier of the United States during the Cold War. Their strategic importance in the 1950s and after was such that they could count on generous military and economic aid from the Americans, aid which was combined with their exceptionally high domestic savings and low patterns of consumption. The combination gave a head start to rapid economic development. Secondly, and also for strategic reasons, they could be – almost had to be – exempted from the pressure to conform to the norms of the open liberal economy. They were allowed, first formally and then informally, to limit foreign imports and also to restrict the entry of the foreign firms that might have proved too strong competitors for their local enterprises. At the same time, they were given relatively open access first to the large, rich US market for manufactures, and later, under some protest, to the European one. And thirdly, the technology necessary to their industrialisation was available to be bought on the market, either in the form of patents, or in the person of technical advisors from Europe and America or through corporate alliances which brought them the technology without the loss of managerial control.

Now, I would argue, these special dispensations are on the way out, and not only because the Cold War is over. The Asian governments will be under increasing pressure from Washington to adopt more liberal non-discriminatory policies on trade and investment. And they will also be under pressure from within to liberalise and to allow more competition, including foreign competition, for the benefit of consumers and of other producers. In short, the exceptionalism of the Asian state during the Cold War has already been substantially eroded, and will continue to be so. As it has been at other times, and in other places, there will be contests for control over the institutions and agencies of government in most of the Asian countries. There will be contests between factions of political parties, between vested interests both in the private sectors and in the public sector. There will be power struggles between branches of the state bureaucracy. Both the unity and the authority of government is bound to suffer.

The neglected factor – technology

The argument in the book depends a good deal on the accelerating pace of technological change as a prime cause of the shift in the state-market balance of power. Since social scientists are, not, by definition, natural scientists, they have a strong tendency to overlook the importance of technology which rests, ultimately, on advances in physics, in chemistry and related sciences like nuclear physics or industrial chemistry. In the last 100 years, there has been more rapid technological change than ever before in human history. On this the scientists themselves are generally agreed. It took hundreds – in some places, thousands – of years to domesticate animals so that horses could be used for transport and oxen (later heavy horses) could be used to replace manpower to plough and sow ground for the production of crops in agriculture. It has taken less than 100 years for the car and truck to replace the horse and for aircraft to partly take over from road and rail transport. The electric telegraph as a means of communication was invented in the 1840s and remained the dominant system in Europe until the 1920s. But in the next eighty years, the telegraph gave way to the telephone, the telephone gave way to radio, radio to television and cables to satellites and optic fibres linking computers to other computers. No one under the age of thirty or thirty-five today needs convincing that, just in their own lifetime, the pace of technological change has been getting faster and faster. The technically unsophisticated worlds of business, government and education of even the 1960s would be unrecognisable to them. No fax, no

7

personal computers, no accessible copiers, no mobile phones, no video shops, no DNA tests, no cable TV, no satellite networks connecting distant markets, twenty-four hours a day. The world in which their grandparents grew up in the 1930 or 1940s is as alien to them as that of the Middle Ages. There is no reason to suppose that technological change in products and processes, driven by profit, will not continue to accelerate in future.

This simple, everyday, commonsense fact of modern life is important because it goes a long way to explaining both political and economic change. It illuminates the changes both in the power of states and in the power of markets. Its dynamism, in fact, is basic to my argument, because it is a continuing factor, not a once-for-all change.

For the sake of clarity, consider first the military aspects of technical change, and then the civilian aspects – although in reality each spills over into the other. In what are known as strategic studies circles, no one doubts that the development of the atom bomb in the middle of the twentieth century, and later of nuclear weapons carried by intercontinental missiles, has brought about a major change in the nature of warfare between states. Mutual assured destruction was a powerful reason for having nuclear weapons – but equally it was a good reason for not using them. After the paradoxical long peace of the Cold War, two things began to change. The expectation that, sooner or later, nuclear war would destroy life on the planet began to moderate. And confidence began to wane that the state could, by a defensive strategy, prevent this happening. Either it would or it wouldn't, and governments could do little to alter the probabilities. Thus, technology had undermined one of the primary reasons for the existence of the state – its capacity to repel attack by others, its responsibility for what Adam Smith called 'the defence of the realm'.

At the same time technology has had its effect on civilian life. Medical technology has made human life both longer and more comfortable. Electrical technology has liberated millions of women from the drudgery that imprisoned previous generations in the day-long labour of preparing food, keeping the family's clothes clean and mended, and houses clean and warm. As washing machines, vacuum cleaners, dishwashers, central heating and refrigerators and freezers spread down the income levels, more people had more to lose from inter-state conflict. Comfort bred conservatism in politics. Moreover, the new wealth was being acquired by the Germans and the Japanese who had actually been defeated in World War II. Acquiring territory was no

old

longer seen as a means to increase wealth. Losing territory did not mean
the state became poorer or weaker. Gaining market shares in the world
outside the territorial borders of the state, however, did enable formerly *New*
poor countries like Japan, Taiwan or Hong Kong to earn the foreign
exchange with which to buy capital goods, foreign technology and the
necessary resources of energy and raw materials. As John Stopford and I
have argued, competition for world market shares has replaced competition for territory, or for control over the natural resources of territory,
as the 'name of the game' between states (Stopford and Strange, 1991;
Strange in Rizopoulos (ed.), 1990). In this new game, the search for allies
among other states goes on, but not for their added military capabilities.
It is for the added bargaining power conferred by a larger economic
area.

Moreover, the search for allies is not confined to other states or
inter-governmental organisations. It is supplemented by a search for
allies among foreign-owned firms. These firms may be persuaded, in
exchange for access to the national market, to raise the finance, apply
their technology, provide the management and the access to export
markets – in short, to take all the steps necessary to locate production of
goods or services within the territory of the host state. In most
developing or ex-socialist countries, the prospect of new jobs and extra
export earnings brought by such investments have become powerful
reasons for a change of attitude toward the so-called 'multinationals'.

The second neglect – finance

Not the least of the TNC's attractions to host states is its ability to raise
finance both for the investment itself and – even more important – for
the development of new technology. Another key part of the argument
of this book is that, besides the accelerating pace of technological
change, there has been an escalation in the capital cost of most
technological innovations – in agriculture, in manufacturing and the
provision of services, and in new products and in new processes. In all
of these, the input of capital has risen while the relative input of labour
has fallen. It is this increased cost which has raised the stakes, as it were,
in the game of staying up with the competition. This is so whether we
look at competition from other firms who are also striving for larger
market shares, or whether we look at governments trying to make sure
that the economies for whose performance they are held responsible
stay up with the competition in wealth-creation coming from other

9

Theoretical foundations

economies. Thus, to the extent that a government can benefit from a
TNC's past and future investments without itself bearing the main cost
of it, there are strong reasons for forging such alliances.

But the escalating costs of technological change are also important for
a more fundamental reason, and not just because it explains the
changing policies of host states to TNCs. It has to do with change in the
world system. The cost of new technology in the production structure
has added to the salience of money in the international political
economy. It is no exaggeration to say that, with a few notable exceptions, scholars in international relations for the past half-century have
grossly neglected the political aspects of credit-creation, and of changes
in the global financial structure.[1] In much theorising about international
relations or even international political economy there is no mention at
all of the financial structure (as distinct from the international monetary
order governing the exchange relations of national currencies.) Briefly,
the escalating capital costs of new technologies could not have been
covered at all without, firstly, some very fundamental changes in the
volume and nature of credit created by the capitalist market economy;
and secondly, without the added mobility that in recent years has
characterised that created credit. The *supply* of capital to finance
technological innovation (and for other purposes) has been as important
in the international political economy as the *demand* from the innovators
for more money to produce ever more sophisticated products by ever
more capital-intensive processes of production.

These supply and demand changes take place, and take effect, in the
market. And it is markets, rather than state–state relations that many
leading texts in international political economy tend to overlook. Much
more emphasis is put on international monetary relations between
governments and their national currencies. To the extent that attention
is paid at all to the institutions creating and marketing credit in the
world economy, they are held to be important chiefly for the increased
volatility they may cause to exchange rates, or to the impact they may
have on the ability of governments to borrow abroad to finance
development or the shortfall between revenue and spending, or between export earnings and import bills.

[1] The notable exceptions include Cerny, 1993; Porter, 1994; Veseth 1990; Wachtel, 1986;
Frieden, 1987; Moffitt, 1983; Calleo, 1982. I should add that we all owe big debts to the economic
historians such as Kindleberger, Cipolla, Feis and de Cecco, and more recently Cain and
Hopkin; to the practitioners such as Volcker and Gyoten, and, not least to journalists such as the
late Fred Hirsch and Yoichi Funabashi.

10

More significant in the long run, however, when it comes to evolving better theories to explain change in the international political economy is the accompanying neglect of the three-way connections between the supply side of international finance (credit), the demand side from firms, and the political intervention of governments as regulators of banking and financial markets and as borrowers or lenders, at home and abroad. There are theories to explain each of the three, but no unifying theory to explain their mutual connections.

For example, it may be asked why so many firms come to financial markets to raise money. It may be to finance a merger or takeover of another firm, to finance the development or application of a new technology or for expansion into a new market. The body of literature known as theories of the firm has produced some answers. One of the best-known is Ray Vernon's product-cycle theory. Although it is now recognised that this theory as first proposed in the late 1960s was over-influenced by the recent experience of US firms setting up affiliates in Europe, and was in any case a rather simplified model of actual corporate behaviour, it did nevertheless have a powerful central idea in it. Briefly, the product cycle begins with the firm introducing a new product or developing a new process in its home market. But when the temporary monopoly rent from the innovation is undercut by its competitors, it starts to export the product to new markets where there is still little or no competition. When that monopoly rent is also undercut by competing exporters, the firm extends the cycle by producing inside the foreign market at lower cost and with greater efficiency. Ploughing back all these monopoly rents into the next technological innovation starts another product cycle (Vernon 1966).

Since Vernon's pioneering idea, there have been other elaborations of the theory of transnational production. One of the best-known is Dunning's self-styled eclectic theory which adds in, as complicating variables, the possible advantages a firm may have in the way it organises production and marketing, the possible advantages – such as cheap labour or access to raw materials – of alternative locations (Dunning, 1988). Both Vernon and Dunning shared with economic theorists a concern with the firm's interest in lowering transaction costs by internalising transactions that otherwise could be effected at arm's length in the market. More politically perceptive of the realities behind corporate behaviour was Hymer's idea that lowering cost was often less important to firms than keeping control (Hymer, 1976).

The point is that such theories helped to explain, at least in part, the demand side for credit. What is needed to complement them is some theory that explains the matching of supply to demand, the expansion of new sources and forms of credit to keep pace with the demand. While there are descriptive accounts galore of the evolution of Eurocurrency markets in the 1960s and 1970s, and of syndicated bank loans to developing countries in the 1970s, and of junk bonds and securitisation in the 1980s, the theoretical explanation of periods of credit expansion has not been well developed. The historians have observed that such periods of expansion often – but not always – lead to booms and bubbles, followed by slumps and crashes. And, of course, economists have developed theories of business cycles and long waves though generally these are couched in rather abstract fashion.

Not only do the demand theories and the supply theories fail to come together, both tend to assume a kind of political vacuum, in which nothing changes in the behaviour of governments to each other and to the operators – industrial, commercial and financial, in the market economy. For example, historians are well aware that financial inflation – excessive creation of credit – is apt to accompany the conduct of war – civil or international. Yet neither the theories of international production nor of banking and credit take account of the dynamics of international relations, any more than the latter take into account the behaviour of firms or financial markets.

Awareness of this failure of inter-connection between bodies of theory relating to political and economic change customarily treated by social scientists in isolation from each other has powerfully motivated the writing of this book. My exploration of the phenomenon of diffuse authority over the global political economy is necessarily sketchy and incomplete. Yet by drawing attention to both the theoretical lacunae in social science and to the empirical evidence of the increasing exercise of non-state authority, my hope is that further work will be inspired to develop at both the theoretical and the empirical level.

Politics, power and legitimacy

There are three premises underlying the argument in this book. Each relates directly to – indeed, challenges – some of the conventional assumptions of economics, social and political science and international relations. The first premise is that politics is a common activity; it is not confined to politicians and their officials. The second is that power over

2 outcomes is exercised impersonally by markets and often unintention-ally by those who buy and sell and deal in markets. The third is that authority in society and over economic transactions is legitimately 3 exercised by agents other than states, and has come to be freely acknowledged by those who are subject to it.

The first two premises require some excursion into matters of theory. As they are essential to the whole argument, they will be dealt with first, in chapters 2 and 3 respectively. General readers may be inclined to skip these two chapters as being overly academic, especially if they already find themselves broadly in sympathy with the main thrust of my argument. However, if they have doubts about it, they may be interested to see where and why my understanding of the nature of power and of politics diverges from the conventional.

In subsequent chapters, dealing with recent changes in international political economy, readers will encounter three general propositions about the patterns of legitimate authority now developing in the international political economy towards the end of the twentieth century. One is that there is growing asymmetry among allegedly sovereign states in the authority they exercise in society and economy. In international relations, back to Thucydides, there has always been some recognition of a difference between small states and great powers, in the way each behaves to others and in the options available to them in their relations with other states. But there has been a tendency all along to assume a certain uniformity in the nature and effectiveness of the control which each state has over social and economic relations within their respective territorial boundaries. The attributes of domestic sover-eignty, in other words, were assumed automatically to go with the regulation accorded each state by its peers. Now, I shall argue, that assumption can no longer be sustained. What was regarded as an exceptional anomaly when in 1945 the United States conceded two extra votes in the UN General Assembly for the Soviet Union – one for the 'sovereign' republic of the Ukraine and one for Byelorussia – now hardly attracts comment. The micro-states of Vanuatu and the Republic of San Marino are admitted to the select circle of member-states of the United Nations. But no one really believes that recognition of their 'sovereignty' is more than a courteous pretence. It is understood that there is only a difference of degree between these and many of the smaller and poorer members of the international society of states who are established occupants of seats in the UN.

The second proposition is that the authority of the governments of all

13

states, large and small, strong and weak, has been weakened as a result of technological and financial change and of the accelerated integration of national economies into one single global market economy. Their failure to manage the national economy, to maintain employment and sustain economic growth, to avoid imbalances of payments with other states, to control the rate of interest and the exchange rate is not a matter of technical incompetence, nor moral turpitude nor political maladroitness. It is neither in any direct sense their fault, nor the fault of others. None of these failures can be blamed on other countries or on other governments. They are, simply, the victims of the market economy.

The third proposition complements the second. It is that some of the fundamental responsibilities of the state in a market economy – responsibilities first recognised, described and discussed at considerable length by Adam Smith over 200 years ago – are not now being adequately discharged by anyone. At the heart of the international political economy, there is a vacuum, a vacuum not adequately filled by inter-governmental institutions or by a hegemonic power exercising leadership in the common interest. The polarisation of states between those who retain some control over their destinies and those who are effectively incapable of exercising any such control does not add up to a zero-sum game. What some have lost, others have not gained. The diffusion of authority away from national governments has left a yawning hole of non-authority, ungovernance it might be called.

This first chapter has presented the broad argument concerning each of the three premises and how each relates to change in the world system. The second chapter defends the second premise concerning the broader and more comprehensive definition of politics, government and authority. It will offer some empirical evidence to sustain the argument that politics on the global scale cannot any longer be conceived as limited to the conduct of inter-state relations. This is the chapter where my understanding differs most from much received wisdom in the social sciences. It is the one most likely to upset and even infuriate my former colleagues engaged in the study of international relations. The third chapter will defend the premise concerning the nature of power. This is fundamental to the central argument, but the premise on which it is based does diverge from some widely accepted notions of power and therefore needs to be argued in some detail, and again with sustaining empirical evidence.

The second part of the book will present some evidence for the three propositions, by describing briefly how half a dozen very different sources of non-state authority actually affect outcomes in the world economy and society. On the basis of this empirical evidence, the concluding chapter will consider what could be done, and by whom, to avert a crisis in the world market economy – a crisis that could be just as disturbing for western liberal society as the collapse of the socialist systems has been for the societies of the USSR and China.

2   Patterns of power

It will be no use my going through the evidence to sustain my three propositions about the shifting patterns of power in world politics unless there is some agreement – or at least comprehension – on the part of the reader concerning two fundamentals – power, and politics. My whole argument rests on a much broader definition of both than is usually encountered by students of politics in the western liberal tradition. This chapter is devoted to the arguments for a broader definition, and against narrower, more conventional ones. The next one is devoted to the definition of politics. What do we mean when we talk about 'political issues' or 'political disagreements'? Are we concerned only with what politicians do, or only about what transpires in political institutions? If you are not interested in such rather abstract notions, by all means skip on to chapter 4. But please do not complain at the end of the book that you cannot accept the conclusions because they are based on ideas that conflict with what is generally understood by the concept of Power, or because they do not accord with commonly accepted ideas about the proper limits of politics, including both the *who* and the *what* – who engages in politics, and what they take responsibility for when they do. At least, consider the case for expanding these conventional notions about power and politics, and for applying the broader concepts to questions of change in the international political economy. Only so, I believe, can the true synthesis of politics and economics necessary to the study of global political economy be achieved. Only so can a sound basis be laid for future research and teaching in the field.

How to think about power

Let us start with the very difficult concept of power. There is a vast literature on the subject; but there is still remarkably little consensus among academics or among more practical people about either semantics or epistemology. On the semantics, political theorists have argued endlessly about words – about whether power is a large generic term which encompasses everything from direct coercion by violent means to the influence exerted through the subtle arts of persuasion; or whether the word should be more narrowly defined so that power is distinguished from authority or influence and is only present when those on whom power is exerted have little or no option but to give in – when, in the *mafioso*'s words, they are 'given an offer they can't refuse'. There then ensues much semantic argument about the interpretation and nuances given in different languages to all the words – synonyms or near-synonyms – used to denote forms of power: *macht* in German, *power* in English, *puissance* in French, *potestas* in Latin, and so on.

For reasons which I hope will become clear, I do not think such semantic discussions are useful, at least for the purpose of observing, understanding and analysing change in the global political economy. And for that reason, I prefer to stick with a larger, more all-inclusive definition of power. Power is simply the ability of a person or group of persons so to affect outcomes that their preferences take precedence over the preferences of others. This definition avoids the logical trap of pinning power to the pursuit of interest – national interest, class interest, corporate interest or whatever. For, as any first-year student of international relations realises, the determination of what *is* the national interest is a highly subjective matter. Different administrations, even different foreign ministers, have had divergent perceptions of what was, and was not, in their country's national interest. As Martin Wight concluded in his seminal essay on power politics, the crucial question for policymakers was the choice between short-term, immediate national interest and enlightened, long-term national interest (Wight, 1948). It still is.

Besides the semantic question, there is the other much-debated (but also unresolved) question about methodology. How can you tell which individuals, or collective associations of individuals are powerful, and why? It is said that it is easy to recognise an elephant – but much harder to define one. The same with power. We all think we can easily recognise the exercise of power when we witness it – though it is often true that those who have to give in to the power of others will recognise power more readily than the top-dogs who have it and use it. Perhaps this is why power is so often defined, either at the local or the international level, in terms of resources, or 'capabilities'. For example, people may say, 'The government has power because it has the police force – and as an ultimate resource, its armed forces.' It also, of course, has codes of law and taxation and the machinery of the courts, and the power to punish by prison or fine those who transgress its decisions. Or, in international relations, they may say, 'Industria is a more powerful country than Ruritania because it has a bigger army.' Or, 'It is more powerful because it has both an army and an armaments industry.' Or, 'It is more powerful because it has oil revenues which give it more money to buy arms and it therefore has better defence forces.' Or, at the party political level, they may say, 'The Blue Party has power in the country because it commands the loyalty, and can get the votes of the landowners, the factory managers, the bankers and the shopkeepers.' In each case, power is derived from resources – material or human, or both.

The problem arises when 'will' is added into estimations of power. If those supporting the Blue Party do not bother to vote, while the farmers and workers turn out in strength to get them out of office, then the party's command of resources goes for nothing. In 1940, the German forces invading France through Belgium and the Netherlands were actually fewer in numbers of men and weapons than those of France. Yet superior tactics and speed, and, not least, the conviction – correct as it turned out – that the French had little stomach for fighting, and trusted neither their politicians nor their generals gave Germany the victory. History is full of stories of large armies – or navies – defeated by smaller, swifter and more determined ones. Of course, it does not always happen. But my point is that if, and when, you have to add will and skill to the kind of resources of men (and women) and material that can be counted, you have added two unquantifiable and often largely unpredictable factors to the equation.

One example of this can be found in an early contribution to the (then nascent) study of international political economy by Professor Klaus Knorr. In a book titled *Power and Wealth; The Political Economy of International Power*, Knorr went through all the constituent resources conferring power on states in international relations. But at the end, he had to confess that capabilities – possession of resources – was only a part of the story (Knorr, 1973) and that past performance was no sure guide to the future possession of power. Moreover, there is the paradox noted by Stanley Hoffman and Kenneth Waltz, that enormous capability is not always translated into power over outcomes. Hoffman described the US as a 'tied Gulliver, not a master with free hands' (Hoffman, 1968). And Waltz, observing the nuclear capabilities of the two superpowers in the 1970s, warned against confusing the use of power with its usefulness. Both states hardly needed to *use* force to gain ends other than their own security; only to be seen to possess it (Waltz, 1979: 191). But then Waltz still did not accept Robert Dahl's idea that power was discernible by control over outcomes (Dahl, 1961). In Waltz' view, powerful states were not always able to make their own preferences about outcomes prevail over the preferences of others. Power in relation to other states – in my terms, relational power – was not the only factor. An example of this paradox, Waltz has said, could be seen in the decisions that concluded the Gulf War. The United States, with its allies, wielded overwhelming military power over Iraq – but did not achieve all of its preferred outcomes – like the removal of Saddam Hussein from office. When it came to outcomes, 'Power is only one cause among others, from which it cannot be isolated', Waltz concluded (Waltz, 1993).

In short, while the theorists in international relations have had many of the same sort of disagreements and confusions on the subject of power as the political theorists, and indeed as social scientists in general, the more recent literature of international political economy has been remarkable for its evasion of these definitional issues. It has given them only rather summary and superficial treatment. Other questions than the nature of power have tended to take precedence in the literature – questions concerning the nature and extent of the subject, its distinctive features and the reconciliation of divergent perspectives upon it. One notable exception, perhaps, has been Joseph Nye's distinction between 'hard' and 'soft' power. In *Bound to Lead*, Nye describes the two kinds of power exercised by the United States – roughly equivalent to coercive, relational power and indirect, structural power (Nye, 1990). He argues persuasively that the declinist school of American writers in focusing on the former paid too little attention to the latter. But the distinction is never precisely defined nor developed into a general theory of power in the international political economy.

One reason for this strange neglect of the nature of power may have been the deference paid (more particularly in America) to economics. Economics claims to be a science – but no such claim is possible if power is allowed into the analysis. Anything as messy as power simply cannot be included in an economic equation, or even a purely economic analysis. A number of scholars have even defined political economy as no more than the application of economic methods and concepts to politics, notably the use of the concept of rational actors and rational choice (Bruno Frey 1984, for instance). But rationality, adapted from economics, has to be – or at least usually is – narrowly defined in terms of action in pursuit of material gain or to avoid material loss, or costs. It is hard to include in it actions which are only made possible because of asymmetries of power. For example, the strong may, and do, use their power to reduce risks to themselves in the long term rather than to maximise immediate gain. Or they may use power to make a trivial gain for themselves at the expense of a large loss by the weak. Real life is full of such uses of power, which by strictly economic logic are not rational.

The other problem with rationality as a basic assumption of economic analysis – and the reason why that assumption cannot be made in the study of international political economy – relates to the purposes, or objectives of those with power in the system. Before the 1950s, liberal economists assumed that rational action, and rational economic actors, were motivated by a single objective or purpose. The seller wanted to sell as dear as possible; the buyer to buy as cheaply. The investor wanted the highest return on capital; the borrower wanted to pay as low a rate of interest as possible. Firms wanted to maximise profits; workers to maximise wages. An American economist, Herbert Simon, then modified this simplistic assumption by introducing the idea of 'bounded rationality' (Simon, 1962). In reality, governments, like firms, had multiple objectives in mind when they took decisions. They were not looking therefore for the best, or optimal outcome, but for one that 'sufficed', which was good enough to satisfy multiple objectives. Simon invented the rather ungainly hybrid word 'satisficing' to describe a decision or course of action that, without being ideal, would plausibly make do. This was certainly an advance, and his concept of 'bounded rationality' has been used by non-economists to good purpose; John Ruggie and Bob Keohane are two examples in international political economy.

As an analytical tool in explaining change in the real world, however, bounded rationality still has serious shortcomings and therefore should be used only with caution. Chief among these shortcomings is its static quality. It assumes that the motivations, or the purposes to be satisfied, remain the same over time – for example, throughout a negotiation, whether between governments, or between firms or between firms and governments. But this, obviously, is not the case. The context of the bargaining changes – a shift in political opinions, an upset in the market – and with it, inevitably, the priorities of purpose for the protagonists. Less important but not to be overlooked is the fact that the protagonists in many situations act instinctively, without always being conscious of their current priorities and purposes.

The hegemonic obsession

Another reason why power has been rather superficially treated in the literature of international political economy may be the tremendous concern – one might almost call it an obsession – with the role of hegemons in the system. This has tended to exclude all other questions relating to the nature and use of power in the world system. It arises, as I have often pointed out, from an awareness and unease with the apparently growing disorder in that system. That awareness, in turn, led to an understandable search for an alternative reason – other than American mismanagement and abuse of power – for the disorders of the financial and trade systems from the late 1960s on.

This search gave currency to an idea borrowed from Charles Kindleberger's history of the interwar world depression that the world economy worked best when one dominant state acted as financial leader or hegemon (Kindleberger, 1973). A market economy needed some kind of stable money to work efficiently. In the absence of any truly international currency, the developing market economy of the nineteenth century had used the pound sterling, partly because its value was fixed in terms of gold, and partly because Britain was a major source of foreign credit and a major open market for foreign goods. The United States played the same helpful role after the Second World War. But in the world depression of the 1930s, because Britain had been unable and the US unwilling to act as hegemon, the whole world economy had suffered – and not so much because of protectionism in trade as because of the absence of a financial leader and lender of last resort with a stable currency. Hegemonic stability theory, many writers suggested, could offer an explanation for the recurrence of international economic disorder from the mid-1970s onwards.

In order to argue that these disorders were the result, not of bad or inadequate American policy choices, but of a loss of power by the United States, it was necessary to find evidence for that loss of power.

Attention to the nature of power was therefore focused almost exclusively on the power of hegemons, and more especially of the United States in the 1970s and 1980s. Other questions of power – whether China was more powerful than India, or Iraq than Iran, for instance, attracted little attention. The only exception was Japan, and whether Japan might be qualifying as the next hegemon in the system. Whether considering the lost power of the United States or the rising power of Japan, the evidence used still dealt only with power derived from resources, not from the capacity to influence outcomes.

Look, for example, at the work of two leading American political economists, Robert Gilpin and Robert Keohane. Keohane defines the power of hegemons as based on 'control over raw materials, control over sources of capital, control over markets and competitive advantage in the production of highly valued goods . . . It must also be stronger on these dimensions taken as a whole than any other country' (Keohane, 1984: 32, 34). The signs of American decline are chiefly seen in the decline of the US share of world exports, and of world GNP, or more narrowly of world production of manufactures. Thus, it was assumed that power was derived from the productive resources of the US territorial economy, and that when this economic base was overtaken and surpassed by other national economies, the mere possession of nuclear missiles and other advanced weaponry would only delay decline. Keohane does admit that there are flaws in the 'basic force model' which parsimoniously reflects 'the tangible capabilities of actors'. A more refined version takes account of the domestic factors affecting the will to maintain order in the international economy. Once again that unquantifiable factor, 'will', is added to capabilities. But where this takes the theory of hegemonic power is rather vague.

Gilpin's magisterial text, *The Political Economy of International Relations*, describes the hegemon's role in generating economic growth as 'the cement that holds the system together' (Gilpin, 1987: 76). The stress here is on the hegemon's keynesian role as leader, priming the pump of world economic growth, where Kindleberger's is on the hegemon's monetarist role, providing stable money. The influence, Gilpin argues, of both Britain as hegemon in the nineteenth century and of the US in the twentieth derived mainly from their economic power. But, like others before and since, he has trouble making clear what exactly 'economic power' means and how economic power is distinguished from political power. Among the properties of economic power, he lists the possession of a large market, and therefore the power to bar entry to it; and the

22

possession of a large capital market giving power through the influence it gives over credit and over the value of the hegemon's currency. Like Keohane, Gilpin argues that the ultimate basis of the economic strength of the hegemon, is the flexibility and mobility of its economy. Like Keohane, he is convinced that the US has lost and is still losing relative power, mainly to Japan but also to Europe, because their economies are catching up or overtaking the productive capabilities of the American economy, defined as the economic activity taking place within the borders of the United States.

Gilpin suggests that it was the lack of resourcefulness, as well as of resources, that caused the decline of British economic power in the nineteenth century, and that the same reasons lie behind the loss of US economic power in the late twentieth century. Both losses undermine the hegemon's will as well as its ability to manage the system. In an earlier book, he had also argued that Britain had suffered from the distractions of foreign investment, and that the United States should not let its multinationals tempt it down the same primrose path (Gilpin, 1975). To do so would risk diverting to others some of the human and financial resources of the country, leaving it the poorer. The whole argument takes us back to a concept of power based on the resources contained within a territorial state, and adds that intangible factor, 'will'. Power is still seen primarily as capabilities, as a property of persons, or of nation-states as organised societies, not as a feature of relationships, nor as a social process affecting outcomes – the way the system operates to the advantage of some and the disadvantage of others, and to give greater priority to some social values over others.

The Gramscian perspective

That is not a criticism that can be made of Robert Cox's courageously radical attempt in *Production, Power and World Order* to apply Gramscian – and some Marxist – concepts to the analysis of power in the international system. As a former specialist in industrial relations (Cox, 1987), Cox's first concern is not with states but with classes – specifically, the workers and, naturally, those who exploit their labour. (In this, he is more like Nicos Poulantzas than his colleagues in international relations and organisation.) He therefore begins with 'the way the world's work is done' (Cox, 1987: 5) – precisely what I have called the Production structure – which involves not capabilities but relationships of power. It is production that 'creates resources that can be transformed into other forms of power – financial, administrative, ideological, military and police power' (Cox, 1984: 5). These relationships, he argues, are the creation of political authority – states – which have imposed certain hierarchies of production on society, which constitute what, using Marxist terminology, he calls a system of accumulation. (The word is somewhat misleading for non-Marxists; what it means is that power and wealth are accumulated through the production structure by the exploitation of some social groups by others.)

When a production structure becomes, as by now it largely has become, a global or transnational one, so does the potential for exploitation. To understand the contemporary 'world order' therefore – whether one wants to maintain it or to change it – requires attention to both the international political system of states and the role in it of dominant states, and to the global production structure. Production; the international political system of states; the international political economy – which he calls world order – these three are visualised as three separate but interacting levels – making a kind of club sandwich – in which 'changes come about through mutually sustaining developments at all three levels' (Cox, 1987: 394). While the hegemonic state and class act at all three levels to maintain the existing order, so those who want change must also act at all three, at the state level, through international organisation and mobilisation, and in the production structure. They must seek to weaken hegemonic power by forming – as Gramsci advocated – counter-hegemonic historic blocs. But while Gramsci was writing of the *blocco storico* in the Italian context, Cox sees the same strategy as valid in a global context. The historic bloc has to be formed and to act transnationally, as well as nationally. The analysis clearly leads Cox to a normative prescription in favour of change; whereas both Keohane and Gilpin and most of their American colleagues are more in favour of maintaining the existing order through the development of more cooperation and coordination among states – the US and Japan in Gilpin's perception, the affluent alliance of all industrial states in Keohane's. Hence their interest in regime formation and maintenance, always provided – it is clearly implicit – that the regimes are chosen, designed and operated under the dominant influence of the United States. Thus, adapting one of Cox's favourite sayings that 'ideology is always *for* something', one might also say that methodology and the treatment of power is also usually *for* something, in that it sustains one perspective, and the prescriptions that go with it, more than rival ones.

It was not my intention to give readers a critical overview of what the entire literature of international relations has had to say about power. The rather brief comparison of Gilpin and Cox has been made only in order to stress the three major points on which my perception of the international political economy, and of the way in which power is used in it, differs from those of most writers on the subject. All three points help to explain a central purpose of this book which is, quite simply, to direct attention to the power of non-state authorities over the structures and therefore over some of the outcomes of the system, and to the extent to which true realism must recognise their involvement in world politics. The other two purposes are to insist on the growing asymmetries of power between states; and on the absence, or desuetude of power over vital aspects of the world market economy.

Structural power

Like Max Weber – and at the local government level, Robert Dahl – I think capabilities or resources are a poor way of judging relative power; it is more 'power over' than 'power from' that matters. Therefore, the exaggerated interest of American scholars in hegemonic power is not only overly narrow, but their tendency to concentrate attention on capabilities based within a geographical area leads them to a wrong conclusion. The authority – the 'power over' global outcomes enjoyed by American society, and therefore indirectly by the United States government – is still superior to that of any other society or any other government.

The point can be illustrated many times over. At the very beginning of the Cold War, the US Congress passed the Battle Act, aimed at preventing the sale to the Soviet Union or its allies of any weapons, machinery or even minerals and other raw materials judged to be 'strategic' – i.e. of potential military value. Almost at once the principal provisions of the Battle Act were adopted by America's allies. A curious *ad hoc* body was set up in Paris which went by the acronym of COCOM, a coordinating committee charged with making sure that the same list of prohibited exports was adopted and administered by all the members of NATO and other US allies like Japan or Australia. The list was added to from time to time, and once in a while items were removed from it – more often as a result of private lobbying in the United States than of objection by allied governments. The nuclear protection given to the allies by US missiles and nuclear weapons was translated into structural power over the rules of the international trading system.

A more recent example can be found in the environmental policy area. Following the accidental oil spill by the *Exxon Valdez* tanker in Alaska in 1992, the US Congress passed an Oil Pollution Act, which applied to all tankers entering a US port no matter who owned them or what country's flag they flew. By January 1995, these ships had to provide the US Coast Guard with a financial guarantee that the shipowners were able to accept unlimited liability for the costs of any oil spill from the ship. In future, they would only be allowed to enter if built with a double hull. Owners of smaller fleets would be automatically barred from trading with the United States. The costs would surely add to prices of oil imported into the United States. And these are only two examples among many of the unilateral exercise of structural power over other states and other market operators.

A second general point is that 'power over' need not be confined to outcomes consciously or deliberately sought for. Power can be effectively exercised by 'being there', without intending the creation or exploitation of privilege or the transfer of costs or risks from oneself to others, for instance. This recognition of unconscious power is one contribution that gender studies has surely made to international political economy. Male partners may not wish or intend the control they have over outcomes affecting their female partners. But as many women are acutely aware, the social structures within which the partnership exists will make sure that such power exists. And social structures, and psychological attitudes rooted in physiological differences are not easily changed overnight. To quote Waltz once again, 'an agent is powerful to the extent that he [*sic*] affects others more than they affect him' (Waltz, 1979: 192). Canadians overshadowed by the United States have long been aware of this truth, so that taking the unintended effects of power relations out of consideration does indeed, as Waltz insists, 'take much of the politics out of politics'.

This is where the distinction between what I have called relational power and structural power is relevant. In relations with others, it is much harder to think of power being exercised by one party over another unconsciously, without deliberate intent. But when you think of power in terms of power over structures, it is easier to understand that relations existing within those structures are affected, even though it may be inadvertently.

The same is true of the power of United States government agencies over outcomes in the international system. Because the US has structural power, it cannot help but dominate relations with others. Just by being there, it influences outcomes. Even when it tries to delegate power to others, it does not always succeed; if those to whom it defers are indecisive or make a mess of things, it is hard to resist the urge to take over. When the Berlin Wall came down in 1989, for example, the G7 heads of state agreed that the reconstruction of ex-socialist countries in Europe was primarily a European interest and a European responsibility. The European Community was designated, with the agreement of President Bush, as the coordinator of western aid and credit. The European Bank for Reconstruction and Development (EBRD) was set up in London with a French chairman, Jacques Attali. Its development strategy – favouring the private sector and 'bankable' projects – was nevertheless set within policy and financial limits decided by the US Treasury. Russia, for example was to be lent only up to the limit of its shareholding – i.e. contribution to the bank's capital. But when it came to actually making loans and grants, individual governments took their own decisions, and as the economic plight of Russia worsened and the risk of political chaos loomed, the United States unilaterally stepped in with a promise of $23 billion in emergency aid.

In Yugoslavia, the story was much the same. First there was multilateral agreement to let the European Community decide what was to be done. But in the light of Franco-German disagreement over Croatia and the member-states' indecision whether to protect as well as to recognise Bosnia, it became more and more difficult for the US to stand aside and to continue to delegate decisions to the Europeans. The fact that the United States still dominated the security structure, and that no other government had the same command of air and naval forces nor the same influence over other heads of state, meant that the earlier American renunciation of responsibility for the Serbian army's massacres of Bosnian Muslims, like the earlier American refusal to use US ground forces in Yugoslavia, was always going to be reversible. American structural power, whether exercised unilaterally or through NATO, was the final determinant of outcomes.

Conclusions about outcomes

The above examples, and the earlier ones of COCOM and the Oil Pollution Act of 1993, prompt several questions. What sort of outcomes result from the exercise of structural power? How does it affect the relative position – power, wealth, autonomy, security – of some states compared with others? And how does it change the system as a whole?

The outcome of a war, whether between states or between factions within states, seems at first a fairly straightforward matter. One side wins; the loser, as they say in boxing circles, collects the second prize. But even with wars, it is not quite so simple. Wars can be inconclusive. Who really won the war in Vietnam? Or the Thirty Years War in the seventeenth century? Nor is the acknowledgement of defeat, as in the case of France in 1940 or Germany and Japan in 1945, the end of the matter. There are other outcomes. In the short-term, for instance, the Germans suffered hardship, food shortages, partition and military government and occupation of their towns and villages by the Americans, Russians, French and British. But in the longer term, the western part of the country at least benefited from the imposition of more even-handed labour relations in industry and of a more competitive regime for big business. Which outcome was more important is a subjective question, one on which those who suffered and those who benefited may not agree. What was the outcome of the American Civil War, for instance?

Or, to take another issue, not of war but of economic sanctions short of war, what was the outcome of these in South Africa? Did they really bring about the end of apartheid and constitutional reform under De Klerk and Mandela? An arguable case can be made for saying it was not so much – or not directly – the sanctions declared by other states against South Africa but the threatened actions of some US shareholders on US banks which started the snowball of change rolling. Chase Manhattan and others began to close, or sell off their South African branches. Financial markets concluded that the effects on South Africa's capital inflow, balance of payments and credit rating would be bad. The value of the rand began to fall. Big business in South Africa saw big trouble ahead. Time for a U-turn, the politicians were told.

Complexity, in a word, is inseparable from the study of cause and effect when it comes to outcomes in international political economy. Political causes and economic causes are as incommensurable as apples and oranges, and so are political and economic outcomes. Within national societies there are winners and losers, and the net benefit to the whole society cannot be assessed without weighing one group's pain against another group's pleasure or profit. Thus, it is not enough to say 'the United States' was victorious in a negotiation like the Uruguay Round or the bilateral bargaining with Japan. The US delegation may have got its way on some matters – but who can objectively tell what the final outcome will be – or for whom on either side?

And if distributional outcomes within and between societies are hard to judge, the systemic outcomes – that is, the mix of values within the whole system – are even harder to assess. Thus, we may say that the United States has had the structural power to determine outcomes in the short term. But when it comes to the longer term, there are many times when the outcomes turn out to be more complex, quite different, even perverse to American intentions. An example here would be the economic success of Japan to which the US postwar occupation and protection surely contributed in several important ways. Being overtaken economically by Japan, as the home of leading car firms or as the largest aid donor to foreign governments, was not exactly what the Americans had originally intended.

The same might be said of the systemic consequences of US policies on the global financial or production structures. The contribution to economic growth may have been intended, but was it anticipated that financial deregulation would lead to such volatility, instability and uncertainty in the system? In the short-term, the deregulation begun in the United States in the 1970s or earlier gave head-start advantages to US-based banks. In the longer term, even US regulators began to worry about the systemic consequences for the stability and welfare of the whole world market economy. Literature, on such matters, may be a sounder guide to understanding than social science. Poetry and drama are full of stories in which the unravelling of a chain of causes and effects is totally unforeseen and often – as for Oedipus Rex, Macbeth or King Lear – profoundly tragic.

Much of the emphasis in this chapter has been on the structural power of the United States. This has been for the good reason that the declinist school in the US has left such an apparently indelible mark on the literature of international political economy. However, the truth is that the main outcome of this structural power has been a shift in the balance of power from states to markets. The United States, using its structural power to lock European, Latin American and now Asian and African economies into an open world market economy, certainly intended to reap benefits and new opportunities for American business. What its policymakers did not fully intend – in line with literary traditions – was the enhanced power that this would give to markets over governments, including their own. This result may make many social scientists uncomfortable. They are accustomed to think of power as pertaining to someone, or some social or economic institution. But markets do not fit this conception. They are impersonal, intangible, not even necessarily to be found in any one place. They do not have rational preferences and can behave unpredictably and in a perverse manner. Moreover, they operate on the 'reflexive principle' as described by George Soros. Following Keynes' earlier perceptions from the 1930s, Soros has pointed out that, in financial markets especially, the market responds to the perceptions of the market-watchers, and the market-watchers' perceptions in turn affect market outcomes. This reflexive principle undermines the basic pretensions of social science to be in any but the broadest (i.e. 'truth-seeking') sense 'scientific' (Soros, 1987, 1994). Objectivity in social science is never absolute. That may be why social scientists find the concept of market power so hard to incorporate into their methods of analysis. Chief executives of multinationals have no such difficulty. For them, the power of markets is an everyday reality.

3   The limits of politics

Anyone who, like myself, has been led by one path or another to the study of international political economy has probably shared my experience of being shot at from both sides – by the political scientists and by the economists. It feels as if one had been caught, defenceless and exposed, in the no man's land between two entrenched armies. On one side, in one set of dug-out trenches, are the armies of Politics and International Relations. On the other, the powerful forces of Economics, led and commanded by generals trained in the neo-classical tradition of liberal economics. Against the political scientists, one is constantly crying for more attention to economic factors, to markets, to prices, to finance. To the others, the economists, one is constantly protesting with equal vehemence the relevance of choices that are essentially subjective and political, the importance of law and organisation for the functioning of markets and to constrain the behaviour of market operators, the role of history and perceptions of history in policymaking. The Germans or Hungarians, for example, are not more rational than, say, Americans, in their pursuit of and veneration for stable money. They just happen to have had a different folk memory of what unstable money and inflation can do to personal fortunes and to social and political relations.

A first step, therefore, in ending this trench warfare between economics and politics and in showing both that it is all just the same one field over which they have dug their opposing trenches, is to show how narrow-minded each specialism has become. I shall make a start by making the case for a much less narrow definition of the study of politics. Indeed, a broader definition is, in my opinion, essential for the

* An adapted version of this chapter was presented as the 1995 Leonard Shapiro Lecture at the London School of Economics and Political Science. It was subsequently published in *Government and Opposition*, vol. 30/3 Summer, 1995.

further development of the study of international political economy. It is certainly necessary to an inquiry such as this into how far authority over social and economic outcomes has become diffused, now that the patterns of power and influence have become so much more complex than they used to be – or used to be thought to be by most political scientists.

It has rightly been observed that the study of politics in most of the twentieth century has been 'colonised' by the state. What this means is that the subject has been so limited that at its broadest political theory concerned only states as political organisms, while in empirical research and teaching attention concentrated on comparative analysis of states – or even more narrowly (as in American politics) on the political institutions and issues of one particular state. One way or another, the state has come so to dominate the subject that almost everything else has been crowded out. Labour unions, business associations, lobbyists are all studied and their behaviour analysed only in so far as they affect the functioning of the state.

But why should we think only (or even mainly) of states as sources of power over outcomes? Why should we imagine that states are the only institutions which exercise authority over others in setting not only rules but norms and customary procedures? Is it not time to ask whether too much of the theoretical discussion of power has been centred on and confined within the state? And whether far too much attention in the literature has not hitherto been paid to the powers of governments? Surely, the time has come for intellectual liberation from this constricting notion?

It is understandable that, out of all the many branches of political science, the study of international relations should have suffered most from this colonisation. The searing experience of two world wars posed the problematic of war. Why did it happen? Could it be avoided? In Europe in the interwar decades, and in America after 1945, international lawyers and diplomatic historians were drawn into developing a new branch of politics – the study of inter-national relations. If you start by inquiring primarily into the problematic of war, it is not surprising that your mental spotlight is on states. Because of their common claim to a monopoly of the legitimate use of violence, it is states which have been most often able to wage war. Although that may now be changing, for most of modern history it has been much more difficult for rebels or revolutionaries to fight wars. And certainly the damage and casualties caused by inter-state wars in the last two centuries have greatly exceeded the damage and casualties caused by civil wars and other kinds of conflict. Therefore, the main issue in the security structure was perceived as how to avoid conflict between states.

But once the security structure is redefined – as many scholars hitherto engaged in 'strategic studies' are now redefining it – as those arrangements providing people with security not just from attack and injury or death at the hands of forces from another state but with security from all sorts of other risks – of long-term environmental degradation, of hunger, of shortages of oil or electricity, of unemployment and penury and even perhaps of preventable disease – then the central role of the state crumbles. Even within its traditional jurisdiction, some states begin to share with private enterprises their once-basic responsibility for security against robbery and intrusion, or for the detention and movement of criminals. And for security from attack from outside, states increasingly depend on the willingness of others to sell weapons or to license technology. Even the United States now requires the collaboration of others to develop its most advanced weapons systems.

The other primary function of the state in modern times has been the control of the currency, of the state money. For much of recorded history, it has been almost as jealously guarded from the rivalry of others as the management of defence forces protecting the state territory and the conduct of relations with other states. The very word used to describe the benefits derived from the state's monopoly over the minting and issue of money – seignorage – reflects the state's claim to an exclusive, superior power. And even when the pretense at monetary independence can no longer be seriously maintained by the national governments of most small and medium states, their governments will still cling to the illusion of autonomy by printing their 'own' banknotes and issuing their own coins. Scotland and Luxembourg are two extreme examples of this. Even the governments of the three major states in the system – the United States, Germany and Japan – cannot be sure that their wishes and policies will prevail over the judgements of the markets.

Nevertheless, it still remains an axiom of most scholars interested in international politics that, to use Caporaso's formulation, 'the primary unit of analysis remains the legally sovereign, if not operationally autonomous, state' (Caporaso, 1989: 9). The trouble is that *primary* too often becomes *only*, so that there is a failure to look at other coexisting – and sometimes conflicting – authorities in the system, and at other

33

arenas of politics in which outcomes are determined and 'power over' is clearly being exercised by authorities other than the state. Gilpin talks repeatedly of the 'fundamentally opposed logic of the market and that of the state' (Gilpin, 1987: 12). But what he means is the fundamentally different motivation of those involved in politics and those involved in buying and selling, trading, investing and arbitraging. His definition, since often quoted, of international political economy as being concerned with the two-way inter-action of the state system with the market economy, and of the market-economy with the state system implies an uneasy coexistence of one system based on economics with one based on politics.

Early writers

The question, therefore, boils down to the essential nature of politics, and to who, precisely, we think of as 'those involved in politics'? For this, it is necessary to go back to some early postwar writers. One of the most influential in political science was David Easton, whose book *The Political System* was published in 1953. He defined politics as 'the authoritative allocation of values in the system', a definition which gets away from particular institutions and specific issues to the heart of the matter (Easton, 1953: 143). As I argued in *States and Markets*, the diagnosis of the human condition, the analytical framework for the study of international political economy, required attention, not so much to specific issues like trade or armed conflict, or to the allocation of values to individuals or groups of individuals, as to those arrangements which determined the *mix of values* reflected in the system as a whole. I reduced these basic values to four – the wealth created; the security provided; the justice dispensed; and the freedom, or autonomy permitted. Every society provided *some* wealth, *some* security, *some* justice and *some* degree of freedom to choose. Differences between national societies, and between the international political economy as a whole at different periods of time, lay in the variable weight, or priority, given to each of these basic values (Strange, 1988: ch. 1). Following Easton, then, one could say that politics could be defined as those processes and structures through which the mix of values in the system as a whole, and their distribution among social groups and individuals was determined.

Now, it is perfectly clear to me at least that it is not states alone which possess the authority to allocate such values. Managers of enterprises, responding to the markets for labour or for physical inputs or licensed technology, will decide to pay some kinds of employees more or less, give them more or less security of tenure. Leaders of opinion – scientists, for example – may have power to persuade citizens or decision-makers that measures should be taken for the sake of greater equity to protect the political or economic rights of some social group considered as disadvantaged by the existing system. Such people – and in part II of the book I shall consider some of the groups who are exercising this kind of value-allocating authority – are clearly engaged in politics, even though they may not realise it. As M. Jourdan learned, one may speak prose for years without realising that one is speaking it.

Approaching the same question, who is 'involved in politics', Bertrand de Jouvenel, a postwar French political philosopher and commentator, suggested a better answer than 'politicians' or just 'people participating in political parties, or social movements with political objectives' (De Jouvenel, 1958). He defined political authority, not according to the institutions or the agents of the state, but according to two basic presumptions: firstly, that action becomes political whenever the help of other people is a necessary condition of an individual achieving his aim (De Jouvenel, 1959: 29); Secondly, that consequently politics occurs whenever a project requires the support of other wills.

From these two basic presumptions, it follows that forming any kind of association of individuals for a commonly agreed purpose is political. Getting people together to contribute to a charity or organise a car pool or a baby-sitting rota is political. Recruiting tennis players to form a club, acquire courts, nets and balls, or recruiting fat people to join Weight Watchers or an aerobics group for those who want to keep fit also involves gaining the support of other wills. Gaining the support of other wills may involve a material contribution, but (as with the baby-sitters) it need not. The essential point is that the initiator cannot accomplish the objective alone; s/he has to have the support of other wills. For De Jouvenel, therefore, political science is 'the study of political life – the capacity to bring into being a stream of wills: to canalise the stream and regularise and institutionalise the resulting cooperation'. It is 'the study of the way in which aggregates are formed and of the conditions necessary for their stability' – it being understood that 'aggregates' are not limited to the collectivities known as states (De Jouvenel, 1953: 25).

The idea of power being derived from the social nature of human beings, from their ability to act in concert, whether hunting or farming or designing aircraft, is not peculiar to De Jouvenel. Hannah Arendt, looking at political institutions rather than 'who-rules-whom' questions, saw them as 'manifestations and materialisations of power'. Power therefore corresponds to 'the human ability not just to act but to act in concert'. Politics of course involves the use of power, but the power so used is derived from the willingness of individuals to act collectively for commonly approved ends (Arendt, 1958: 181ff).

I would only add to De Jouvenel's wide but perfectly logical definition of politics that the study has to comprehend not only the bringing into being of a stream of wills, but also the consequences while the association lasts, and if and when it disintegrates, how and why it does and with what results. Such questions – all political – can be asked of the rise and fall of an alliance of states, the rise and fall of a coalition government, the rise and fall of a political party. By the same logic, politics enters into, indeed is inseparable from the rise and fall of a large enterprise engaged in a variety of productive or distributive operations. From the moment when its originator conceives the enterprise, he or she needs the supporting wills of creditors, employees, managers and salesmen to achieve the dream. Bargaining, persuasion, the offer of inducements, the threat of negative sanctions, the inspiration with a common vision – all these activities are little different from what politicians do when they seek election. If business people in action simply told their financial backers or their employees that the enterprise would reduce transaction costs by internalising them they would not get very far. The cold logic of economic theory will not get people acting enthusiastically in concert to compete energetically with rival firms.

Conceptual problems

This broader definition of politics suggests the way in which at least three important conceptual problems might be resolved. Each has been acknowledged by the leading writers in international political economy, but so far there has not been much constructive thinking about how to deal with them. One conceptual problem arises from the separation of domestic politics and international politics implicit in most of the literature of political science and in the organisation of university courses. The problem is how to re-unite the two since by now it is generally recognised that the origins of international conflicts and cooperation are more often than not domestic (Grieco, 1990; Milner, 1988; Funabashi, 1989).

Extending the focus of analysis from states to all forms of authority allows us to ask how, and by whom values are allocated and political decisions taken – in the wider sense outlined above – to affect outcomes. At one and the same time, we can ask about authority within states and outside them as well as just in their relations with each other. We can avoid the perennial temptation in the study of international relations to 'reify' the state, that is, to treat it as one 'thing', a unitary actor, as if France, say, or Japan, were a discrete personality. In any situation, we can look within the state to see whether it is the Chancellor of the Federal Republic or the Bundesbank, the Finance Ministry or MITI that speaks respectively for 'Germany' or for 'Japan'. Analysts of foreign policy have long recognised the significance of shifts in the internal balance of power – between State and Treasury, or State and Defense in Washington, for example – in determining the conduct and course of American diplomacy. All I am suggesting is that scholars in international political economy should take the same logic a step further by redefining the nature of politics, and of political authority.

The second conceptual problem has also been universally recognised but never satisfactorily resolved. It is how to relate in one synthesising study the political system of states and the economic system of markets. Gilpin starts with this question: 'The parallel existence and mutual interaction of "state" and "market" in the modern world create "political economy" . . . I use the term "political economy" simply to indicate a set of questions to be examined by means of an eclectic mixture of analytical methods and theoretical perspectives' (Gilpin, 1987: 8–9).

Gilpin's basic equation, therefore looks like this:

$$S(States) + M(Markets) = P/E(Political\ Economy).$$

That is the basis for an analysis of how states affect the production and distribution of wealth – the world economy – and how markets affect the distribution of power and welfare among states – 'the impact of the world market economy on the relations of states and the ways in which states seek to influence market forces for their own advantage' (Gilpin 1987: 24). For Gilpin, three questions arise from this two-way interaction. Firstly, how is market interdependence affected by the presence or absence of political leadership – the hegemon question? Secondly, how does the interaction of political and economic change affect the geographical location of economic activity? And thirdly, how does change in the world market affect,

37

and conversely is affected by, the regimes created by states to govern these activities?

By focusing mainly on the role of states, he finds that almost everyone dealing with these questions falls into either a liberal, a nationalist (or mercantilist), or a Marxist school of thought. In this view, he echoes a trend in the study and teaching of international politics to offer students a choice of three *prix fixe* menus, three contending perspectives – sometimes called pluralist (liberal), realist or neo-realist (nationalist) and structuralist (critical) – on the world system. Since each perspective derives from political opinions based on subjective value-preferences, there is little prospect of synthesis between them. Many students have found this imperative to 'pay your money and take your choice' between the three menus somewhat frustrating and unsatisfactory.

Extending the definition of politics beyond states to all sources of authority, to all with power to allocate values, however, allows the two worlds of markets and states, of government and business, to be treated as one, rather than as two as in Gilpin's equation. An alternative equation would replace states(S) with multiple authorities – A (n). And it would replace the generic market(M), with multiple markets – M(n). This is because in reality, as international political economists are well aware, some markets are more or less 'free', some entirely or partially managed by governments or by cartels, and sometimes by dominant firms. So in place of P/E, by which Gilpin means the distribution of wealth and power among states, we have the variable mix of basic values – security, wealth, justice and freedom – incorporated in the system. We could express that as V(n). But we also have as an outcome the allocation of those values not just among states or nations but among classes, generations, genders and multiple social groups and associations. The latter could be expressed as Soc(n), if by society we understand society to represent multiple cross-cutting, overlapping social groupings. The alternative equation could be the following:

$$\frac{A(n)}{M(n)} + \frac{M(n)}{A(n)} = \frac{V(n)}{Soc(n)}$$

There are a number of major advantages of this more comprehensive analytical framework. In the first place, it gets over the 'actor' problem which has long bedevilled the study of international relations. As argued above, the notion that the state is the sole unit of analysis, or even that it is the primary actor in international relations, is untenable when it comes to international political economy. It does not hold good even in international political issues.

For example, how can the security problems of the Middle East be analysed without taking into account the important part played by the Palestine Liberation Organisation(PLO)? How can the major changes in Italian politics in 1992 and 1993 be explained without going into the internal politics and economic roles of non-state authorities like the Sicilian mafia, the Camorra – and indeed, the Vatican and the P2? Yet, if guided by commonsense, the PLO as an authority capable of negotiating with the US, even with Israel, is admitted within the charmed circle called politics, why not the Colombian drug barons? There is no question but that they are 'recruiting others to their objectives' or that their authority over the farmers and processors is generally acknowledged and seldom challenged with impunity. The conceptual contortions which writers on international relations get themselves into when dealing with such problems all arise from this idea that states are primary actors. Exactly how, in any situation, you distinguish primary actors from the others – presumably 'secondary' actors – is never made clear. And the same false assumption underlies a long, tedious (and inconclusively sterile) debate among the theorists about what they call the 'agent-structure' question, i.e., do the actors (agents) create the structures or the structures constrain the agents?

Secondly, the more comprehensive analytical framework gets over another hitherto unresolved conceptual problem. It concerns the agendas of political economy – the definition of the core political questions in a market economy. Gilpin, as shown above, sees these agendas as pertaining to the interests of states. And for 'states' he takes the United States as a typical model. Those issues which concern the government in Washington, and which involve the governments of other countries are the core issues of international political economy – the rules governing international trade, the management of exchange rates between currencies, the property rights of foreign investors, the arrangements for interstate transport and communication and so forth. Because Gilpin recognises that the power of the United States, its ability to get its own way in relations with other governments, is bound to be affected in the long run by the health or otherwise of the US economy, his perception of the agenda of international political economy does not stop at what is generally understood by 'foreign economic policy' issues. Like other economic patriots in the United States, Gilpin adds the issues of industrial policy (see Zysman, 1983; Tyson, 1992; Reich, 1983; Prestowitz, 1988; Thurow, 1992). For example, should semiconductors be produced under our jurisdiction or in another state? And if they are mostly made by foreign firms and imported, what is to be done about it? Are the rules governing global financial markets such as give opportunities to our financial enterprises? And if not, again, what can be done to open up more opportunities, more closed markets?

But this is only a small step in the right direction. The fact is that the United States is by no means typical of all states in its perceptions of the agendas of political economy, domestic and global. Most other governments, especially in developing countries, would include a much larger range of issues. If we conceive of a continuum representing the intervention of state in economy going from maximalist at one end to minimalist at the other end, the US is (and for the most part has always traditionally been) well on the minimalist side of the continuum.

Moreover, there is no intrinsic reason why scholars should limit analysis to those issues which most governments, at most times, have acknowledged as being part of the agenda. This is particularly so now that issues like abortion and contraception, euthanasia, animal breeding and husbandry, the property rights of 'traditional' musicians, and many other social issues that once were addressed by local or national authority, are now overspilling national frontiers, and involving the interaction of multiple authorities and multiple markets. All these and many more surely belong in the agenda of political economy.

To go back to the definition of politics, if 'political' relates only to the typical concerns of most governments, the agenda is limited. But if 'political' includes all action requiring the cooperation of others, the agenda is much more comprehensive. What resources should go into limiting the spread of AIDS? How can the preservation of rainforests, or for endangered animal or plant species, be weighed against the need for economic growth for poor people? By extending the limits of 'political', we include the notion of a world society that is buffeted and sometimes bruised by both the political system of states and by the economic system of markets. At the least, we should include in the agenda any issue on which some government, or some non-state authority, at some time, has thought it necessary to intervene. This may be a pointer to the next question: how to assess the changing locus of authority in the international political economy.

Methodological options

There are several ways in which this broader and more comprehensive approach to the study of international political economy could be developed, and its comparative advantages over simple comparative politics or comparative economics could be demonstrated.

One way would be to organise material on the basis of markets, or sectors of the international political economy. By examining the role of state and non-state authority in the working of specific markets, the balance between political authority and market forces could be assessed, and the consequences for a variety of social groups presented in such a comparative way that the variation between sectors along the free-to-managed continuum would appear every bit as great as the variation between national economies along the same free-to-managed continuum. Just think of the difference between the almost totally managed market in diamonds under the control of De Beers and the almost totally unmanaged market for pirated compact discs, or for small arms. There is much to be said for this empirical, sectoral approach and I have advocated it and tried it out myself (Strange, 1976: Strange and Tooze, 1981). So have a growing number of perceptive international political economists. Some sectors have been more thoroughly researched than others; oil, textiles and cars are particularly popular subjects for analysis. But there have also been valuable studies of world markets for shoes, for civil aircraft, for wheat and other primary commodities, and for services like tourism, shipping or telecommunications.

Two problems arise with the sectoral method, if adopted wholesale to present a holistic picture of the world market economy and the role of authority in it. One is where to stop. How many markets have to be analysed in depth to give a reasonably accurate and comprehensive picture of the mix of values and the who-gets-what in the system as a whole? The other problem is how far it is necessary to subdivide each market into its different parts. Even for something as straightforward as wheat, there is one market for hard durum wheat and another for soft wheats, as there is one for arabica and another for robusta coffee. The market for malting barley exists alongside and overlaps that for feed barley. When it comes to manufactures, the picture is even more complex. The car market, for example, is a bundle of markets for car parts, from tyres to windscreens and computers. The authorities involved with one component may be quite different from those involved with others. Markets in services are even more complex. Trying to sum up the net systemic change on the basis of this method is very difficult.

The second method is like that now under development by the institutional economists. By analysing in turn the intervention of a number of institutions from national governments and international organisations to private foundations and business associations, a better picture of the intervention of authority with enterprise is possible than when analysis is confined to government agencies. The problems here, however, are three-fold. Firstly, the description of these institutions can be dry and tedious. Secondly, assessing the relative importance of various institutional sources of authority on different issues and at different times is not easy, so the dynamics of authority-market relationships are hard to capture with a method that tends to a rather static vision. Thirdly, the accent on organisation may distract attention from market-authority dynamics. That is, changes within the market, especially in demand and supply but also sometimes in technology affecting products or process, can have very marked effects on the power exercised by authority over the market. The ups and downs of OPEC influence on the oil market are a classic illustration of the point.

A third method, or way to proceed, is the one which I have chosen to explore in part II of the book. It is not so much exclusive of the other two as supplementary to them. It might be called functionalist, if the word had not been so widely used in the study of international organisations. It starts from the various functions of authority in a political economy, and asks who or what is exercising those functions or responsibilities, and with what effect of outcomes. If we imagine the same sort of free-to-managed continuum as before but do not limit the intervention of authority to states or agencies of states, the method has the advantage of great flexibility. It can be applied to all forms of authority, from that of parents in a family, or elders in a tribe, or priests in a religious community to the managers of a firm or leaders of a mafia or bosses in a political party. In any situation and on any issue, the question it starts with is who, if anyone, is exercising authority – and with what purpose, by what means and with what consequences. My hypothesis, as explained in the last chapter, is that on many issues most states have lost control over some of the functions of authority and are either sharing them with other states or with other (non-state) authorities. The outcome in some cases is that no one is responsible for authority functions, even though they may pretend to be. It presumes some general decline in the power of most states and some gain in the authority of world markets and of enterprises operating in world markets.

This shift away from states and towards markets is probably the biggest change in the international political economy to take place in the last half of the twentieth century. It is most marked in matters of production, trade, investment and finance – in what I would call the production and financial structures. These are the ones which have most impact on people's daily lives. I shall argue that one of the major shifts resulting from structural change has been the increased power and influence of the multinationals – more properly called transnational corporations (TNCs) – and the networks they set up and operate. The next chapter, therefore, will explore in historical perspective how far and what ways TNCs are encroaching on the authority of states in relation to society and economy, while assessing the explanatory theories offered for these changes.

4   Politics and production

If there is one change, above all others, which has affected politics at the highest inter-state level and, at the other extreme, the life chances of individuals throughout the world, it is change in the production structure of the world economy. That is to say, in what goods and services are produced, how, where and by whom. This change is not so much the emergence of the 'multinationals' so-called – they have been around for a long time; it has been the change from production mostly designed and destined for one local or national market, to production mostly designed and destined for a world market, or at least for several national markets. In short, it is not the enterprises that are multinational. (The word was always a misnomer, anyway.) It is the market. Production for the larger world market has transformed innumerable national or local enterprises into transnational corporations (TNCs).

A major hypothesis of this book is that the shift from state to markets has actually made political players of the TNCs. The argument is not that they influence the foreign policies of states or are, in any general and important sense, the 'powers behind the throne', even though in special circumstances they may be so. Rather, it is that they themselves are political institutions, having political relations with civil society. These political relations are even more important than their political involvement with other firms or with specific governments. They are important at every stage of production when firms act as technical or organisational innovators, as consumers of others' goods and services, as producers and sellers, and as employers.

The paradox is that this has not happened entirely by accident. The shift from state authority to market authority has been in large part the result of state policies. It was not that the TNCs stole or purloined power

44

from the government of states. It was handed to them on a plate – and, moreover, for 'reasons of state'.

This is better understood if we put the shift into a longer historical perspective, as did two of the classical writers on international political economy – Fernand Braudel and Karl Polanyi (Braudel, 1975; Polanyi, 1944). Their writing makes it clear that the relation of market authority to political authority has never been stable for long, and that at different times and in different places the pendulum has swung away from one and toward the other and back again, often in ways unforeseen by contemporaries. We may not be able as yet to see how exactly this pendulum may swing back in the future from markets to some form of authority – not necessarily that of territorial states – but history does offer some reassurance that, somehow, sometime, it probably will. Meanwhile there are some senses in which TNCs themselves are acting as political authorities.

The purpose of this chapter, therefore, is to explore in more detail how far and in what ways, TNCs have encroached on the authority of the state; to ask why this has happened, and finally, to look at some of the political and social consequences of this shift. One hypothesis is that there is not much left of the territorial basis for authority. States are legally and conventionally defined by the territorial limits of their authority. Sovereignty has been defined in international law as 'the right to exercise (in regard to a portion of the globe) to the exclusion of any other state, the functions of a state.' (Picciotto, 1992; 307).[1] International law is less precise on what those functions are, and on whether these *de jure* rights can or cannot be exercised *de facto*. When the shift of power is to other authorities – authorities whose basis is not their command over territory but their command over the nature, location and manner of production and distribution of goods and services, this clearly raises some new questions about the nature of sovereignty and the dispersion of power and political control.

Among those who study international business, it is now generally acknowledged that TNCs have become the 'central organizers', the 'engines of growth' of economic activity in the world economy. They are the 'driving force' of international transactions, including trade (*World Investment Report*, 1992: 1, 6). So much so, that 'a part of economic decisionmaking power over who gets what, when, where and how is

---

[1] Picciotto (1992) quotes from a 1932 Hague Court report in an international arbitral award in the *Island of Palmas Case. Netherland vs. United States*.

shifting to TNCs' (ibid.: 306). (The echo of Lasswell's classic definition of politics in that remark will not be lost on students of international relations.) Indeed, the same UN report makes the point that the outcome of competition between states in years to come will be determined more by the TNCs than by domestic firms operating only within the boundaries of individual states (WIR: 301). That in itself is a big change.

But we have to ask just what this means in terms of power and politics and the locus of authority in the system. We can be clear, from the start, what it does not mean. It does *not* mean that sovereignty is at bay in the sense that TNCs are displacing the state – the sort of implication of those simplistic comparisons that were made in the 1970s between the GNP of middle-sized states and the turnover of General Motors or IBM. When Kindleberger remarked then that the nation-state was just about finished (Kindleberger, 1970), it was a gross exaggeration. No one seriously expects states to disappear, at least not in the foreseeable future. It is something else to argue, as I shall, that the progressive integration of the world economy, through international production, has shifted the balance of power away from states and toward world markets. That shift has led to the transfer of some powers in relation to civil society from territorial states to nonterritorial TNCs. Less importantly, it has also affected the limits of cooperation, and the competition, between states and thus to shifts of power as well as wealth between states. Finally, it has led to the emergence of some no-go areas where authority of any kind is conspicuous by its absence. But before explaining how and where this has happened, we should note some of the most important recent trends in the internationalisation of production.

Trends for TNCs

No one knows the precise extent to which production has become international – designed for and destined for world markets and conducted in more than one country. The UN's Transnational Corporations and Management Division – formerly the UN Centre on Transnational Corporations – offers a round figure for 1992 of 35,000 TNCs with some 150,000 affiliates. But this counts only the major enterprises in the major investing countries. It gives the book value of foreign direct investment worldwide as $1,700 billion – but book values are the sum of historic costs of investment or acquisitions and therefore often grossly understate market values. And in any case, one of the major trends of recent years has been to new forms of investment (NFI) in other countries (Oman, 1989). These include franchising deals, joint ventures, buy-back and licensing agreements. In all these, the capital is often raised by the local partner, while the foreign-owned firm (FOF) supplies capital only (or mainly) in the invisible form of the costs sunk in developing new technologies and/or management expertise, and in developing and publicising a brand name or a corporate reputation. The local partner benefits from the foreign firm's past efforts in building up the trust and confidence of consumers and investors and thus gains the access to domestic and export markets which otherwise would be a long, costly and risky business.

Thus, the statistics for foreign direct investment of the old kind, in which funds actually cross the exchanges from A to B, are only the very roughest of indicators of what has been going on. On this at least, both firms and governments are agreed (Stopford and Strange, 1991: 14–16). For example, it is possible that an apparent decline in the growth rate in FDI in 1990 compared with the high annual average growth rate in the 1980s may simply have reflected a shift from conventional direct investments abroad to the new, invisible and largely uncounted (and probably uncountable) investments in licensing, joint ventures, franchising and so forth.

Partial as they are, FDI figures are still impressive. Between 1985 and 1990, the *average* annual increase in FDI was 34 per cent, while the comparable (nominal) average annual rise in world exports was 13 per cent a year and for GDP, 12 per cent. In 1990, the total stock of known foreign direct investments was $225 billion. And sometime around the mid-1980s, it is generally agreed that the total of international production – output of the affiliates of TNCs outside their home base – overtook the volume of world exports of manufactures. Indeed, by 1990 the goods and services sold by foreign affiliates of TNCs were almost double world exports, if intra-firm trade is excluded to avoid double counting. One estimate for 1985 was that the TNCs accounted for 20 per cent of world production and trade (Robock and Simmons, 1989); by the mid-1990s it may have risen to as much as a third.

More and more, the goods passing from one country to another are not in any sense of the word actually 'sold' or 'bought'. They are only moved by order of corporate managers between different branches of the same TNCs. Contrary to the teaching of conventional international trade theory, they are moving not because of any comparative advantages in market terms of one country over another but because the management of a transnational company has decided on a production strategy that involves such movements. Overall, it is thought that by now well over a quarter of all worldwide trade is now intra-firm trade. In particular countries, and in certain sectors, the figure is much higher. As much as 40 per cent of Mexico's trade with the US in the early 1990s, for example, was done by the affiliates of US firms. In the late 1980s and early 1990s, foreign affiliates accounted for over 50 per cent of manufactured exports from Malaysia, the Philippines and Sri Lanka. In Colombia, thanks mainly to the growing practice of FOFs sub-contracting offshore production, exports of clothes grew in only four years by over 50 per cent, and of shoes by over a third. Morocco and Slovenia are two other countries where domestic firms have substantially boosted national exports by arranging to produce under contract for foreign TNCs. One estimate of German trade with the Czech Republic in the mid-1990s, for example, suggested that over 70 per cent consisted of manufactures – mainly textile products – sent to be processed with the aid of cheaper skilled labour before returning to Germany. Some of the biggest facilitators of offshore production in recent years have been the Japanese trading companies, or *soga shosha*. Their operations in the late 1980s already accounted for 5 or 6 per cent of world trade – not surprising, as they offer not only low interest loans to finance trade (usually with Japan), but also advice on marketing and business contacts, again usually with Japanese firms. The nine largest *soga shosha* have over 3,000 foreign affiliates, over half of them in developing countries.

Taking a somewhat longer historical perspective, there have been three major changes in international production over the last fifty years or so that are worth noting for their political significance. One is that whereas in the early part of the twentieth century, the majority of TNCs were engaged in minerals and plantation agriculture, these operations are now much the least important. Even where the original investment was in primary production, most of the companies still engaged in this are apt by now to have diversified into processing, manufacturing and even services.

Take BAT (British American Tobacco) in Brazil, for example. Growing tobacco for the local cigarette market is now only a small part of their business, even though BAT has practically a monopoly of the Brazilian market. Manufacturing the paper for cigarettes took the firm into other paper products and packaging, as well as into research into largescale timber production and management. They immediately become much more welcome. Employing plantation labourers or miners at wages not much above subsistence levels was always bound to provoke angry accusations of exploitation. In other parts of the world, taking copper or oil out of the ground to sell on world markets, keeping prices down for rich consumers, could easily be represented as robbing the country, and future generations, of their national heritage. Little wonder that, as long as less developed countries saw themselves as forever destined to export raw materials cheaply and buy manufactures dear, their politicians and scholars should see TNCs as the authors of their poverty and impotence. Today, opinions are much more divided.

Dependency, to be sure, still exists. If anything, it is harder than ever for poor countries to be truly independent of the capitalist world economy. But dependency is no longer equated with the relegation of local labour to menial tasks in the fields or the mines. The Malaysian factory worker, whether producing cars with the help of Japanese technology, or air-conditioners for the Japanese market, is likely to be better off, and have better prospects for the future than his father or grandfathers. Thanks to foreign firms, there are new career opportunities open to himself and to his children either as managers or as entrepreneurs. The foreign firm has not only proved that it can be the engine of growth – in incomes, in jobs, in exports, in skills – it is also perceived as such. It is a general rule that the older the FOF, the more expatriates will have been replaced by local managers. Between FOF and host government, there may still be conflict over the terms and conditions of entry; but the bargaining that ensues is a clear recognition of symbiosis.

As a result, nothing is more striking in recent world economic history than the U-turns of at least thirty Asian, Latin American and even African governments on the matter of policies toward foreign investment and toward state vs. private ownership of enterprises. In the first half of the 1980s, there were only fifteen national expropriations, compared with 336 in the first half of the 1970s. As the UNCTC commented, 'Not many developing countries would now see the activities of TNCs as impinging on their sovereignty [and] there are clear indications of a new pragmatic approach which comes from the growing belief that developing countries can negotiate agreements with TNCs in which the benefits of foreign investments are not necessarily outweighed by the cost' (UNCTC: 314). In the years since that comment was made, almost every developing country, including Cuba, Myanmar and Vietnam as well as India, Turkey and all the former socialist countries of the Soviet bloc have revised and liberalised their policies toward foreign enterprises, and have done their best – not always with great success – to sell off state-owned enterprises to private owners. One very striking move has been in Tunisia where the 1994 Code for foreign firms assured them of maximum freedom from administrative restrictions.

The second politically significant change in international production is that it has become genuinely 'multinational', in the sense that firms engaged in international production of goods and services now originate from many countries. Time was when the TNC was seen as a pre-eminently American phenomenon. This perception prevailed in North and South America, less so in Europe where the British, French, Dutch and Swiss had all had their 'multinationals' at work around the world for many years – even decades.[2] The high point of this perception of TNCs as a mainly American phenomenon was probably reached with the total nationalisation of US-owned copper companies by the Allende government in Chile in 1971.[3] The American multinationals were widely blamed for the subsequent fall of Allende, although the major responsibility undoubtedly lay with President Nixon and the CIA. The whole incident, however, conveniently served to confirm Latin American suspicions that US firms were a tool of US imperialism; that the government was only (in Marxist language) the executive committee of the bourgeoisie, providing American capitalism with the political support necessary for the systematic exploitation of developing countries.

That perception has given way to reality, even in Latin America. Throughout the 1970s, nationalisation, and even progressive exclusion as envisaged by Decision 24 of the 1970 Andean Pact, prevailed as official policy goals. But meanwhile European and Japanese firms were joining the Americans in setting up or buying up affiliates in Latin America, as elsewhere. By the 1980s, many of them had become well established. When foreign bank loans dried up and the cost of debt service and repayment became a major problem for many countries, the reinvested profits of foreign firms were doubly welcome.

And in the US itself, the perception of international business as a primarily American phenomenon was under equal correction. As US protectionism mounted, especially against Japan, Japanese TNCs

---

[2] Two major Anglo-Dutch TNCs, Unilever and Shell are not only genuinely bi-national in structure but were already well established in several host-countries in the 1920s.

[3] Allende's nationalisation only completed a process begun 4 years before when both Anaconda and Kennecott had been forced to sell minority shares in the company to the state-owned Codelco.

hastened to invest and produce inside the United States, as did the Europeans. FDI became a two-way street.

Nor were the developing countries left out. Taiwan firms, for instance became major investors in South Africa, especially in the 'homelands'. Indian hotel chains expanded abroad in Asia and the Middle East. Two major airlines operating out of Hong Kong – both privately owned – took market shares from their triad-based competitors.

A third trend in global production may be the most politically significant of all. But it is the least recognised and the worst documented. It is the switch in employment, and in trade, from manufacturing to services, a change every bit as revolutionary as the earlier shift from agriculture, forestry and mining to industrial manufacturing. It is a shift in the production structure that is most evident in the rich industrialised countries. But it is one that fundamentally affects the whole world market economy. Peter Drucker has suggested that only one third of the extra wealth produced in the whole world economy in the last half-century has gone into extra material goods. Another third has gone in increased leisure for American, European and even Japanese workers. And the final third has gone into improved education and health care (Drucker, 1990: 171). These two non-material thirds are the base for the long and diverse list of services now offered and traded, both within and between national economies. That list includes transport services on land, sea and air; communications services by mail (conventional and electronic), by telephone and cable, fax, computer link-ups, data base information services; financial services, not only in banking but in insurance and re-insurance, asset management and the provision of complex financing arrangements, leasing and franchising deals; advertising and public relations; auction services in art, furniture and property; publishing and marketing of books, music, films and videos, magazines and news; international legal services, accountancy and management consulting. It also covers a wide range of medical and education services – even professional designing in architecture and construction.[4] Tourism and hotel services are also counted in the total of invisible exports, although – except for travel agencies – these differ from the rest in that they are not so predominantly a service sold to enterprises in the poor countries by enterprises in the rich ones, because more of the services are locally provided and customers come from the rich countries.

[4] The British Consultants Bureau estimated total fees earned by British architects for foreign contracts in 1994 at $3 billion (RIBA *Journal*, June 1995: 10–13).

This North–South asymmetry between sellers and buyers of services echoes the old asymmetry between manufacturing production in the North and primary production in the South. But it is in many ways more subtle and probably harder to escape. What is obvious is that no enterprise in a developing country can operate in and sell on the world market without making use of more than one of these services. Even the simplest export cargo has to be insured before it leaves harbour or airport. Even if locally insured, all but the most predictable of actuarial risks have to be usually laid off (i.e. re-insured) with one of the big international reinsurance firms who alone are big enough to take them on. Any financial arrangement involved in trade or investment also probably requires the services of a foreign as well as a local bank (see below, ch. 9).

In short, by opening up their economies to the world market, developing countries have certainly increased their chances of competing successfully in exported manufactures – but at the price of accepting increased dependence on the financial and marketing services provided by large firms in the developed countries. True, there are some new niche opportunities – software production in India is an example – which open up for them; and the foreign firms selling services will have their local offices or partners with job opportunities for what Drucker calls the 'knowledge workers'. But the social gap between them and the counter-culture of unskilled factory workers is bound to widen, in developing countries just as it has already in the United States, Europe and Japan. And while industrial labour was able to organise to improve its bargaining power with management, organising the new knowledge workers to bargain collectively is much more difficult because the diversity of their skills makes it impossible to fix a standard price for their labour. And in any case, they are not so conscious of the need for labour unions because their knowledge makes them so much more mobile both between firms and between countries. Thus the shift in employment and in trade from manufactures to services reinforces the other factors eroding the political authority and power of organised labour. And in doing so it undermines the neo-corporatist base of state power in those countries which have depended on tripartite negotiations between government, employers and unions to maintain social cohesion and support for the government.

Obviously, there are other political implications for states and for political parties that are, as yet, only dimly perceived. But there can be little doubt that this shift in the production structure will have social and political consequences every bit as far-reaching as the industrial revolution had in the past. Drucker is not alone in pointing out the impact on the national state of the technological changes in the dissemination of news by voice, pictures and digital signals. Censorship, police power and state control over information flows all belong to the past. That is clear. But what the social innovations will be that will follow the technology, just as surely as banks, conscript armies, post offices and civil services followed the industrial innovations of the nineteenth century, still lie hidden in the future.

Meanwhile, I have little doubt that these three trends add up to a substantial shift of power from territorial states to world markets, and indirectly therefore to the major operators in those markets, the transnational corporations. At this point, some readers will doubtless object that the evidence for the three main trends certainly shows a shift in the economy but that states surely remain the primary actors in the world system, and that the mere proliferation of TNCs does not mean that, either collectively or individually, they exercise more political power.

So, to meet this objection, let us return to the two theoretical points, about the nature of power and the limits of politics, that were made in earlier chapters. Power, it will be recalled, is to be gauged by influence over outcomes rather than mere possession of capabilities or control over institutions. Politics is to include all activities by which others are persuaded or coerced to collaborate in the achievement of aims designated and desired by another. The broader definition of power opens up the question, what outcomes? The broader definition of politics opens up the related question, what kind of aims?

The objection that, despite their growth, TNCs still exercise no significant political power by comparison with states can be sustained only if these two questions, what outcomes?, and what aims?, are both answered in very narrow terms. That is, if the only outcomes to be considered are those affecting international security – peace and war between states – and if the only aims relate strictly to the maintenance of international peace between states. No political theorist studying national or comparative politics would conceivably accept so narrow a definition. No political campaign manager would advise a candidate to fight an election solely on issues of security and order, excluding all the other issues of possible interest to the voters – of trade policy and monetary policies as they may affect economic growth and employment, or of social policies as they may affect people's housing, health, education and welfare chances. Why should world politics be any different? There, too, economic and social issues matter no less than security issues, as governments are only too well aware. Outcomes arising within the production structure, the financial structure and the knowledge structure no less than those in the security structure are part of the stuff of politics in the world economy.

In the production structure which is the subject of this chapter, there is evidence to support at least four major hypotheses. All of them sustain the argument that TNCs have come to play a significant role in determining who-gets-what in the world system. The first is that states collectively have retreated from their former participation in the ownership and control over industry, services and trade, and even from the direction of research and innovation in technology. On the max-min continuum of state/non-state decision-making over what is produced, how, by whom and where, the median line can be said to have moved from left to right.

The second hypothesis is that TNCs have done more than states and international aid organisations in the last decade to redistribute wealth from the developed industrialised countries to the poorer developing ones. Investment and trade have created many more jobs and done more to raise people's living standards than official aid programmes.

The third hypothesis is that in the important area of labour–management relations, TNCs have come to take away from governments the major role in resolving, or at least managing, conflicts of interest. And the fourth is that in fiscal matters, firms have increasingly escaped the taxation of corporate profits by governments and themselves are in some respects acting as tax-farmers and collectors of revenues.

Privatisation

The first hypothesis, that states collectively have moved out of the production of goods and services, hardly needs saying. In the sixth of the world that the old Soviet Union leaders used to boast was under socialist management the transition to private ownership is under way and is unlikely to be easily reversed – even if many of the new 'private' enterprises are in fact being run by former state managers wearing different hats. The change may be slow but it is inexorable as long as the state in Russia and central Europe no longer has the confidence nor the command over resources to take direct responsibility for production and trade.

Moreover, before the collapse of 1989, *all* research and development for Soviet industry was state-run and state-controlled, with the lion's share going to production for the armed forces. Much of the finance for that R&D has now vanished; how much of it is being replaced by R&D for civilian production by private enterprises is unknown. But the scale and importance of the shift is undeniable.

Elsewhere, in India, Brazil, Turkey, mainland China and many other developing countries, strenuous efforts are being made to privatise state-owned enterprises and to put both the development and the production processes into private hands. Though not all the desired sales go through, there is no visible movement in the other direction (Stopford and Strange, 1991: 121–3).

In America and Europe, too, there has been a retreat by government from involvement in both production and subsidised research in manufacturing. Take, for example, the semiconductor industry in the United States. In 1958, federal funding covered an estimated 85 per cent of overall American R&D in electronics. Between then and the early 1970s, the government continued this strong support, covering roughly one-half of the industry's development costs (Tyson, 1992: 89.), mainly for defence purposes. Thereafter, the US government's interest in the military applications of semiconductors was overtaken by the expansion of production for a rapidly growing civilian and global market. For this, the US government intervention was somewhat indirect, through the Sematech project. This was a cooperative, inter-company venture set up in 1988 to develop and disseminate advanced semiconductor processes technologies as a means of keeping up with Japanese competition. Although inspired and encouraged by the government, only half its $200 million a year budget was paid for by taxpayers, federal, state and local. The rest was funded by the firms. They continued to collaborate after 1993 when its five-year support by the state ended. Otherwise, US government policy concentrated more on the trade balance, especially through the SemiConductor Trade Agreement of 1986 with Japan. Yet Tyson's detailed and illuminating account of this agreement only claims partial success for it – 'manipulated' rather than managed trade was her description (Tyson, 1992: 106–54). She argued that the national interest still required support from the government for Sematech, but conceded that market forces, bringing increased competition and many new entrants like the Koreans, had caused prices to fall and the nature of competition between firms to change.

In Europe, governments had smaller defence budgets and less leverage over industry. But in the 1960s and 1970s, many were much more directly involved in supporting and subsidising private firms. Increasingly in the 1980s and 1990s, however, they have given up much of their former support for 'national champions' – firms given favourable treatment by the state in order to help them maintain a dominant presence in the home market and a competitive share in the world market. Even in France, where the bureaucracy and politicians clung longest to the idea of national champions, the government's influence has waned as the larger firms have found it necessary to expand their operations in the US and elsewhere (Savary, 1984: 157–90; Sally, 1992).[5]

Not surprisingly, at the European Community level, there was a deliberate effort in the 1980s to take the national champion strategy to a higher, communitarian level, by seeking to build European champions. This was done through a subsidised research and development programme for semiconductors. This comprised support for the ESPRIT consortia of firms engaging in pre-competitive R&D, the JESSI collaborative project and some support from inter-European strategic alliances between particular firms. The aim was to help European firms keep up with the Americans and the Japanese. But the results have been disappointing. The firms gladly took the subsidies offered but, as with Air France and other state-subsidised airlines in Europe, the subsidies did not guarantee competitiveness. Their collaboration never produced a really European champion in world markets (Lawton, 1995, van Walsum, 1994). The 1990s would see a retreat from unilateral and collective state intervention in support of European firms.

Meanwhile, the experience of support for European champions had revealed the problem – also discovered in the US – of deciding what was a European firm. The EC had excluded the British firm ICL from the ESPRIT programme after it came under the control of Fujitsu even though the firm still operated in Europe. And when it came to the car industry, the EC willingly accepted the European affiliates of Ford and General Motors but could not agree that European affiliates of Nissan or Honda were no different. The contradiction added to other arguments for keeping the state out of involvement in the market. These

[5] Savary's book was originally published in French in 1981. A supplement to it which was added when the English translation was published in 1984, noted the growing tendency of large French firms to expand faster abroad than at home, even though this added to their risks. Sally's 1992 thesis confirmed this trend and noted the weakening influence of French government over corporate strategies in the chemical sector.

European policy dilemmas also highlighted the extent to which the internationalisation of production is slowly but surely undermining the whole concept of nationality. While some writers on international business protest – with reason – that 'multinational' is a 'misnomer and that the TNCs are really only national firms operating in a world market' (Hu, 1993), the social signals of change tell another story. It is perfectly true that every firm has to have a corporate headquarters, a national base from which to operate; that boards of directors rarely include more than a token 'foreigner' (and not always even one); and that firms habitually look to their home governments for political and sometimes financial support. Yet at the same time, while corporate headquarters may stay 'at home' the financial 'holding' may find it advantageous to go abroad. The holding company for Mercedes-Benz, for example, is registered in Switzerland. There are a growing number of TNCs for whom the home market is *not* the most important part of the business. Northern Telecom is a Canadian company which employs more people in the United States, and earns more profits, than it does in Canada. The business done by several large chemical TNCs at home is dwarfed by the total amount of production under their control in other countries. So, while their executives may occasionally turn to the home government for support, this will not stop them at the same time turning for help and support to other governments acting as host to their offshore operations.

Moreover, their relations with governments are often less important than the negotiations they conduct with other firms. The story of foreign firms' attempts to break into the Japanese market despite the many informal barriers keeping them out shows clearly that while media attention has concentrated on the diplomacy between the US and Japanese governments, many of the big breakthroughs in the past were negotiated by (especially) US firms with Japanese firms (Strange, 1995; Mason and Encarnation, 1990; Encarnation, 1992).

Relocating manufacturing industry

Looking back to the 1960s, it is hard today to appreciate how deeply gloomy were the general expectations held then for the modernisation and industrialisation of Asia, Latin America and Africa. In Africa, the outlook outside of the Mahgreb and South Africa is still not bright. But in Latin America and Asia, the process of industrialisation had progressed by the 1990s beyond the wildest dreams of the 1960s. The difference between what most economists, most governments and international bureaucracies expected to happen, and what has actually happened, especially but not only in Asia, is enormous. The general assumption all along, by the government representatives of both rich countries and poor ones was that the dynamics of the world economy would keep manufacturing industry in the countries already industrialised. The 'Third World' so-called would remain the poor world. The only hope for it lay in a massive increase in foreign aid and a radical change in trade policies. This was the burden of the argument by the 1970s Commission named after Willy Brandt and set up by him with the help of Robert Macnamara at the World Bank. Yet the Brandt Reports fell on deaf ears in America, and state aid programmes instead of becoming more generous became even stingier and more directed to helping export industries than satisfying poor people's basic needs. A much-praised report for the World Bank by the economist Wassily Leontief in 1977 called *The Future of the World Economy* proclaimed there were no physical barriers to sustained economic growth in developing countries – but it was not very optimistic about the prospects for change in the policies of the rich countries and the institutional arrangements that existed to help them. Leontief's input–output calculations led him to foresee a large and probably insurmountable payments deficit as a major obstacle in the path of economic progress and industrialisation in developing countries.[6]

Where everybody went wrong was in assuming that change could come only at the level of state policies. True, state policies in the host countries were crucial to success. Domestic saving had to be kept high by one means or another. Government had to be stable and reliable. Workers had to be both plentiful, cheap and literate. But if such conditions were met, structural change and the response of firms in the industrialised countries to it could – and did – work wonders. This was the argument developed in *Rival States, Rival Firms* (Stopford and Strange, 1991). Given accelerating technological change, the greater mobility of capital and the improvement in transport and communications, the attractions of shifting their production to developing countries

---

[6] At about this time, Walt Rostow was one of the few economists who took a more optimistic view, arguing that the latecomers to modernisation could still catch up, as the Japanese were then doing. But for politically correct reasons, Rostow was never taken seriously by other liberal economists. And even he thought population growth would hold progress to a crawl and that only government action to check births and increase resource transfers could make a difference (Rostow, 1978. See also a comparative summary of Leontief's and Rostow's predictions in the *Economist*, 19 August 1978).

was going to prove irresistible for manufacturing firms in America, Europe and Japan (and later in Korea, Taiwan, India, Brazil etc.) They, and not government aid programmes, were going to accelerate the modernisation of developing countries. Sometimes it has been done by the sale of patent rights, more often by the licensing of patented technology, by joint ventures with local firms, and by strategic alliances in which the TNC offers quick, dependable market access through its established brand name or through its distribution networks of dealers and retailers.

Managing labour relations

The conventional political wisdom in Europe and America from the 1930s or earlier through to the end of the 1960s or later was that the protection of workers from their employers was a major responsibility of a modern state. Either – as in the New Deal in America – the state set strict new rules guaranteeing the workers' rights to organise in defence of their interests and incomes. Or, as in Japan and many parts of Europe, the state initiated and supervised corporatist arrangements by which the interests of labour were reconciled with those of management and investors and with the overall economic strategies of the government. Typically, annual negotiations were held at which targets were set for prices (and therefore inflation rates), wages and profits. In a nutshell, for most of the twentieth century in most industrialised countries, relations between management and labour were considered a necessary aspect of public policy.

But in recent years, neo-corporatism has encountered new difficulties. National economic management has become subject to upsets in financial markets, and to economic forces beyond government control. It is not only in the US that job security in manufacturing industry cannot be guaranteed by anyone, least of all the government. And it is not only in recession-hit sectors of industry that the *political* management of labour relations has shifted from the offices of government ministries to the boardrooms of transnational companies.

Instead of wages and working conditions being fought over within the context of state laws on industrial relations, or within institutional arrangements of a neo-corporatist nature. much more of the bargaining now takes place within the firm. As the company has extended its operations to locations in a number of other countries, it has been up to management to establish some political balance between the claims upon it of its workforce at home and the claims upon it of workers, backed in some cases by their governments, in its foreign affiliates or partners. Firms, just like states, can be conceived as social institutions for the coordination of potentially conflicting interests. The managers of Volkswagen in Wolfsburg, or of General Motors in Detroit, or of Matsushita in Tokyo, may decide that corporate strategy requires investment in the newest plant to be made in the Czech Republic, in Brazil or in Malaysia. In due course, new workers will have to be hired, new suppliers engaged. The old workers, and the local suppliers at home, will have to be convinced to cooperate, not resist. No less than getting voters to believe in a party nominee, managers have a political task in getting their employees to see that the longterm success of the firm (and their own prospects of employment) is the imperative. They have to be persuaded that internationalising manufacturing is not a zero-sum game in which if the foreign affiliate's workers get more jobs and more pay, the workers at home get less of both.

A lot of academic analysis of labour relations and employment issues has not yet recognised the importance of this shift. And governments, especially in Europe, have been slow to change. The social chapter in the Maastricht Treaty was obsolete even before the treaty was signed.

Tax issues

No analysis of the political role of TNCs in the world economy would be complete that gave no attention to the issue of taxation – both to the role of firms as tax-avoiding elements in national political economies, and to their more subtle role as tax-gathering organisations that accumulate revenues from their operations in the world economy and then take politically important decisions about how to allocate them. Let us take first the changes that have affected the power of states to raise revenue from corporations.

As Picciotto observed, 'Taxation is the point of most direct intervention between government and citizens, the state and the economy' (Picciotto, 1993: xiii). From the earliest times, rulers have looked for ways to get ordinary people to pay for the costs of government – preferably with something over to spend on themselves. And from earliest times, people have tried to avoid being taxed. But what has changed is: firstly, the needs and demands of governments; secondly, the means used by governments to raise revenue; and thirdly – thanks to the growth of trade and international production – the (declining) ability of governments to exercise exclusive rights to tax within their territorial borders.[7]

Of course, taxation was never a problem for centrally planned economies like the old USSR or the PRC. The state that owned the means of production and distribution could very easily exploit its monopoly control to appropriate labour, materials and credit for whatever purposes it chose – including a lavish lifestyle for party leaders. Even in market economies, governments sometimes conscripted soldiers and ran state monopolies (of salt, tobacco or alcohol, for example) for profit. For most of history, however, rulers of all kinds used the immobility of peasants to tax land, and the control of borders to raise revenue by tariffs and excise duties. Both were relatively easy to administer, but not very efficient in yielding revenue.

Income tax – a means of direct rather than indirect taxation – was introduced in Britain in the Napoleonic wars, when it supplemented the time-honoured resort to inflation to pay the (rising) cost of fighting enemies. (A capital levy which might have been another option would have been politically resisted and hard to impose by force.) But for a century or more in the most economically advanced country, Britain, no distinction was made between individual and corporate income. Only in the First World War – again a costly enterprise – did the British government impose a special excess profits tax on firms. It did so again in the late 1930s, discriminating against distribution as compared with reinvested profits. It was not till 1965 that a tax specifically aimed at corporations was introduced.

Already by that time the increase in world trade and international investment had revealed a basic conflict of interest between governments. Those whose firms were exporting capital claimed the right to tax 'their' firms wherever they operated for profit. Otherwise, such firms would have had an unfair advantage over stay-at-home enterprises. But their host governments also wanted to tax foreign firms so that they had no better treatment than local ones. The firms, caught between the two, had strong incentives not just in avoiding being taxed twice over on the same income but for actually understating their foreign profits to both governments. Aware of this, both governments also had a common interest in seeing that they did not get away with

---

[7] Actually, rights to tax have seldom been exclusive to the state. In the past, too, priests as well as rulers demanded money, as tithes or by overcharging for 'services rendered'; and local landlords and barons, not to mention robbers, pirates and highwaymen competed with monarchs and emperors for tax revenues. The game is an old one; just the competition takes new forms.

such tax evasion. Could they find a way to resolve their conflict of interest so as to serve their common interest in raising revenue? A case, if ever there was one, for an international regime!

It has never been achieved. There are only bilateral double taxation agreements between pairs of governments, constituting a loose and laboriously constructed system for the coordination of tax jurisdictions (Picciotto, 1992: xiii). This ramshackle system has in fact generated a kind of epistemic community of people whose careers actually benefit from its shortcomings. For fiscal experts, academic lawyers, management consultants and officials have to constantly negotiate with their opposite numbers on a case-by-case basis, and what is more, to do it in secret to avoid complaints of inequity and special treatment.

This lack of agreement between states on a set of common global principles for taxing business profits has been apparent since the early days of the League of Nations. Its Finance Committee made a first report on it in 1923. Then a 1933 report, written by a delegate of the US Commerce Department – even though the US was not a member of the League – identified even then the possibilities for firms of avoiding tax by transfer pricing and the use of tax havens. By the 1980s, the number of transnational firms intent on avoiding tax and the number of tax havens helping them to do so had grown enormously (Johns, 1983). The need for a proper universal tax regime was greater than ever. But the 1988 model convention carefully drawn up by the OECD in collaboration with the Council of Europe was strenuously resisted by business interests. It was rejected by the governments of Britain, Germany, Switzerland and Australia and has remained therefore a dead letter.

As Picciotto observes, 'The greatest constraint on the state's assertion of its right to tax business stems from the international mobility of capital' (Picciotto, 1992: 309). So that while international lawyers insist there is no limit on a state's *right* to tax, the open world market economy means that its actual *ability* to collect taxes outside its territory is severely limited. This is so whether it is a government trying to tax profits from the foreign operations of its own firms, or a government seeking to tax the profits of foreign firms operating within its formal jurisdiction. Of the two, the greater loss is probably that of developing countries. They cannot get much tax from low wages and have all the more need therefore to tax profits. A general system of arbitration would surely redress somewhat their bargaining weaknesses. And their tax officers would gain access to all sorts of useful information from a global tax regime and with it would be able to confront much more effectively the transfer pricing, understated profits and overstated expenses now customarily claimed by foreign firms.

The one serious attempt by a host state to assert greater tax claims on foreign business was made in the late 1970s by the state of California. Circumstances there were peculiar in that the state had large and rising costs for welfare and for infrastructure to cope with a population swollen by immigration (by Americans as well as Mexicans and other Hispanics). Its voters were rich and tax-resistant. Yet a number of Japanese, European and other foreign firms were so eager to get into the US market that they were prepared to sustain short-term losses in the expectation of long-term gains. Normally, such initial losses would keep local tax liability low. The unitary tax however proposed to assess them on the basis of their total, global profits, divided according to the percentage of global operations located in California.

In the end, the bid failed. Some firms left. Others threatened to leave, and at a time when jobs in defence industries were being cut and military bases closed. More important, the federal government (and its courts) were unwilling to concede control over fiscal policy to the states.

The social and political consequences of this situation are almost entirely overlooked in the large literature on foreign investment and international production.[8] Yet it is clear that the failure of governments to devise a common tax regime imposes serious costs on all of them. Picciotto concludes that the strengthening of an international institutional basis for international taxation is an urgent necessity. Yet there is little reason to suppose that major players are going to change their mind. Meanwhile, one obvious consequence is that the national tax burden falls increasingly on the individual citizen, and to a growing extent, through the speed of value-added forms of indirect taxation, on small local businesses. While government spending stays high, states are increasingly tempted to resort to borrowing, usually by issuing bonds, to meet their bills. The dangers of this addictive habit have been well described by another tax expert-historian, Michael Veseth. His book, *Mountains of Debt* vividly described the perils of government borrowing first by the rulers of fourteenth-century Florence, and later in the nineteenth century by Britain. The US, now the world's largest

[8] A notable exception was a 1975 monograph by Robin Murray, *Multinationals and Nation States* (London, Spokesman Books). This had a short chapter on fiscal policy making the point that tax havens and transfer pricing by TNC's greatly weakened the ability of the state to enforce company taxation.

debtor, Veseth argued, ought to learn from their mistakes before its fiscal deficit becomes unviable (Veseth, 1990).

It was a Harvard Business School professor, Lou Wells, who first likened the practices of large firms to those of eighteenth century tax farmers. These were enterprising characters who paid (among others) the French government for the right to collect taxes in the name of the king. What made the concession worthwhile, of course, was that the tax farmer could line his own pocket in the process. No one could check up on how much he could actually extract from the suffering peasants. But they and the state coffers were the poorer.

In our own times, most governments hold corporations liable to pay taxes on company profits. But there are no clear, universally applied rules on how much they actually pay as a proportion of sales or value-added. Tax is calculated after various expenses are deducted. The oil companies are an extreme case. In the 1950s, the US government allowed them to deduct from their tax liability to the United States the amounts paid in royalties to the governments of the oil-producing countries in the Middle East. The predictable result was that they paid no American tax, and in due course little or nothing to European governments either. The amount of tax paid on North Sea operations, for instance, was a matter of arbitrary negotiation with the British and other governments.

Banks too have been allowed by governments (led, of course, by the US government) to use profits to build up reserves to compensate for their imprudent loan practices. High and rising interest rates set by the markets have increased their income from loans, and increased volatility and uncertainty has added to their income from management fees of various kinds. But the amount of tax paid over to the state has not increased accordingly.

More generally, the passing of power from shareholders to managers has gone on unchecked since it was first observed in the 1930s (Burnham, 1943; Berle and Means, 1932). One consequence – perhaps especially marked in the Anglo-American financial systems – has been a marked rise in the rewards to managers, both in terms of salaries, of severance payments – golden handshakes or parachutes – and of stock options, to say nothing of the perquisites of office in first-class air travel, expense accounts for restaurant bills and luxury hotel accommodation and not least the regiment of chauffeurs, gardeners, masseurs, social secretaries, even doctors, dentists and lawyers – who in olden times would have made up the retinue of a landed aristocracy. All that the corporate executives lack today is a personal chaplain – but perhaps his role is now taken up by the company psychiatrist.

Conclusions

From all the above, we can conclude that while TNCs do not take over from the governments of states, they have certainly encroached on their domains of power. They are increasingly exercising a parallel authority alongside governments in matters of economic management affecting the location of industry and investment, the direction of technological innovation, the management of labour relations and the fiscal extraction of surplus value.

5   The state of the state

Scholars in international relations spent a great deal of time in the last thirty years arguing about, comparing and analysing various paradigms, or conceptual perceptions, of the international system. In the 1970s they were also arguing about methodologies – how to study and research international affairs. These debates continue.

But by the closing years of the twentieth century, the major debate in international studies is a new one. It is between those scholars who think that, even after the end of the Cold War, very little has changed, and those who are convinced a great deal has changed (Krasner, RIPE, 1994; Strange, RIPE, 1994). Since the central hypotheses of this book belong in the latter camp, and since the fundamental argument is really about the role of states in the international system, serious consideration has to be given to the views of those who maintain that, in essence, there has been, and still is, continuity in the international system from its inception. Some would go so far as to say it all started with the Sumerian city-state in the 3rd millennium BC and continued right up to the collapse of the Soviet empire nearly 5000 years later (Watson, 1993; Buzan, forthcoming). That *longue durée* view of human history is perhaps extreme – the historical sociologists emphasise that in ancient Mesopotamia as in ancient central America, state authority owed so much to religious superstition that it has little in common with the modern secular state. But there are many more scholars who take the more modest position that the essentials of the international society of states – the Westphalian system, as it is often called – have not radically changed since the middle of the seventeenth century. With the end of the Cold War between the American and Russian superpowers, they argue that a bipolar balance

* A shorter, earlier version of this chapter was published in the *Tsukuba Review of International Political Economy*, vol. 1, no. 1, 1995.

of power between states has merely been replaced by a multipolar balance – or, others argue, by a sort of unipolar system, since with the disintegration of one superpower, only one, the United States is left.

Paradoxically (or perhaps understandably), the alternative view that human society is undergoing major structural changes that also affect the place and function of states in their relations with each other is more evident among scholars who are *not* specialists in international relations. This has long been perceived by the historical sociologists (Mann, 1986; Hall, 1986; Chase-Dunn, 1989; Sklair, 1991). Recently, it can also be seen in current work by the geographers – perhaps because they have always been more interested in maps of physical geography than of political geography (Dicken, 1992; Corbridge and Thrift, 1994). It is evident among some lawyers who argue that states are not the only sources of legal authority, either today or in the past (Teubner, 1993; Weiler, 1994). It can be found in much recent work by scholars concerned with management and the organisation of business, who see the strong development of networks of economic enterprises, transcending state frontiers, confusing state agencies and replacing the hierarchical firm as the dominant model for the production of goods and services (Michalet, 1993; Kobrin, 1995). This insight is significant for the authority of the state since it has hitherto been the state which conferred 'corporate personality' on the firm, even though this was always little more than a convenient fiction. If individual firms are no longer the 'engines of growth', so to speak, in the national economy, and networks work across state frontiers, then the link between nation-state and national enterprise is substantially weakened. It almost seems as though the resistance of writers on international relations comes from their vested interest in an academic discipline which would hardly exist as a separate specialism if states were shown to be less dominant than they used to be.

For international political economists, already acutely conscious of working in a no-man's-land between politics and economics, the breakdown of protective professional barriers between one speciality in the social sciences and another, presents no new threat. They have already learnt to live dangerously in the midst of intellectual diversity. The notion that major structural changes have so affected the world economy and world society that the nature of world politics – aka international relations – has changed is no problem. They can concede that, to outward appearances, the world of states may look no different. But if it is true that, behind the facade, the reality is very different and states are more vulnerable to markets where once markets were regulated and controlled by states, then this only means that the problematics of international political economy are more numerous than (and certainly different from) the old problematics of the study of international relations.

For those unfamiliar with the literature of international relations, some clarification may be necessary of the three or four main points of difference between the nothing-has-changed professors of international relations and the maybe-a-lot-has-changed writers in international political economy. Firstly, all the standard texts in international relations insist that states are the primary 'actors' in the international system. If the cast list in the human drama includes other entities, these 'actors' play only bit parts. They do not greatly influence the course of dramatic events (Morgenthau, 1956; Holsti, 1967; Waltz, 1979; Bull, 1977). International political economists, for the most part, do not agree. Depending on the issue, it may be that banks or the oil companies, or the drug barons of Colombia, or large multinational enterprises are just as important as states in determining the who-gets-what questions that have always lain at the centre of the study of politics.

Secondly, writers on international relations for the most part have assumed states to be unitary actors. That is, that in relations with other states, governments adopt a united front, based on an agreed consensus concerning the national interest of the state. If the further assumption is made that states are not only unitary actors but also rational ones, then international relations can be analysed according to the logic of rational choice and satisfactorily understood with the help of game theory borrowed from economics. Some writers, it is true, have conceded that in reality governments may be playing two-level games at the same time. They are bargaining to get their way with other governments and, at the same time, bargaining domestically with their social constituents, or with other political parties, in order to remain in power as representatives of the state (Putnam, 1988). But problems of logic arise if, instead of two-level games, it is conceded that the heads of government may be playing any number of simultaneous games, and playing each of them as a rational actor. For rationality means having the same preferences, presumably based on a certain priority of preferred outcomes in which some core values or standards of conduct are ranked above others – loyalty to friends above honesty perhaps, or fair play above personal gain. Yet in playing many games simultaneously, it may well be that what is rational in one relationship may reflect exactly opposite preferences to what seems rational in another relationship. Rationality on the part of a unitary actor then becomes an absurdity. And indeed, most scholars in comparative politics, together with a good many in particular aspects of international relations do recognise that the long separation of international relations from domestic political relations has been totally artificial. Governments that are weak at home cannot act as decisively or effectively as those with a strong domestic power base. Attitudes in international negotiations on human rights, on refugees and migration, on environmental protection and any number of other issues will be largely determined by the balance of political forces within the country (Keohane and Milner, forthcoming).

The third point of difference between international relations and international political economy concerns the core question of the study – what the French call the *problematique*. The primacy of states as the main actors in international relations is only defensible if the premise is accepted that war and peace and the resolution of inter-state conflicts is the primary issue in world politics, and the main reason why people should study international relations. Since it is states that make war, and whose conflicts of interest may lead to war and to the deaths and wounding of millions of people, that is reason enough for the study of the relations between them.

That premise, however, is one which many international political economists do not accept. Security is not the only issue for world economy and world society. Who gets rich and who stays poor, who has access to doctors, medicines and hospitals and who has not, whether rain forests, or tigers, are protected, and whether the ozone layer is progressively damaged by CFC gases are also important *problématiques*. Moreover, violence to a person or damage to property can be caused in other ways than by wars between states. Indeed, both can be caused by agents of the state – like the Stasi in east Germany or the KGB in Russia – acting against their own people. Dissidents in China have more to fear from their own state than from any possible foreign invader. Therefore, I have argued, the structures that provide security have to be conceived in a much more comprehensive way. Inter-state war is only part of the problem. In many parts of the world today, civil war, ethnic conflict or simple crime within states, if unchecked, may offer much greater threats to life and property than inter-state war.

There are other matters affecting world society and economy, where it is obvious that states are no longer always the primary, let alone the sole, actors. In the three other major structures of the international political economy – the production structure, the financial structure and the knowledge structure – actors other than states, the players of 'bit parts', will often play more decisive roles in determining what gets produced where, and by whom; in choosing who gets access to credit and who gains and who loses in the casinos of international finance; or in persuading others to share fundamental beliefs about society and economy or to decide what knowledge is sought for and acquired and by whom, and to whom it is, or is not communicated. On all these issues, states may provide a framework of legal rights and duties within which other actors influence outcomes. Or they may be merely the arena, the stage or the circus roof beneath which the action is played out. That is not the same as being always and on all important issues the *primary* actors, as writers on international relations have often claimed.

The fourth and last point of difference concerns the relations between the state and the individual man or woman. The final argument of the realists when they assert that nothing, fundamentally, has changed is that individuals identify so closely with 'their' state that for them their primary loyalty belongs to the state. Their identity is first and foremost a national identity – as a German, an Italian, a Brazilian or an Australian. Others would contest this, arguing that in real life, subjective perceptions of individual identity are much more complex. In real life, people often identify themselves, first and foremost as members of a family; 'My name is so-and-so; I am the son (or daughter) of such-and-such'. They may also identify themselves as coming from a particular village or town, or a region. In Europe especially people are more likely to tell you they are Sicilian or Bavarian or Scottish than that they are Italian, German or British. The passport they carry is less important to them than their fellow-feeling with people from the same town or province. Ask them more about themselves and they will often identify themselves by profession or occupation, or by religious or political affiliation or even by the football/baseball team they support. Identity, in short, is cultural and geographical as much as it is national. Chinese especially identify with a large, ancient and important culture that spreads far beyond the Peoples' Republic not only to Taiwan Singapore and Malaysia but to 'Chinatowns' in San Francisco, London, Manchester, Melbourne and Vancouver.

In very few territorial states, however, is 'national' identity entirely natural and organic. In most, it has been deliberately engineered and cultivated by the political community of a ruling elite. In this respect, Japan is exceptional in that the society was sufficiently homogeneous that it was not necessary to invent or impose a common national identity on the great majority of people. In Europe, North and South America, Africa and the Indian sub-continent it was different. After the French Revolution the rising middle classes took over government from an aristocracy which had relied heavily on feudal loyalties to maintain their wealth and power. They appropriated the state, so to speak, for the nation, and in the name of the people. But in doing so they used force as well as cultural means – like free schooling, national flags and anthems and colourful historical myths – in order to assimilate ethnic or religious minorities. The strength of the state in relation to its neighbours depended on its social cohesion and this did not allow strong competing identities. Forging American national identity in the United States was necessitated less by fear of neighbours than in Europe, but instead there were the exigencies of assimilating large numbers of polyglot and often illiterate immigrants in whom respect for established authority, symbolised by the American flag, had to be implanted. Much the same was true in Brazil or Argentina or Australia. In Africa, the boundaries of states were largely inherited from European colonial powers and it was a matter of chance which tribal or other groups managed, after independence, to appropriate the powers of government in the state.

The crucial question, however, is not whether the feelings of identity with a particular nation and its state are spontaneous or artificial. It is, firstly, whether the feelings confer legitimacy on the authority of the state above all others; and, secondly, whether, given feelings of identity, and given the acknowledgment of legitimacy, the state can also count on the individual's loyalty. To put it another way, I have feelings of identity with other citizens of State X. I acknowledge it has legitimate authority over us. Do I therefore give it my loyalty to the extent of saying 'My country, right or wrong'? The progression from the first to the other two statements is not necessary nor logical. Some people in some states for example, may feel the sense of identity, but may acknowledge the legitimate authority of the state only because they are obliged to do so, and because the penalties of challenging that legitimacy are too severe. They obey the rules laid down by the state, and conform to the policies decided by the government because that is the line of least resistance; anything for a quiet life. But it may not follow from conformity and acquiescence that their primary loyalty is to the state, or that there are no limits to the sacrifice the individual is voluntarily prepared to make in showing that loyalty.

It is at this point that realist thinkers in international relations make an extreme claim. They hold that despite interdependence and globalisation and all that, the individual human being still identifies with the society living inside the territorial borders of the state, acknowledges the latter's legitimate authority and *therefore* is loyal to the state to the point of sacrificing life itself for the good of the state. Now, this may have been true in the past. Europeans, including committed socialists, answered their country's call in the First World War, and many died as a result. They did so again in the Second World War, and in Japan especially there was no shortage of young men ready to die in suicide attacks on the enemy.

Today it is much more doubtful that the state – or at least the great majority of states – can still claim a degree of loyalty from the citizen substantially greater than the loyalty given to family, to the firm, to the political party or even in some case to the local football team. The exceptions are the few states whose very survival is under great immediate threat – Israel, Chechenya, Bosnia, possibly North Korea. It may be true, as the realists insist, that the global company does not call on its employees to face death for the good of the firm – though some, such as war correspondents in the media, may do so, and though the firm very often calls on its employees to work long hours, to change the work they are used to doing, to go and live in places far from home, among strangers and in strange climates. But then in today's world, the state does not ask citizens to die for it either. The loyalty given to the state is, in general, no different in degree from the loyalty given to the employer. Apart from professional soldiers, people in stable political societies do not expect to have to sacrifice their lives for anyone – except perhaps their families.[1] Loyalty of the kind that is ready to die for a cause is more often found among ethnic or religious minorities – the Tamil Tigers, the Irish republican militants or their Ulster loyalist counterparts, the Palestinians or the Kurds – than it is among the ordinary citizens in the average state. In short, the realists' claim that there is a fundamental difference of degree, or of intensity, between the loyalty owed and given to the authority of the state and the loyalty owed and given to other forms of authority cannot be easily sustained. On some issues, and in some circumstances, state authority will be given priority. On other issues, and in other circumstances, it will not.

To say this is not the same as saying the state as an institution is disappearing, that it is on the way out, or that it is being ousted by the

---

[1] And in the US, for example, public opinion is visibly unhappy if even a few of its professional soldiers are killed when US armed forces are sent abroad.

multinationals or any other kind of authority. It is only saying that it is undergoing a metamorphosis brought on by structural change in world society and economy. This metamorphosis means that it can no longer make the exceptional claims and demands that it once did. It is becoming, once more and as in the past, just one source of authority among several, with limited powers and resources.

To test this assertion, let us consider in more detail the ten more important powers or responsibilities attributed to the state, and still claimed for it by many political leaders.

1. The right to sacrifice the lives of individual citizens clearly related to the state's responsibility for defending national territory against foreign invasion. If all were at risk, it is only logical to conclude that some may have to be sacrificed *pro bono publico*. The decline – at least in most developed countries – in the citizen's sense of obligation to the state referred to above is directly related to the general perception that the risk of foreign invasion is minimal in many societies, declining in most. Professional armies are maintained in case of need – but this may be for intervention overseas or, in some cases, to support the government in power against dissident minorities. In general, territory is no longer a crucial factor in determining the prosperity of the national society. Competition for world market shares has replaced competition for territory as the name of the game between states (Strange, 1990; Stopford and Strange, 1991). At the same time, war has become more costly, both in lives and in resources. The perceived need for the state as an institution necessary to defend society against violence within or beyond its territory still exists, but in many societies at a much lower level.

2. The second basic responsibility of the state is probably to maintain the value of the currency. Adam Smith and the classical political economists looking back on some of the monetary messes of the eighteenth century, certainly thought so. The market economy cannot function without a stable medium of exchange, and it cannot grow unless savings are secure against depreciation. The IMF today surveying the record on economic transition in the ex-socialist countries agrees; in its view, the Baltic republics managed the transition successfully because of their control over inflation, while Russia did not and mainly because of the failure to manage the currency and restrict the money supply (IMF Survey, 3 April 1995). Yet while responsibility formally rests with the individual state, the record of recent decades suggests that this responsibility is now both a national and a collective one. Inflation in one important economy can easily spread to others. The inflation affecting the United States in the 1970s spread to all but the strongest industrial countries like Germany and Japan. It affected the prices of most commodities traded on world markets. The main reason for France and Belgium linking their currencies so firmly to the Deutschemark in the 1990 – and thus incidentally admitting their inability to maintain the value of their respective francs without outside assistance – was to convince the markets that they were seriously committed to stable money.

3. Choosing the appropriate form of capitalist development is generally thought to be a major responsibility of the state. Variations of the capitalist model are primarily the result of political choices by governments past and present (Crouch and Streeck, forthcoming). Models diverge on two major issues: how far the state intervenes in the market economy by ownership and control of the means of production and distribution and by acting as the regulatory authority over private enterprise; and how far it assumes responsibility for social welfare. The issue of divergence was first raised in Andrew Shonfield's *Modern Capitalism* (Shonfield, 1963). More recently, Michel Albert in France has drawn a sharp distinction between what he calls Rhenish capitalism and the Anglo-Saxon variety (Albert, 1990). American authors especially have drawn equally sharp distinctions between 'western' models of capitalism and 'Asian' ones, of which Japan is the prototype, and Korea, Taiwan and Singapore are regional variants (Tyson, 1992; Prestowitz, 1993; Hart, 1993; OTA, 1993). In the Asian model, the state more actively intervenes to protect domestic enterprises from foreign competition, to provide them with ready access to capital for expansion, while using what political measures seem necessary to the government to maintain political stability and confidence in the economic future.

In the economic literature on development, too, there has been much discussion over the role of public policy in developing countries in choosing between import substitution and export orientation (World Bank references: Prebisch, 1950; Ariff and Hill, 1985; Krueger, 1988; Cline, 1987; Porter, 1990). The weight of argument by professional liberal economists, and by officials of the IMF and World Bank has been strongly against import substitution and protectionism, even though the east Asian record of success in gaining market shares suggests the either–or choice is over-simple. As Singer has argued, export-orientation is often possible only after an earlier phase of import-substitution (Singer, 1989).

For present purposes, however, the question is not so much which opinion or interpretation was the correct one, for any particular economy or at any specific time, as whether or not the governments of states still have as much freedom to choose the national development strategy as they have had in the past. Put another way, are the differences between forms of capitalism likely to persist in future, or are the forces of structural change pushing all governments along a path to greater convergence between models of capitalism? If the evidence of convergence suggests the latter, then the freedom and responsibility of states to choose between variants of capitalist development is reduced.

That evidence is to be found in various places. In the development literature, the U-turns of government in the last ten years in many developing countries, from India to Mexico, from Tunisia to Myanmar, are incontrovertible. Trade has been rapidly liberalised; public enterprises have been privatised; foreign firms made welcome. In the management literature, especially in US business schools, Japanese methods of management are analysed and western firms are strongly recommended to adopt just-in-time stock control, consensus-seeking among groups of workers and managers, a longer-term corporate strategy and a more research-oriented use of human and financial resources. Conversely, in Japan, the pressure from business associations led by the Keidanren on the state bureaucracy to deregulate and to open the economy to foreign competition has visibly grown in recent years. The trend to convergence, moreover, is strongly reinforced by the coincident trend toward strategic alliances between firms in each of the main industrialised regions of the world. The Mitsubishi-Siemens-IBM networking agreement is one among many in which major enterprises agree to work together to develop new technology and exploit market opportunities.

4. Correcting the tendency of market economies to cyclical booms and slumps has been another major responsibility assigned to the state, and accepted from the 1930s onwards by governments of many developed countries. 'We are all keynesians now!' President Nixon was supposed to have remarked in the 1970s. But by then the capability of any individual government to prime the pump of economic activity was already shown to be much restricted. The oil price rise of 1973 brought

75

on the 'stagflation' recession of the mid-1970s and a down-turn in growth rates, from which European governments struggled to escape. The Volcker–Reagan change of monetary policy in 1981/2 while it certainly checked inflation also imposed deflation and depression not only on indebted developing countries but on the world economy in general. Attempting to buck the trend, President Mitterrand in France planned massive investment in public works and state enterprises financed in part by foreign capital. The result was negative. Financial markets were reluctant to help and French capital took flight abroad. Keynesian counter-cyclical measures no longer worked at the national level. And at the global level, cooperative agreement was lacking on how much counter-cyclical action was desirable; and, if desirable, how it was to be done and where the funds were to come from. An ideal opportunity occurred with the collapse of the Soviet empire and of the state-trading arrangements under the auspices of Comecon. A Marshall Plan for east and central Europe could have been devised and put into effect – except that there was no support for it forthcoming from the United States, the governments of the European Community were divided and in particular the Germans were distracted by their own problems of German unification. Moreover, the central Europeans themselves proved highly resistant to any suggestion that they should act collectively in the mutually preferential way the western Europeans (under pressure from the Americans) had in the postwar period.

5. Providing a safety-net for those least able to survive successfully in a market economy – the old and the young, the sick and disabled, and the unemployed. If the state was no longer so important to civil society as a shield against military attack, it was perhaps still essential as a shield against economic insecurity.

It is certainly true that the welfare function of the state has been the chief reason for the expansion of state bureaucracies, and the rise in government spending as a proportion of GNP, in many countries. Even in the United States where the federal government has never assumed responsibility for health care or for unemployment to the extent that is commonly accepted in Europe, the government has substantially extended its intervention in the market in order to protect the consumer, the natural environment, the factory workers and others by means of increased regulation of private enterprises. It is this extension of state intervention that persuades many people that the role of the state is in no way declining but, rather, is actually increasing.

The question for the future, however, is whether that extension has not reached its limit, inasmuch as state budgets will no longer allow the addition of new standards of welfare spending and new expansions of the bureaucratic machinery to administer welfare programmes and to enforce protective regulation. If indeed, the state's provision of military security is no longer considered crucial and is therefore likely to decline, while its provision of economic security has reached its highest point, it could be that the net value of national government to society is headed for decline.

6. The above open question relates to the sixth attribute of the state – its responsibility for taxation. That responsibility has been jealously guarded from encroachment by international organisations from the earliest international public unions of the nineteenth century to the squabbles in the Budgetary Committee of the United Nations. The only international organisations that were not kept dependent on national contributions, determined by national governments, were the international banks whose functions allowed them to charge for their services, and a few rare exceptions like the Rhine and Danube Commissions which could levy tariffs on river traffic to defray their expenses.

Yet as argued elsewhere in this book, the power of governments to raise revenue is no longer an exclusive monopoly of state power; it is shared with powerful criminal associations (see chapter 8). Nor is it anything like so unconstrained as it was in past times. The internationalisation of production and the incorporation of enterprises in multiple countries, including tax havens, has insulated a great deal of international business from the exactions of the tax authorities (see chapter 4). The tax paid by corporations in practice nowadays is the consequence of *ad hoc*, secret bargaining between the firm and the two or more tax authorities claiming a share of its profits (Picciotto, 1992). Their rivalry ensures that governments cannot increase the amount of spending financed by taxing business. Nor can it in most cases significantly expand the amount financed by direct or indirect taxation of the individual. Voters in America, Europe or elsewhere do not elect parties that look likely to raise income taxes. And the competition between states for private investment sets a limit to the revenue that can be raised from indirect taxation, either by sales or property taxes.

7. The seventh responsibility claimed by states is linked to, but distinct from, its overall development strategy. It is responsibility for the control

77

over foreign trade, especially imports. This is one policy area where there is a particularly substantial gap between the claims of states and the actual outcomes in trade. The question is how much is imported, from whom and at what price. But on this the literature of social science, both in economics and international relations, is mostly very misleading. It suggests that the amount, direction and content of international trade is the result of state intervention by tariffs, quotas or non-tariff barriers of various kinds. The fears, voiced by the world's media almost without exception, that disaster would follow if the delegations to the multilateral trade negotiations in the Uruguay Round failed to reach agreement were based on those assumptions. Yet they have less basis in fact today than they had even in the 1930s. Even then, economic historians, including liberal economists, were not convinced that the protective tariffs put on in the depths of the world depression had much effect on the direction, volume and content of trade flows. Today they have even less. The content is determined by firms and their response to markets. The direction likewise is a consequence of demand and competitive supply, and the ability of governments to penalise imports from particular sources is very limited. The United States government has attempted to get agreement by the Japanese government to quantitative targets on Japanese exports to the United States – but with little success. And this is not because the Japanese government resisted, but that it had little control over the aggregate result of multiple corporate decisions. The one serious attempt at managed international trade – the Multifibre Agreement on trade in textiles and clothes – became such a shambles of deceit and diversion through third parties that it had to be abandoned.

As to the volume of trade, the figures produced from Geneva by the GATT secretariat tell a story very different from the conventional beliefs of liberal economists. Since the late 1970s, there has been increased protectionist intervention in defence of American and European markets against Asian imports. Yet Asian imports and world trade continued year on year to rise. The only hiccup in the statistical series followed the onset of the debt crisis for indebted developing and socialist countries. Credit to them dried up. So therefore did their ability to pay for imports. For the same reason, exports from countries like Brazil were so badly needed to take the place of foreign credit that, with government help they increased. That example makes the point that while the major changes in trade are finance-driven and demand and supply determined, government intervention can have some effect on trade flows – but only at the margin.

8. If the state has powers over the economy and over society they are mostly exercised within its territorial borders. Despite a good deal of variation in the manner and the means – public or private – by which it is done, governments have taken responsibility for the building of the economic infrastructure, from ports and roads, to posts and telegraphs. Even if railways were privately owned and financed, governments intervened with helpful legislation to help their construction. In most modern states, too, the state has provided schools to educate children and has supported scientific research and nurtured the growth of tertiary education in universities, technical schools and within firms. Some of this concern with infrastructure has been more in the nature of nation-building than aid to enterprises – support for the national language, for instance, or the preservation of national monuments, art collections and historic buildings. It is at this domestic level that the state can contribute most to the competitiveness of its own firms and of foreign firms operating inside its borders. Its success as a trading state can be enhanced more by indirect, infrastructural intervention than by subsidy or trade protection (Rosecrance, 1988); Cerny, 1992).

The key questions here are what kind of infrastructure, and how . much help the state is prepared to give, in the form of credit, of statutory assistance, of official approval, in setting it up. Take railways, as an example. In the nineteenth century, all the industrialising states recognised the importance of the railway as a new, reliable and fast means of transport, enlarging markets and increasing the potential division of labour. The French and Germans in Europe, the British in India, could also see the strategic value of a railway system in moving armed forces to where they might be needed. Even where governments, as in the United States, looked to private enterprise to find the necessary capital, they never hesitated in revising the laws on landed property so that landowners could not easily obstruct the infrastructural investment.

Today, the infrastructural need in modern economies is for faster, cheaper means of communication. Once again, governments recognise the need to adapt the legal system to accommodate the new technology. State-owned PTTs (agencies responsible for Posts, Telegraph and Telephones) have to be privatised and given greater freedom to rearrange pricing systems for their services. This time, however, governments are in a weaker bargaining position in dealing with private interests. Some of those interests are foreign firms and have the accumulated experience, capital and technology necessary to technological change that the old PTTs lacked. Governments who see the need to improve communications as an element necessary to the competitiveness of firms in the national economy are much weaker than they were in dealing with the railroad barons. Pricing tariffs, for instance, may go against some of the social and geographically marginal users that the state in its own interests of self-preservation used to subsidise. Its weaker position no longer allows it to do so.[2]

9. Competitiveness in the world market requires a competitive environment in the national market. This is an aspect of global structural change which has directly affected the responsibilities of national governments. In the past, it did not matter so much if a government allowed public or private monopolies to dominate the local market. Indeed, it was one of the prerogatives of power in the absolutist state in the early stages of capitalist development to confer monopolies over trade at home or abroad (as with the Hudson Bay Company or the Dutch East Indies Company). And there was often a symbiosis between the monopolists and the state, as in the British East India Company. Later, governments gained control over other levers of power by setting up state-owned monopolies not only in basic industries like coal or steel or shipbuilding or armaments but in consumable staples like sugar, alcohol or tobacco.

But monopolies have always tended to resist change, to prefer the comfort of their privileged position to the challenges of adapting to change. This was well explained by the American economist, Mancur Olson in 1982 (*The Rise and Decline of Nations*). When that challenge comes from foreign competitors in world markets, and the national market is too small to yield profits enough to finance new investment, national monopolies are no longer such an attractive option for governments. The South African case is instructive here. The economy was long dominated by four very large 'trusts' or conglomerates. By the 1990s, the policy of apartheid that they had supported, if not initiated, was proving too costly (Sampson, 1987; Lipton, 1985; Sampson, 1995). It was costly in terms of the exchange rate of the rand and the restricted opportunities for the trusts in markets outside South Africa. Nelson Mandela's new government had two transitions to manage; bringing an end to apartheid in all its aspects, and subjecting the trusts to competition from new enterprises, foreign and local.

Under similar pressures, the European Community was also obliged

---

[2] See below, chapter 7 on Telecoms. The dilemma is particularly acute for governments of countries like Greece or Indonesia with a population dispersed in archipelagos of islands, where the demand from users is too low to cover the high costs of including them in the infrastructural communications system.

to give up its earlier attempts to nurture 'European champions' in place of national ones to resist the challenge of Japanese and other Asian competitors especially in semiconductors and electronic consumer goods. Its experience with the JESSI and ESPRIT programmes demonstrated that protecting or subsidising national firms could not ensure that they held on to market shares even in their home markets. Japan has been the most resistant to letting foreign-owned firms compete with its protected enterprises like Asahi Glass in manufacturing or the major banks and securities houses in the financial markets. But in the long run, as in Brazil for example, pressure from other domestic users of intermediate goods produced under monopoly or protected conditions will be inexorable – and more effective than the bullying *gaiatsu* practised by successive US administrations in relations with Japan (Strange, 1995).

The conclusion for state power is obvious. Structural change has greatly increased the costs if it has not yet quite removed the options of protection of national champions and the award of monopoly privileges hitherto available to states. It is not that some international institution or regime has made new rules that have to be obeyed. It is that the world market economy has just made such options increasingly costly to the whole economy on whose growth and viability the powers of government ultimately depend.

10. Marxist writers always counted as the most important attribute of the state a special kind of monopoly – that of the legitimate use of violence against the citizen or any group of citizens. Every government appoints a minister of defence in charge of its armed forces.[3] No government can easily tolerate private armed forces over which the state has no control. Even Irish republican politicians sympathetic to the irredentist objectives of the Irish Republican Army and its militants in Sinn Fein have recognised the threat it constitutes to state power. Hence the anxiety to conclude an agreement with the British over the future of Northern Ireland.

In a subsequent chapter, the powers of organised criminal associations – or 'mafias' – are examined in greater detail. Their use of violence in pursuit of profit is perhaps the greatest threat to the state's monopoly

---

[3] In the United States, the President is the commander in chief of US armed forces, although constitutionally only the US Congress can declare war. This ambiguous aspect of the separation of powers enshrined in the Constitution has been the source of a continuing tug-of-war between President and Congress for most of the past 100 years.

of the use of force to emerge in modern times. Nor is it confined to any one country. It is not just an Italian, or a Colombian or a Russian problem. And the reason lies in the global security structure in which a world market exists and has never been subjected to effective control, not only for small, portable weapons, but for explosives, tanks, missiles and the materials necessary for nuclear bombs. When the entire subway transport system of a major city like Tokyo can be brought to a standstill by some hitherto unknown pseudo-religious sect led from outside the country, it is clear that state control over the use of violence is under threat. Once again, the reasons are ultimately to be found in the world market. The mafias, and the terrorists are only the instrumental symptoms of structural change.

Conclusions

The value of an exercise like this, looking at the functional responsibilities of the state in general terms, is that it does bring out the element of secular change, not in the outward appearance of the state, but in its actual performance of specific tasks. The general impression left is that the domain of state authority in society and economy is shrinking; and/or that what were once domains of authority exclusive to state authority are now being shared with other loci or sources of authority.

One indication of this shrinkage is that certain social groups which states in general, or certain states in particular, used to protect and sustain, are now much more exposed to global structural forces of change. An obvious example, at least in social democracies, are labour unions. Governments in the first half of the twentieth century increasingly intervened in the economy to secure the right of unions to organise and to represent their members in collective bargaining with the employers. The right to strike was enshrined in national law. Unions were even allowed to insist on closed shop agreements with firms, forcing employees to join the union as a condition of employment. The statutory rights of labour unions were even sustained when it was publicly known that a union – like the American Teamsters – was a criminal organisation whose leaders kept power by intimidation. In many European countries and in Japan, the state went further than offering legal protection. It incorporated unions in the machinery of government. Neo-corporatist arrangements in which tripartite negotiations between government, unions and employers annually negotiated targets for inflation and growth, wage increases, fringe entitlements and other aspects of social policy, briefly became the norm in developed economies.

By the 1990s, the protective shield was proving ineffective. Unions were powerless to stop managers of multinationals moving production to other countries where labour laws were minimal and neo-corporatist mechanisms were non-existent. When BMW set up a plant in South Carolina it did so without the union representation on the board required by German law. When Kodak located an administrative office near London it did so on a non-union basis, despite the fact that the local authority was Labour-controlled. In the 1970s, an attempt was made to match the transnational strategies of large corporations with a link-up of labour organisations. Led by Charles Levinson and the International Metalworkers Union, it tried to get labour unions in rich countries to support strikes by labour unions in poor ones. The results, predictably, were dismal. Better a job without a union, decided workers in developing economies, than no job at all. Why help those who take our jobs away from us, asked members of unions in the developed economies.

In the European Union, member states badly needed the support of organised labour and socialist parties for the Single European Act and the Maastricht Treaty. The result was the Social Chapter and the declaration of neo-corporatist principles protecting workers against, among other things, wrongful or summary dismissal. By the mid-1990s, such promises looked increasingly unreliable. The response of managers in many firms was to engineer a major shift in employment policy. More part-time workers and more employees under short-term contracts freed the company from the statutory obligation to pay large sums in compensation to employees declared redundant. Even in Japan where lifetime employment was accepted as a fundamental social principle, and where firms in many sectors had long enough pockets to keep employees on their payrolls even though there was nothing for them to do, the signs of change were already apparent in the aftermath of the collapse of the bubble economy. Year-end bonuses shrank dramatically and though the job might be secure, at least for the time being, the salary that went with it was not.

A similar argument can be made concerning the declining power of the state to secure the interests of special social groups – landowners, pensioners or shareholders, for example – or of certain professions once regarded as the pillars of national society – the military or the church in Europe, for example. None of these has been insulated from the forces of structural change in the world economy and society. Nor have governments been able to shield them from erosion of their power, their privileges or their entitlements.

While it is not difficult to find empirical evidence of change, the shift in political theory is much less apparent. A great deal of political theorising is resistant to notions of change. The state remains the focus of analysis, and its institutions and processes are sufficiently unchanged, so that many political scientists – even perhaps the majority – are reluctant to admit that, behind the unchanged facade, the reality of state authority is not the same as it once was.

In fact, there are – and have been for some time – dissenting voices challenging conventional wisdom. A very early one, Hans Schmitt, writing in the 1970s about boundaries of authority, observed that while state authority used to extend to the territorial frontiers, and to coincide with the limits of the national economy and of national society, there were reasons to doubt whether this was still the case. In matters of investment, of currency and of labour markets, this was no longer always the case. Firms increasingly took investment decisions that extended their authority beyond the limits of the territorial state in which they first emerged as successful enterprises. Transactions within the state were increasingly conducted in currencies other than those issued by the local monetary authorities. More people were seeking employment in labour markets different from those of the nation-state in which they grew up (Schmitt, 1972).[4]

While Schmitt was probably the first to notice that the *territorial* character of the state was undergoing profound structural change, he was not alone in thinking that the *purposes* of states were also changing. Paradoxically, Robert Gilpin, who in the 1990s was one of the major defenders of the realist view that the state remained at the centre of the international system, had noticed as early as the 1960s the growing concern of national governments – or at least of the government of France – with science, technology and industrial competitiveness. His *France in the Age of the Scientific State* – as the title suggests – recorded the efforts of Gaullist policy in the 1960s to maintain and improve the country's scientific and technological reputation and achievements (Gilpin, 1968). In the French case, of course, scientific excellence was the necessary complement to military strength and to monetary independence, not exactly a substitute for either. It was in accord with Servan-Schreiber's message that state policy should be geared to helping European firms in general, and French ones in particular, to

___

[4] The article in question attracted little attention from the academics, perhaps because Dr Schmitt was then an official of the International Monetary Fund, the institution where he later rose to be head of the European desk and then special assistant to the Managing Director.

meet the challenge of American firms on their home ground (Servan-Schreiber, 1967).

Another step in the same direction was Richard Rosecrance's *The Rise of the Trading State* (Rosecrance, 1986). He argued perceptively that governments were having to give increased attention to their balance of payments, and were developing policy instruments to encourage exports and to keep manufacturing enterprises competitive with those of their rivals.

Philip Cerny, who like Gilpin started as a specialist in French politics, took the discussion of the changing nature of states and their concerns a stage further. In his *The Changing Architecture of Politics*, he argued that while the welfare state was encountering fiscal and other difficulties, the 'competition state' was taking its place. The state was being 'sucked in ... to the competitive rat race of the open world economy' (Cerny, 1990: 228). In Europe both British and French governments found it necessary to intervene to restructure important industries, to support scientific and technological research, and to liberalise or deregulate sectors hitherto protected from competition.

Even more radically critical of conventional theory of the state, David Dowd brought a historical Marxist perspective to his analysis of the changing role of states in the world economy. 'The rise of monopoly capitalism within nations', he wrote, 'carried with it the great expansion of the power of the state, whereas the rise of "global capitalism" *transforms* the already great power of the State, in the process reducing some of its activities (those concerned with social as distinct from corporate well-being') (Dowd, 1993: 385). As examples of the retreat of the state, he cited the greater importance of private credit and lending compared with government credit and lending, both within states and between them, and the replacement of the state by the market as the main source of armaments.

Two British economic journalists attempted a radical interpretation of recent political and economic developments affecting not just the British but all governments. Matthew Horsman and Andrew Marshall from *The Financial Times* and *The Independent* called their book *After the Nation-State*. It went further than most in looking to change in the world economy for explanations of change in the authority of the state. It is worth quoting from their conclusions because they are broadly consistent with my own:

neither the nation nor the state is about to disappear . . . there are no substitute structures that can perform all the functions traditionally associated with the nation-state. At the same time people are not prepared to give-up a state-centred nationalism altogether, even if they are prepared increasingly to divide their loyalties . . . patterns of allegiance are shifting and multiple loyalties will be the inevitable result . . . What we are seeing then are the outlines of a global system that has been in the making since the French Revolution; in the process, the principal defining element of it – the autonomous nation-state – is losing its privileged position . . . this involves political and social change on a very grand scale: the map is changing, literally and metaphorically. (Horsman and Marshall, 1994; 264)

Horsman and Marshall identify two changes in the behaviour of states which reflect their altered role: firstly, governments get civil society to accept international rules, even though these have been made without consent and by essentially undemocratic processes; secondly, governments manipulate democratic processes within the state by various means including a willingness to move decision-making down to the local and up to the transnational level. By these means, the state ceases to be the sole vehicle of public policy. Their suggested explanation of why this change has taken place, going beyond the cliches of interdependence and globalisation, is that 'the creation of risks has outpaced the development of trust' (Horsman and Marshall, 1994: 212). Since risk is a concept more familiar to economists, and trust is a concept more familiar to students of politics, society and psychology, it is not surprising that in the divided world of specialised social science, the two have not been juxtaposed in this way. Yet it is obvious that the time element in each is different; risks can occur suddenly and are quickly perceived, while trust is slow to build and is not quickly destroyed. People, therefore, are inclined to continue to trust the state to take care of them, while being acutely conscious of increased risks emanating from the market economy.

This is not inconsistent with the explanation in this book, which is that, as the nature of the competition between states has changed, so has their nature and their behaviour – both towards civil society within the state and towards each other in their international relations. The result is that authority over society and economy is undergoing another period of diffusion after two or three centuries in which authority became increasingly centralised in the institution of the state. It is nothing new or unusual that the nature of an individual state is subject to change. The French Republic after the revolution, the French Empire after the Terror were both radically different in their ideologies, in their institutions, in their domestic and foreign strategies from the French state under the Bourbons. The federal government of the United States underwent almost as radical a transformation during the Second World War, when it became temporarily the manager of a largely state-planned and substantially state-owned economy (Vatter, 1985).

What is new and unusual is that all – or nearly all – states should undergo substantial change of roughly the same kind within the same short period of twenty or thirty years. The last time that anything like this happened was in Europe when states based on a feudal system of agricultural production geared to local subsistence, gave way to states based on a capitalist system of industrial production for the market. The process of change was spread over two or three centuries at the very least and in parts of eastern and southern Europe is only now taking shape (Anderson, 1974a and 1974b). In the latter part of the twentieth century, the shift has not been confined to Europe and has taken place with bewildering rapidity (Dicken, 1992).

Part II
The empirical evidence

6 Authority beyond the state

Perhaps because of the limitations of conventional political science, as noted in chapter 3, there has been surprisingly little attention paid to non-state authority in society – except perhaps by the sociologists. One result of this neglect is that there is no simple definition that encompasses all the various forms of non-state authority in world society and economy. Nor is there any agreed taxonomy that classifies non-state authority according to some common criterion.

The problem of definition clearly cannot be solved in institutional or organisational terms. There is too much variation between the constitution of, say, a mafia and a partnership in accountancy for that to be feasible (see below). Non-state authority, therefore, can only be determined on the basis of outcomes. It may be exercised directly, by relational power, and indirectly by structural power. The *capo* of the mafia, or the chief executive of a multinational, mostly exercises relational power. A banker, or an insurer mostly exercises structural power. Indeed, so does any association, organisation or institution other than a state whose decisions indirectly affect the choices of others in society in ways comparable to that produced by the actions of state agencies. Structural power is exercised both by states and by non-state authorities. In both cases, authority over social or economic relations is exercised whenever the choices open to others are changed. If, for example, the options open to others are extended, so that more choices are available, or if they are narrowed so that fewer choices are available, then it is likely that authority has been exercised structurally to produce that change.

(Of course, choices can also be narrowed or extended by the forces of nature. Floods, earthquakes, climatic change, raging lions or poisonous rattlesnakes can cause people to change their behaviour, to accommo-date their choices accordingly. However, since this is an analysis within social science, it seems sensible to exclude the authority of nature, even though logically people do respond to it. It is a different matter when human authority, by intervening with natural forces, affects the choices of others, as for instance, when the operations of a chemical enterprise pollute the natural environment – the air, sea or rivers – so that risks of taking certain choices of where to live or work are affected.)

Using this definition, based on effect on outcomes, still leaves a bewilderingly wide variety of forms and sources of non-state authority. Since the same authority may be exercised at different times, or for different sections of society, with both great effects and rather modest effects, it is hard to classify according to impact. A possible alternative, suggested here, is to classify in relation to the authority of states. Although this too gives no basis for prediction, since the relationship of state to non-state authority is seldom static, it does perhaps better answer the problematic of change, and the causes of change, that has underlain a great deal of theorising in the field of international political economy (Keohane, 1984; Strange, 1994).

Suppose a continuum between one extreme in which non-state authority sustains and reinforces the authority of the state, and, at the other extreme, a non-state authority which contests and challenges, or threatens to supplant that of the state. The place of either on the continuum is not, and cannot be, objectively determined. It depends entirely on the perceptions of the state, whether it regards the non-state authority as an ally, a helpful partner in the ordering of society or the management of the economy, or whether it regards it as an enemy, a rival for legitimacy and power. A strong, highly authoritarian state is apt to be more jealous of its monopoly of power than a weak, decentralised state. There is not necessarily anything very rational in the perception of either of these of the seriousness of the threat, or of the helpfulness of sustaining, or adjunct, authority. As in international relations, where there is the potential for conflict between states, much has always depended on the mutual perceptions of the parties. Such perceptions are necessarily subjective. So they are in state/non-state relations. But although perceptions may change, as in the case of the Italian state's perceptions of the threat posed to it by the Sicilian mafia, they do not usually change very fast or very radically. It is possible, therefore, to choose examples from both ends of the continuum and from the more ambiguous middle, where relations might be compared –

in international relations terms – to an armed truce, or a state of wary co-existence.

That is what I propose to do in the pages that follow. As an an example of a rival, or counter-authority, to the state, I have chosen the Italian mafia which bears certain resemblances to other outlaw organisations such as the Chinese triads, the Colombian drug cartels, the Japanese yakusa or the thousands of new mini-mafias that have sprung up in the former Soviet Union.

At the other extreme, as examples of non-state authority that is not only tolerated by state government but is actually welcomed, legitimised and approved by it, I have chosen two major transnational professions – accountancy and insurance. Both were originally adjuncts of state authority, governed by institutions to whom national governments delegated a special kind of functional power necessary to a capitalist system of accumulation and production. What has happened as the businesses both serve came increasingly to operate across frontiers, time zones and currency areas is that these professions are able to operate more independently of state authority, yet with a great impact on the lives and options open to others. Both lay claim to a kind of professional status in society and therefore to a degree of moral authority comparable to that of the more established professions of lawyers and doctors.

A rather similar kind of moral authority, supposedly based on specialised expertise, is exercised by the international bureaucracies employed by inter-governmental organisations like the International Monetary Fund, the World Bank or the European Commission. For some of the more powerful states, these bureaucracies are also welcome adjuncts to the authority of the state, so that a very real symbiosis exists between the national bureaucracy and the international one. For the citizen of many smaller, poorer, weaker states, however, the international secretariats look more like enemies, instruments of a new kind of collective colonialism devoted to the preservation of the capitalist system and the hierarchies of power represented in it, even at considerable cost to their material welfare, the dignity and sometimes even the survival of individual men, women and children in a neo-colonial society.

I have included the international bureaucracies in my selection of non-state authorities partly because of their important role in the international political economy. But also because the conventional literature of economic liberalism, spilling over into the extensive literature on international regimes, has shown so strong a tendency to uncritical approval of any evidence of cooperation between states, whatever its social and economic consequences for people. This liberal ideology is criticised, and rightly so in my view, by post-modernist writers for its unwarranted and often unconscious assumption of the priority of certain values over others. One does not have to be a follower of Michel Foucault or for that matter to write in the dense and convoluted prose that characterises much post-modernist criticism, to see the built-in bias.

Between the two extremes of non-state authorities welcomed and opposed by states lie certain non-state authorities whose relation to governments is variable or ambiguous. An example explored below is those powerful associations of international enterprises, the transnational cartels, which draw up rules – systems of governance in the current parlance – and actively exercise direct authority over markets and in some respects over their members. These, as I shall explain, operate in a shadowy area in which their role, depending on circumstances can be very ambiguous. Some, as in the electrical sector, are known to exist even though governments often shut their eyes to the fact, pretending that they do not. Others, as in shipping, are tolerated, though with official disapproval as contravening declared principles of free markets and an open, liberal economy. A few, as in steel, uranium or aluminium, are actually given formal legitimacy by means of inter-governmental agreements.

Other examples are the transnational social movements, often reflected in NGOs – non-governmental organisations. Some of these have been given institutional status in the United Nations Charter with the right to represent their views and even to be consulted by UN agencies with common interests. Both the number of NGOs and their membership have grown fast in recent decades. By the late 1980s, the UN's Yearbook of International Organizations listed over 4,500. To take two well-known examples, the World Wildlife Fund increased its membership from fewer than 100,000 in 1983 to over a million by 1991, and its annual revenues from $9 million to $100 million; Greenpeace membership increased over the same period from fewer than 1.5 million to 6.75 million, and its revenues similarly quadrupled from $24 million to $100 million. For their membership, and for governments, such NGOs have the authority and legitimacy of popular support allied to technical expertise and sources of information. At times, they have been useful to state agencies. At other times, they have been an embarrassing the unwelcome irritant to politicians who do not want to act as quickly or strongly as the NGOs want. Amnesty International is one non-governmental organisation which is actively opposed by many of the governments whose imprisonment of political dissidents without trial it actively publicises and criticises. Perhaps because of their close association with established inter-state organisations such as the UN, most of the influential NGOs have been the subject of quite extensive academic interest and research (Princen and Finger, 1994). For that reason, I have not added them to my select list of examples.

That is only one of the several large areas of non-state authority I have left unexplored. All of them, however, serve to illustrate the underlying argument of the book that the centre of gravity in world politics has shifted during the last quarter century from the public agencies of the state to private bodies of various kinds, and from states to markets and market operators. A fuller and more comprehensive analysis would require a very much more extensive survey of the extent and limits of non-state authority than is possible in one short book. And for that, I am not at all well qualified.

For example, I am not qualified in any sense to write about religious authority, though I can recognise that in most of the major religions, like Islam, Judaism or Christianity, there are powerful sources of authority over human behaviour. There is even more intrusive authority over their members in a great many of the smaller religions: consider such sects as the Mormons or Jehovah's Witnesses (or perhaps extremists like the Branch Dravidians in Texas or the Awm Shinrikyo in Japan) or religious orders like the Jesuits, and quasi-religious organisations like the Freemasons. Both the internal politics, and the economics of any of these transnational religious authorities would be a research project in itself.

The transnational authority exercised within and by powerful families, too, is a subject of great importance for social historians and biographers. And this is especially so as Asian economies grow and become more prominent and successful within the world market economy. For it is axiomatic that enterprises in many countries from Turkey to Taiwan are built around family relationships and the authority exercised by fathers over sons, and incidentally daughters and sons-in-law.

There have also been a few powerful political organisations that have operated not just within one country but across national borders. The Communist International or Comintern is the prime example, both in the interwar and the post-1945 period: in one sense, a foreign policy tool of the Soviet Union, in another, the organised form of a secular ideology operating in a particularly hierarchical and authoritarian way.

Another, more regrettable omission – but one which is also due to my lack of expert inside knowledge – is of those transnational authorities who, more than states, manage various multinational sports and thereby affect the options open to the participants, spectators and those who provide the necessary finance. The political economy of football has been less seriously researched than the psychology of the game and its devotees. Yet when it comes to the millions and millions of people who follow football, mainly but not exclusively in Europe, Africa and Latin America, most of them might judge football authorities more important to their everyday lives, interests and enthusiasms than the authority of states. Each game or sport, moreover, has a different kind of authority, or mix of authorities. Compare tennis, for example, where national governing bodies like the All-England Lawn Tennis Association based at Wimbledon in South London, maintain a certain independence while coordinating their activities with other national bodies, with golf where there is a certain accepted hierarchy of authority at least when it comes to the interpretation of rules. Again, in baseball, US authorities dominate others but have to cope with players' organisations that are effectively a labour union. Cricket, on the other hand, used in the past (and really until the mid-century) to reflect British class distinctions, with players treated differently according to whether they were judged 'gentlemen' – i.e. amateurs – or 'players' i.e. 'professionals.

Most complex of all, and most truly multinational, athletics has been an arena of bitter, highly politicised conflict (and of substantial economic profits and losses) ever since 1896 and the revival in modern form of the ancient Greek Olympic Games. In this arena, the governments of states and the local authorities of cities have competed hard to be chosen as the venue for future Olympics. They were the suitors, the candidates; the Olympic committee were the arbiters and judges. The results of past choices have had important political repercussions – Nuremberg in 1936, Moscow or Los Angeles in the context of the Cold War. Politics led to the exclusion of South Africa, and the withdrawal of Soviet Union. There were also economic consequences for states and cities, and their taxpayers; Montreal was landed with a huge burden of debt in consequence of the 1976 games, while Los Angeles in 1984 made a profit through professional promotion and use of sponsors, and despite much lavish spending.

Nor are sports and athletics the only social activities in which non-state authorities play a significant regulatory role. In the world of art, the market has been effectively dominated over several decades by two London auction houses, Sotheby's and Christie's. Both were sharp enough, back in the 1950s, to anticipate the rapid expansion and internationalisation of the fine art market and to respond technically and organisationally to the challenge. Both quickly became truly multinational in terms of the localisation of auctions and the use of multiple currencies in the bidding. Their say-so, not that of states, decides whether this work or that is the work of a known and sought-after artist and whether it is genuine or a fake. There are times when they have been fooled. Yet their authority is rarely, if ever, challenged.

This is less true in the market for music, more particularly 'pop' music. Here, as in accountancy or insurance, the market is truly a world market and here too it is dominated by a handful of leading producers of recorded music, such as Philips, Sony-MCA, Time-Warner and Bertelsmann. They have produced and marketed recorded music first on discs, then on cassettes and at the time of writing on compact discs. In the future, it may be that compact discs give way in their turn to music produced by computers. Authority of these leading firms has been derived in part from their mastery of technology, in part from their financial resources and developed systems of marketing and distribution. But it has also depended on the support and collaboration of states in the promotion of an ideology of property rights. These are claimed not for the composer or the performer but on behalf of the manufacturing firm. The irony is that the US government which has led this fight for the protection of copyright against 'piracy' was itself a latecomer to the idea. Only in 1947 did the US, under pressure from the Europeans, at last sign the International Convention on Copyright. In the nineteenth century, US publishers had ruthlessly pirated the work of popular foreign (mostly British) writers of whom Charles Dickens was a notable example. By the 1990s, the piracy problem had become more acute than ever, and especially so in music rather than in books because of the size and profitability of the world market. This was because there are no language barriers to music and because the technology of compact disc production made it impossible to tell a pirated disc from a legitimate one. There was no perceptible difference in quality between the original and the copy, unlike cassettes where copies were of lower quality. In the Uruguay Round of multilateral trade negotiations a major objective of the US delegates was to get universal acceptance of the principle of intellectual property rights. By this means, any bilateral pressure the US government might put on China, for example – as it had in the past put on Taiwan or Mexico – would be reinforced and legitimated by a multilateral declaration.

From a political economy point of view, what has been at stake is not the current profitability of the major firms but their prospects of even greater profits in the future. As the demand for recorded pop music grows in poor countries, so does the purchasing power to satisfy it. This is underlined by the fact that sales of pirated music in the US market, for example, are probably less than 5 per cent of total sales. But in China, at the time of writing, they may be as much as 85 per cent. The loss is notional more than actual. But in a market of a billion consumers, a lost opportunity to profit from such sales is acutely felt by the big firms. But for the composer, and for the performers, it is largely immaterial, since they are mostly rather weak bargainers with the major firms and tend to be tied to them by contract.

The professions

Yet another kind of non-state authority is exemplified by the two service businesses – insurance and accountancy – whose key role in the world market economy I have briefly outlined below. It would be tempting to explore the role of a number of other professions in world society. The subject has engaged the attention of sociologists for much of the past century, in which great changes have taken place in both the reality and in popular perceptions of professional authority (Carr-Saunders and Wilson, 1933; Johnson, 1972). But again, the subject is beyond my grasp and competence. Yet it is clear that the large transnational law firms – Coudert Brothers, for example – which operate simultaneously in different national capitals and in different national legal systems, play an important part in the negotiations of international deals and contracts. It is also clear that in medicine, there are research centres, clinics, medical schools and hospitals whose reputation confers on them an authority that transcends national frontiers and that works not only over the customers – the sick – but also over the suppliers – among whom the large transnational pharmaceutical firms occupy an important role in the world economy.

This example illustrates a common feature of non-state authorities. It is the frequent symbiosis, not only (as noted above, p. 92) between such authorities and states, but also between complementary non-state authorities. Banks have such a symbiotic relationship with accountancy firms, for example. Sports associations have them with the commercial sponsors of events or of famous players. Telecom enterprises have them with both their equipment suppliers and their TNC customers.

The task of the international political economist, therefore, is to try and untangle the complex web of overlapping, symbiotic or conflicting authority in any sector or on any who-gets-what issue. The regime literature, with a few exceptions, has from its beginnings in the late 1970s tended to oversimplify by concentrating on state authority, thus underplaying the structural authority exercised by markets and the authorities and operators involved in markets, whether it is music or medicine, telecommunications or tennis. In sea-use issues, for instance, the relevant authorities affecting sea trade run from the International Maritime Organisation and Inmarsat, through state-related port authorities to the P and I Clubs to which shipping firms belong. In issues related to fishing, governments share authority over the business of catching and selling fish with inter-governmental fisheries commissions and fishermen's associations and the political parties in electorally important regions. The total, aggregated impact of inter-governmental, state and sub-state authority, together with that of diverse non-state authorities is the product not so much of an orderly, static 'regime', as of a complex pattern of interlocking, interacting bargains among them all. These bargains may be relatively stable, or relatively unstable. They are often potentially very vulnerable to changes in technology and changes in the market, in conditions affecting supply or demand. The job of the political economist is to identify, if s/he can, firstly, the points of greatest vulnerability to existing bargains, and secondly, the potential distributional and value-mix consequences of both the existing complex web of bargains and of conceivable alternative webs.

7 Telecoms: the control of communications

A classic, extreme example of one process by which authority has shifted massively away from the governments of states to the corporate management of firms is to be found in telecommunications. At the peak of their power over society, states claimed, and exercised, the right to control the substance of information – by censorship, for example, of books or the press – and to control the means by which information was communicated – post, telegraph and telephone. In the last decade or so, a rapid decline in this power has set in, set off by a combination of technological change, demand in the market and policy changes in the United States driven by economic interests but legitimised by the economic ideology of private enterprise.

The result of the shift has been to narrow the options open to supposedly sovereign states, and to extend the opportunities – and risks – of those enterprises engaged in the supply of services and of the hardware by which the services are offered on the market. Another result has been to concentrate authority over this economic infrastructure in the governments and firms of the developed countries, and especially in those of the United States. Other governments have been forced by a combination of technological and economic change to give up their exclusive control for the sake of maintaining the competitiveness in world markets of the national economies for whose welfare they are held responsible. Yet another result has been to put technological advance at the service of transnational business, especially large enterprises, and at the expense – quite literally – of small business and of the individual citizen.

* For this chapter, I am indebted to Michael Hepburn for valuable research assistance, and to Giorgio Natalicchi for expert advice based on work for a doctoral thesis for New York University.

Technology

None of this would have happened without rapid technological change. But it has not been one single invention or technological advance. It has been the result of a coincidence of at least half a dozen. These advances have combined to create new products and services and to bring down the unit costs of messages. An understanding of these technological changes is essential to any analysis of the political economy of the business and of the political and social as well as economic consequences resulting from change (Codding, 1952).

Firstly, there have been great improvements in transmission systems. Thirty years ago, telephone systems buying copper wire were staple customers of the big multinational firms like Kennecott, Anaconda, Roan Selection Trust and Rio Tinto Zinc. Today, for the fast-growing new networks fibre optics offer a better alternative. More expensive to install than copper wire, they are much less expensive per message. The extra capacity, or bandwidth, of fibre optics allows thousands of messages to be carried simultaneously over the same strand of glass. It is also easier to maintain and keep secure from interference. Even on copper wire, new data compression techniques speed up transmissions to 10 megabites per second or more.

Secondly, large digital switches have allowed an increase in the capacity of connections to the point where the needs of an entire region or even a small country can be served from just one switching point. Computer-related technology also allows these switches to give more sophisticated services, such as repeat calls.

Thirdly, the invention of the cellular or mobile phone that operates within a limited radius but without wires (hence, cordless) has created a whole new market. In 1994, there were already over 24 million subscribers and business was booming, especially in the ex-socialist countries lacking the developed infrastructure of America, Japan or Europe.

Fourthly, there are the earth-circling satellites. First developed by the superpowers for military surveillance purposes in the late 1950s, they had become big business for civilian use by the 1970s, thereby recouping some of the costs of military competition for both the US and the USSR. In a strange piece of Cold War cooperation, both joined with others to buy shares and set up an international syndicate enterprise, Intelsat. Its first geo-stationary satellite carried 240 simultaneous conversations across the Atlantic. By 1989, the sixth Intelsat satellite could carry

120,000 circuits working in both directions. Distance being no determinant of cost, the result has been to bring a dramatic fall in intercontinental telephone and data transmission charges. Annual rent charges for a whole circuit fell to almost a tenth between 1960 and the 1980s (Dicken, 1992: 107).

Fifthly, computers and the more efficient telephone transmissions systems combined to render telex message systems obsolete, just as telex had done the same for the telegraph system in the 1960s. Once, large, slow and costly, these quickly became small, fast and cheap and by digitalising information were able to compress data that, by other means of communication would have taken a long time to pass from A to B. Then, by the late 1980s, fax (facsimile message) was becoming the commonest system of communication for business users. By 1993, fax terminals numbered 25 million. This added considerably – around 15 per cent – to the volume of traffic on telephone lines. Even faster was the growth of electronic mail, which allowed terminals to give instant access to anyone connected with another terminal. By the 1990s, a million new users joined the system every year – but the nature of the technology meant that almost all were employees of big business, government or universities. The privileges of what Drucker calls the 'knowledge workers' were greatly enhanced by comparison with those of manual workers in agriculture or industrial manufacturing. The innovation of electronic mail, at the time of writing, was rapidly replacing conventional mail, telex and fax. Individuals with computers can pass messages to each other in real time, with no intervening authority at all, except that of the organisations subscribing to the system who can allow or disallow individual access to it. Cable TV networks, owned by the network operators and therefore independent of telephone systems are another alternative open to business users. Video links connecting TV screens with telephone lines and computers are already the next step. And after that voice recognition will link users to computers without the use of keyboards.

Technological change has not only been rapid, and increasingly so. It has been expensive. The combination of shortening life cycles of new technology and increasing cost of investment in development raises the *ante* in the competitive game between enterprises in the market. It is these aspects of technology that account for the paradox that the old national telecoms, in order to survive, are almost forced to forge strategic alliances with enterprises of different nationalities – to create, in effect, genuine 'multinationals'. Examples (at the time of writing) are the joint venture between Britain's privatised BT and the American MCI; the cooperative arrangement called Unisource between the Dutch, Italian, Swedish and Swiss telecom operators; the trilateral deal between the US long-distance telecom firm, Sprint, with the German and French state monopolies; and the looser links established by AT&T with a number of operators called 'WorldPartners' (*Financial Times*, 19 January 1995).

Demand

Technology by itself has little consequence without a demand from the market. In this case, the rapid internationalisation of production, at double the rate of growth in world trade by the mid-1980s, created a demand for rapid, reliable and plentiful communication between headquarters and offshore affiliates, distributors, and suppliers. Integration of financial markets was made possible by improvements in communication systems; and financial integration itself contributed to those improvements by providing the Telecoms with rich customers well able to pay for large international transfers of data. The rapid spread within national markets of mobile phones over only three or four years, and in Asia as well as Europe and America, is one aspect of technology meeting a mass demand. Where state policy used to determine the structure of the communications sector, it is now much more driven by market demand. And as the relocation of manufacturing has been made possible by improved communications, so the service sector has been able to expand, taking advantage of the efficient flows of information. Examples are to be found in the running of airlines, of travel agencies, of carhire and hotels, and in transnational linking of retailers with suppliers. Political representation mirrors the technological changes. In Europe, for example, a new pressure group has been formed, the European Virtual Private Network Users' Association, to push for two things: more sophisticated services – such as video and audio-conferencing on demand – shortcode dialling, company calling cards, and, of course, price cuts that could be as big as 40 per cent to corporate users. Since it is firms, not individuals, who are the big users, the state-owned public telephone operators, or PTOs, have to heed their interests.

Thanks largely to corporate customers, there was a five-fold increase in international traffic over the decade 1984–94 – or so available statistics suggest. Between 1984 and 1991, exports of telecom equipment rose by

17 per cent, although capital investments of public telephone operators increased by only 11 per cent, suggesting that national PTTs that had tended to rely on their own local suppliers of equipment were now importing it (ITU, 1994: 12). The total size of the market was estimated at over $530 *billion* by 1992, of which equipment sales accounted for only a quarter and telecom services 75 per cent. (ITU, 1994: 1). The revenues of 15 leading public telephone operators are now greater, at $10 billion each or more, than the GDP of many small countries and level with the largest TNCs in manufacturing industry (ITU, 1994: 16). In short, Telecom has proved a highly profitable business, at least for some. It generates cash on an unprecedented scale. There are at least 15 PTOs with revenues of more than $10 billion a year (ITU, 1994: 16). No wonder competition is hot.

US policy changes

A third necessary condition of change was the deregulation of telecommunications by the US government in 1984. Privatisation of the Telecom operations of the British post office, British Telecom, followed soon after. While most other governments had kept their state monopolies of postal, telephone and telegraph (hence PTT) services, the US federal government appointed a Postmaster-General but had from earliest days delegated the operational management of telephone and telegraph service to private monopolies – the Bell telephone company, the old Western Union and American Telegraph and Telephones or AT&T. The alternative – a federal government service – would most certainly have been fiercely resisted by the individual state legislatures. The decision by the Reagan administration to deregulate and to break up the AT&T system put pressure on the companies to compensate by seeking profits from new markets outside the US. The American lead was only belatedly followed by other governments – but followed in the long run, it had to be. The chain of causation was well summarised by Dyson and Humphries (1994: 242):

> By dint of its economic power and technological leadership, the United States has managed to transform the agenda of the international political economy of communications towards deregulation to match the domestic characteristics of its own economy . . . Asymmetrical dependence has revealed itself most profoundly in the role of the United States as initiator of agenda change to which the European Community and its members must respond.

Here, indeed, is a clear instance of structural power being exercised indirectly through the market. It is market forces which appear to be inexorable, pushing national PTTs in Europe and Japan to deregulate and to privatise state monopolies in Telecom. But the market forces have been unleashed by US policy choice, and US firms, subjected to acute competition and vigorous demand at home, have had a head-start in gaining market shares in transnational communications from hitherto sheltered national PTTs.

Consequences

The dominance of corporate demand in the market has had direct effects on the cost structure of the sector – the crucial political economy questions of 'who pays? who benefits?'. As a recent analyst of the business observed, 'The terms and conditions of access to telecom services are instrumental in determining who can participate fully in the social, cultural, political and economic life of society' (Mansell, 1993: x). The key issue is whether the whole costs of the Telecom infrastructure are equally shared among all the users, for instance by a standard charge (as it were for overheads) on each call; or whether the notional 'costs' of long-distance calls are treated separately from the notional 'costs' of the local calls. In the latter case, the long-distance caller pays only for the additional capital overheads of the long-distance network, even though something like 70 to 80 per cent of the overhead costs are common. By artificially separating the basis for tariffs for local and long-distance (including international) calls, the PTOs effectively lower costs to business users. With more revenue from corporate users they are better able to meet the competition of new operators. By leasing whole lines to banks or big companies, they can cut prices even more drastically. And another device, referred to as de-averaging, gives lower prices on 'thick' (heavily used) lines as compared with 'thin' ones, thus discriminating price-wise against rural and in favour of urban users (Hills, 1994: 177). According to Hills, de-averaging was defeated in the Congress, while the debate over 'who pays' was still under discussion by European governments (Natalicchi, 1995).

Even without such discriminatory pricing policies, the dominance of corporate users' interests over household users' interests results from the combination of new technology and vastly increased business demand. The effect has been generally felt in the more rapid fall of international and long-distance calls than of local ones. The power of governments which, for social policy reasons, might want to keep rural areas and lonely old people fully integrated into the communications system at minimal cost has clearly diminished.

So has the control of governments. By means of their ownership of state monopolies, PTTs used to have control over the design and availability of such communications. No longer. The prospect in the mid-1990s is for a mere handful of global corporations to take the place of many mostly publicly owned national operators, and to dominate the business world-wide. Governments everywhere are being forced, willy-nilly, to bargain with these transnational operating firms over the terms on which national systems are incorporated into the global network and the ways in which they develop. In these negotiations, and because of their access to credit and command of the technology, the bargaining power of the large PTOs, often acting in strategic alliance or consortia with one another, is far greater than that of governments of most countries. Even the government of a country with a potential market as large as that of China no longer has the option of controlling and running its own communication system; the range of options open to it has narrowed to picking the foreign partners and negotiating with them the best terms of the alliance.

The story also underlines the power of markets over states. By the mid-1990s, North America and Europe accounted for three-quarters of all Telecom revenues. OECD countries accounted for 85 per cent of these revenues (ITU, 1994: 2). At the beginning of 1993, they had 15 per cent of the world's population – but 71 per cent of the telephone lines. And of the OECD countries, the United States was way ahead of the rest. Nine of the fifteen top PTOs were based in the US, five in Europe, one in Japan, the state-owned NTT (ITU, 1994: 16). In addition, the four long-distance service firms – AT&T, Sprint, MCI and the Japanese KDD – which use the PTO lines all have annual revenues of more than $1.5 billion (ITU, 1994: 20). Their cash reserves give them another kind of bargaining power. The political consequences of this shift from governments to markets are plain. The gap dividing rich people from poor people, big business from small business, was widening. And this was apparent both within national societies and between them in world society.

What is perhaps more controversial is how these changes have affected international 'regimes' as reflected in inter-governmental organisations. Much of the relevant literature tends to underplay the dynamic forces working on these organisations. In telecommunications the question arises whether, through them, US structural power is being converted into relational power over other states, legitimated by economic orthodoxy (Hills, 1994: 170). The evidence for this new (and more sophisticated) version of the old dependency theories is drawn from discussions in the International Telecommunications Union (ITU), with supporting evidence from Intelsat, the World Bank and the GATT's Uruguay Round. ITU grew out of one of the oldest of the nineteenth-century public unions and from coordinating arrangements between state PTTs concerning communications by telegraph, expanded into telephone and radio communications. But it had also always been peculiarly open to private firms and to government regulators in states (like the US) where the telegraph was in private hands (Murphy, 1993: 112). Thus, it was not seen as a great departure from traditional ITU practice when, after World War II, the real work of transnational standardisation and regulation came to be done in working parties and committees in which private firms, rather than national delegations, played a key role. The plenipotentiary conference in which government delegations sat, became largely formal and irrelevant. A point worth stressing here is that this is only an extreme case of a common experience. In many international organisations, the delegate's seat is occupied by a government official; but behind his seat there is often a 'technical adviser' – an *éminence grise* drawn from some interested firm or business association. Much academic analysis on regimes and international organisation overlooks and thus under-rates the part played in inter-state bargaining by private interests.

Over the period 1945–1995, in fact, this shift of decision-making power from governments to business firms substantially affected the policy decisions taken in the organisation. This was done in part by budgetary means; ITU contributions were voluntary and consequently a decision to help telecom development in poor countries was easily negated by the refusal of large delegations to allocate money to it. Partly, it was done by a 1989 restructuring which drastically curtailed, according to Hills, the powers of the numerical majority of LDC representatives. Through the Business Forum in which multinationals are given representative and not just observer status, it may not be long before they are also given voting rights. Hills describes the process as the 'beginning of a form of privatisation of international institutions'.

Meanwhile, Intelsat which was set up in the 1960s to finance and operate earth-orbiting communication satellites on behalf of participating governments as shareholders, from being highly profitable began in the 1990s to suffer competition. This came first from privately owned submarine optic-fibre cables. Secondly, it came from privately-owned satellites. Provided they could find a willing partner to launch the satellite, there was nothing to stop private enterprise from breaking the original Intelsat monopoly. An early challenge from Luxembourg, the Astra satellite, leased space to commercial users. A later one, IRIDIUM, due to start operating in 1996, was a multinational syndicated venture involving Motorola, Bell Canada, Raytheon, Mitsubishi, Sprint and Sony. Such competition had led to a US–UK bid to sell off Intelsat to private enterprise. This was defeated by the other shareholders, but a takeover bid, or a loss of business could still mark another victory for markets over governments.

The tension between public unions and private business is not new. Fundamentally, it is about who pays for technological innovation and who benefits. In telecommunications, the balance of benefit in the last two decades of the twentieth century would seem to have gone to the private sector firms at the expense of governments and their publicly owned and controlled enterprises. The efforts of states, individually and collectively, to use their countervailing powers in the interest of society as a whole and including the weak and the poor seem to have failed, at least for the time being. But capitalist societies in the past have acted sometimes quite successfully to stop an unbalanced concentration of wealth and power, to ensure more equitable distribution of wealth and entitlements. Nor has it been out of pure idealism. The economic history of Latin America or Africa, compared with some east Asian societies, has shown that capitalist societies in which wealth and entitlements were rather evenly distributed in society were often more politically resilient, more adaptable and more stable than those in which a small rich elite prospered while the masses suffered deprivation and hardship. A leading contemporary economist, Amartya Sen, argues that the long-term viability of the capitalist or market economy actually requires a more even social distribution of what he refers to as 'entitlements' – access on reasonable terms to food, to clothes, decent housing, medical care, education and some income security. The market will not always provide such entitlements without help from political authority. This view is in accord with the views of sociologists like Ralf Dahrendorf who emphasise the prevailing inequality in world society of 'life chances' for the individual. Neo-liberal economists do not see this inequality as 'market failure'. Yet in most societies, the political contest has always been between those who gave priority to the short-term advantages of financial and technological bargaining power and those who saw the longer-term advantages of social and political legitimacy as a result of their enlightened concern for the broader interests of civil society. In our own times, that contest continues – but this time on a global scale. Here, the diffusion of power among so many governments, and from them to non-state authorities makes it more difficult for policy-makers to take the long, more socially and economically enlightened view. Yet it would be rash to assume that it cannot be done or that current trends in telecommunications will extrapolate forever-or even far into the next century.

8 Organised crime: the mafias (in collaboration with Letizia Paoli)

Like transnational enterprises, organised criminal gangs – mafias, for short – have been around for a long time. Neither is a new phenomenon. Yet in both cases, what is new is their number; the expanding extent of their transnational operations; and the degree to which their authority in world society, and in world economy rivals and encroaches upon that of governments (Naylor, 1993: 13–51; Arlacchi, 1992a, b).

Cosa Nostra, which is probably the best-known, and the original exemplar of the term, 'mafia', also provides the model of organised counter-government. It engages in activities declared criminal and illegal by the government of the state, but at the same time imitates, in mirror fashion, many of the characteristics of formal state government.

For example, its authority – like that of a state – is exercised through an established power structure, by means of which obedience is rewarded and disobedience punished, occasionally by the use of violence and always by the threat of violence. In both state and mafia, the path to power may be achieved by force, quelling and discouraging opposition. Or it may be by peaceful persuasion exercised through some kind of electoral process. For instance, up to the 1960s, most of the Sicilian mafia groups elected the head of each *cosa* every year, and major decisions were taken collegially.

Both states and mafias own and operate economic enterprises, although for both the survival of the organisation takes precedence over profit maximisation. Like a state, too, a mafia is an economic parasite, in the sense that it raises revenue from civil society by demanding payment for protection. Governments call this taxation to pay for public goods when they do it, extortion when the mafia does it. The only big difference is that in many states, but not in all, the rules on taxation are

110

clearly laid down in advance and the demands for payment are not, for the most part, arbitrary and *ad hoc* as are those of the mafia.

Today, both mafias and nation-states are under pressure from the forces of globalisation. For each to survive in the competition for shares of the world market, economic rationality means taking less account than in the past of kinship (or ethnicity) as the basis for a shared sense of community and the basis of legitimate authority. Yet for both this may be at the expense of social cohesion and the authority conferred by the sense of a common identity.

Mafias, however, are not the only associations challenging state authority and treated by states as being on 'the wrong side of the law'. Some time ago, two French social scientists observed (Baechler, 1975; Chesneaux, 1965) a significant overlap between mafias, terrorist organisations, bands of pirates and brigands and urban criminal gangs. As Baechler pointed out, revolutionaries often tend to engage in bank robbery and other crimes in order to finance their subversive activities. The Chinese Triads were founded three centuries ago with the express aim of fighting the foreign Ch'ing dynasty and restoring the Mings, even though today their political purpose is forgotten (Morgan, 1960, 1982). Conversely, mafias often exploit ethnic or regional discontent to recruit members.

From local to global

What is new and of importance in the international political economy is the network of links being forged between organised crime in different parts of the world. While the Sicilian and American Cosa Nostras were the growing point, as it were, of this network, they no longer operate alone. There are half a dozen other major transnational criminal organisations, most of them connected to Cosa Nostra by informal agreements and shared interests. In Italy, there are the two most important criminal coalitions, the Calabrian 'Ndrangheta and in Campania, the Camorra. Outside Italy, there are contacts and business deals with the Chinese triads, and the Colombian drug cartels. The expansion of illegal markets has fostered a wider and more frequent interaction among the major organised gangs, Drugs, arms or illegal immigrants often pass through the hands of up to ten or twelve different operators attached to various national gangs. Inter-group bartering of illegal commodities has also become very common since such deals help conceal the origin of the profits from the state authorities. As various criminal groups (like the multinationals) have expanded their activities outside their home territories, the illegal markets within state boundaries have joined together horizontally to form a single world market. For example, as a consequence of long-term emigration fluxes and their expulsion from mainland China after the Communist Revolution, the Chinese triads are nowadays to be found in Hong Kong, Malaysia and Singapore, Thailand, Burma, the Philippines, Australia and New Zealand, the United States, Canada and several European countries.

The transnational diplomacy between national mafias has been made easier by a trend to more concentration at the national level. In Japan, for instance, it seems there has been a process of steady centralisation and coordination among the groups that form the yakuza. According to the very precise estimates of the Japanese police, in 1992 the Yamaguchi-gumi syndicate succeeded in including almost 40 per cent of the affiliates of the yakuza and in dominating over 1,300 smaller groups, while in 1980 it had held only an 11 per cent share (National Police Agency, 1989; Japanese Embassy in Rome, 1993). In Italy too, criminal society is evidently undergoing the same process of networking and concentration. Criminal groups of Sicilian, Calabrian, Campanian and how Apulian origin seem to have interwoven a thick (and relatively peaceful) network of illicit businesses, trading goods, information and funds.

The newcomers to the global network are the numerous mafias that have grown up inside the former Soviet Union. Their rapid growth, wealth and influence has been made easier by the dismantling of the Party apparatus and the security forces, the disarray, weakness and lack of resources of law enforcement agencies and the opportunities opened up by the rapid and largely unprepared transition to a market economy. Some of the internationally most active groups, like the Chechens, are based on ethnic and territorial bonds (Serio, 1992). One estimate cited in 1995 by the chief prosecutor of Florence suggested that organised criminal groups in Russia then controlled 35 per cent of the commercial banks, 40 per cent of former State-owned industry, 35 per cent of private enterprise – and as much as 60 per cent of commerce and 80 per cent of joint ventures with foreign firms (see *La Repubblica*, 28 January 1995).

The truth at the time of writing is open to a certain amount of guesswork. The late Claire Sterling, an American author who wrote extensively on the subject, went so far as to allege a *pax Mafiosa* – an agreement or a series of *ad hoc* understandings linking the American Cosa Nostra, the Sicilians, Chinese triads, Japanese yakuza, Chechen,

Georgian and other mafias from the old USSR (Sterling, 1994). She recounted the 'visible signs of the planetary attack force forming among the most powerful crime syndicates'. What she described is essentially the penetration of the United States by all of the other criminal gangs, and of Europe by both the Americans and the rest. Much of the evidence is derived from press reports or interviews. What is incontestable are the escalating crime statistics and the ease of transport of goods and people across national borders in Europe and Asia, from the Atlantic to the Pacific. So, whether the alleged *Pax Mafiosa* exists as a formal organisation or just as a loose network of bilateral deals does not matter. Either way, there is some kind of anarchical 'international society' of mafias as there is of states. And it is abundantly clear that during the past half-century there has been a transition of organised crime from a counter-society whose economic base was local and regional, to one whose economic base was first transatlantic, and now is clearly global.

The magic of the market

Change in the market best explains how and why the leaders of organised crime who began, for the most part, poor and rural have ended up very rich and cosmopolitan. It was not so much that the demand for drugs was new, but that it became very much bigger than in the days when the League of Nations set up its Narcotics Commission and discussed ways to stop the traffic in narcotics – mainly opium – from Iran and points east into Europe and America (Lowes, 1961). At that time, as records show, there was incomprehension among the Asians of the westerners' concern over a trade that, to them, seemed rather less harmful than the trade in alcohol. That was also the time when the Volstead Act prohibited the production and sale of alcohol in the United States, thus opening new opportunities for organised criminal gangs to make large profits from the supply and sale of illicit booze on the black market.

Still larger profits could be made from the demand for illicit drugs. For whatever political and social reasons, including perhaps the Vietnam war, the 1960s in the United States saw the growth of a mass market not only for marijuana/cannabis but also for cocaine, heroin and eventually their synthetic chemical equivalents like LSD or Ecstasy. In the next decades the market became global. Indications of this growth on the supply side of the market are to be found in the figures published by the United Nations on world-wide narcotic drug seizures. Annual heroin seizures increased from just over one to more that 21 metric tons; cocaine seizures increased from 2 to just over 300 metric tons, while those of cannabis starting from 2,000 tons in the early 1970s, multiplied from three to ten times, reached the record figure of 53,000 metric tons in 1987 (UN, 1993; Ministero dell' Interno, 1994). Assuming that in the long run the quantities seized account for an approximately constant share of the overall volume of narcotic drugs flowing through world markets, then the heroin market recorded a twenty-fold increase and the cocaine market a fifty-fold increase over the last twenty years. The assumption is confirmed by evidence collected by a Financial Task Force on Money Laundering, established in 1989 by the seven most highly industrialised countries. Its very conservative estimates of the trade in Europe and the United States valued it between $120 and $150 *billion* a year (FAIF, 1990). A report of the European Parliament estimated that the bank interest alone from the $100 billion laundered profits from drug trafficking amounted over a decade to more than $800 million (Assemblée Nationale, 1993).

The state–mafia symbiosis

A key factor in the growth of organised crime groups has been the repressive policies of national governments. Demand from the consumers in the market has been one side of the coin when it comes to the profits of organised crime. The other has been the role of the state. This explains both the profitability of the drug and other illicit international trades, and the changing attitude of governments – notably the Italian government – toward organised crime.

Profitability is always increased when a trade in goods or services is declared illegal. This has been true of gambling, prostitution, alcohol, guns, pornography and, of course, drugs. Barriers to entry are raised because risk is increased and the means to manage or reduce risk are not available to all. A monopoly rent results for the supplier. It is hardly surprising that organised criminal gangs – like other transnational enterprises – have seen new opportunities for profit in diversifying their activities. The same organisation could be used to defy state controls and to trade in an illegal market for arms, for illegal immigrants, or stolen cars past the state controls and distributed into the market. Reliable estimates suggest that between 1991 and 1994 at least 25,000 Chinese entered the United States illegally. Profits to the Chinese triads were estimated by *Time* magazine from this business – a modern form of the old slave trade – at $2.5 billion a year (*Time*, 1993).

Where the large profits reaped from the international drug trade have been politically important was in their disruptive effect on the old cosy relationship between state government and local systems of corruption based on criminal extortion (Guzzini, 1995). The Italian mafias had operated as a kind of shadow system of government, maintaining order and delivering votes, that saved Rome a certain amount of trouble. For decades, the state in effect delegated to the *mafiosi* the functions of social intermediation, and arbitration, protection of property and persons and the preservation of order (Arlacchi, 1988: 21–43). Many traditional mafia bosses in turn were openly protected by the political and administrative establishment of the time. They exercised their power in the firm belief that they were acting in the name and on behalf of the state. A 1993 report approved by the Italian Parliamentary Commission on the Mafia put it plainly:

> in practice, the relationships between institutions and mafia took place, for many years, in the form of relationships between two distinct sovereignties: neither would attack the other as long as each remained within its own boundaries . . . an attack (by State forces) would be made only in response to an attack by Cosa Nostra, after which they would go back to being good neighbours again.   (Commissione, 1993)

Without the vastly greater profits from the transnational trafficking, and without the possibility of laundering (i.e. hiding) the dirty money in legitimate business, none of the organised criminal associations in Italy or elsewhere would have become so rich. Their wealth brought power, and this threatened the stable coexistence of state and non-state authorities. The Christian Democrats could no longer afford to tolerate their rich, parasitic and unpredictably violent partners in political and economic crime.

To this must be added the impact of cultural modernisation on public and political attitudes. Beginning in the 1970s and accelerating through the fifteen years 1980–1995, Italian politicians had begun to conceal and cover up their links with the mafias for fear of damaging their political reputations with other voters. Representatives of the Italian state in Rome began to think better of their delegation of authority to the mafia as the latter tended to act more and more blatantly outside the law. A new generation of well-trained magistrates, themselves mostly Sicilians, were courageous enough to initiate an open break between state and mafia. This was made easier in the mid-1980s when the judicial system allowed local magistrates to conduct 'maxi-trials'. For the first time, the prosecutors collected evidence against 700 defendants, alleging the existence of a *criminal* association calling itself Cosa Nostra (Arlacchi and Paoli, 1995). The legal process was slow but ultimately effective, both in breaking down the rule of silence (*omerta*) imposed on mafia members – thus allowing the *pentiti* to testify with immunity against their former bosses – and in uncovering the secret links between politicians, banks, businesses and the mafias. Laws were passed to dissolve town councils infiltrated by the mafia. A special police force was set up to deal with organised crime. And the way was opened for penal prosecutions of members of parliament. In January, 1992, the Italian Supreme Court confirmed first-degree murder charges against all the major defendants in the Palermo 'maxi-trial', sending them to high-security prisons.

What remained far from clear was whether state or mafia had suffered most from the conflict. The mafia, after all, still had its legitimate businesses bought with laundered money, and a continuing source of profit from the transnational traffic in drugs. While the direct exchange of votes in return for an official 'blind eye' to mafia extortions had discredited the Christian Democrats and ended that aspect of mafia infiltration of the polity, that was not the only damage done to the state. The subsidiary practice by which officials awarded construction and other public contracts to the mafiosi, or approved their fraudulent applications for state or EC subsidies, was not so easily cleaned up. It may be that though the state had put many leading mafiosi behind bars and many corrupt politicians had been punished and banished from political life, the government of the country was still burdened with the legacy of its past symbiotic relationship with the mafias. It has not proved easy to reverse decades of political malpractice while at the same time wrestling with unresolved problems of finding the money for its welfare system, especially the pension schemes, and of adapting the economy to the competitive pressures coming from integration in the European Union and the world market economy.

Sociologists have argued that criminal gangs, like underground resistance movements in wartime or recalcitrant groups in prisons, tend to emerge when state authority, for whatever reason is already weakened, and the government has lost or failed to obtain the consent of the governed (Cressey, 1969: 171). Similarly, an analyst of Chinese secret societies in Singapore and Malaysia wrote that 'our findings suggest that the emergence of local Chinese secret societies is not related to the political deprivation of Chinese immigrants, but to the inadequacy of legal protection given to them' (Lau Fong, 1981: 4). When national governments are weak and criminals are rich, something close to civil war results. In Colombia, between 1984 and 1990, the Medellin drug cartel had the means to arrange the deaths of a minister of justice, a state general prosecutor, four presidential candidates, dozens of governors, mayors and local administrators, not to mention 300 judges and prosecutors, and more than 2,000 police agents (Ministero dell'Interno; 1993: 31–7).

Financial connections

Another striking feature of the last forty years has been the much larger intermediary role played by financial operators. Their expertise in financial markets helped to cover the tracks of the criminal money-launderers and to cover up their political connections (Paoli, 1993; Lernoux, 1984; Walter, 1989). It is not by chance that some of the most important tax havens and off-shore centres are situated at the cross-roads of the principal routes of the illegal narcotics trade. Panama and the Bahamas are well known for their financial clearing of the transactions in cocaine between Latin America and the United States (United States Senate, 1992, 1983). Hong Kong plays a similar role for the heroin coming from the South-East Asia towards the West (Gaylord, 1990: 23–7) while Switzerland, Liechtenstein or Gibraltar shelter the illegal proceeds of the heroin produced and exported by traffickers from Turkey and other Middle East countries (Ziegler, 1990). In such places, large movements of 'hot', highly speculative, money are inextricably mixed with the smaller shifts of ill-gotten dirty assets.

The fact is that while financial crime has grown enormously and everywhere has become the stuff of novels and newspaper headlines, it remains, legally and morally, an indeterminate grey area. The dividing line is seldom clear and is nowhere the same between transactions which are widely practised but ethically questionable and those which are downright criminal. The grey area may include a range of conduct between the more or less normal use of inside information for personal gain to the law-defying, conscious collusion with known criminals.

The need to use such secret or covert financial channels is not only a prerogative of organized and economic criminal groups – but also of terrorist and revolutionary groups and indeed of many individuals and economic operators engaged in activities which are not necessarily illicit. Investigations into the biggest financial scandal of the last fifteen years, the bankruptcyof the Bank of Credit and Commerce international, showed that BCCI was engaged in 'reserved' or illicit financial services for a very varied group of clients, including Colombian narco-traffickers, Middle East terrorists and Latin American revolutionary groups, as well as tax evaders, corrupt politicians and several multinational companies (United States Senate, 1983, 1992).

Where the illegal trade in arms is concerned, the confusion of roles reaches its climax in the former Soviet Union and its former satellite states. The combined military arsenals of the Warsaw treaty countries was immense. Much of that arsenal is in process of being dismantled by the democratic regimes that have come to power since 1990. But it is common knowledge that much has gone to the illegal arms bazaar (Almquist and Bacon, 1992: 12–17). A part of this arsenal has been sold by unscrupulous traffickers, in collaboration with former soldiers and intelligence agents, to developing countries, revolutionary and criminal groups. There are also well-founded worries – especially after the seizures accomplished in the summer of 1994 by the German police – that chemical, nuclear and biological weapons are also being marketed by criminal groups of the former Soviet Republics and sold to non-democratic governments and movements (*Time*, 1994).

Conclusions

The theoretical implications of this political economy analysis of organised crime, incorporating as key variables both changes in the authority of the market and changes in the authority of states and non-state authorities, are far-reaching. It suggests that the models of international society conventionally accepted in the realist, the neo-realist and in the neo-liberal literature of international relations may have been rendered obsolete by changes in the world market that have *indirectly* eroded the authority of states.

Ever since the Westphalian treaty in Europe, it has been held that the determination of what was and what is not 'the wrong side of the law' lay in the last resort with the governments of territorial states. It was up to them to decide what actions or associations of residents within their borders were within the law and what were beyond it – illegal, criminal. In recent years, however, the majority of such governments have taken two intrinsically conflicting decisions – on the possession and sale of stupefying or hallucinatory drugs, and on financial transactions through the banking system involving clean and dirty money. The first has been declared the wrong side of the law. The second has been tacitly admitted as being on the right side, inasmuch as only the most feeble attempts have been used to make the banks responsible, as criminal accessories, to the laundering of money acquired by criminal activities – whether bribes, robbery or illegal trafficking. The contradiction between the two decisions, that selling drugs is illegal but handling the financial proceeds of the trade is not, is putting the entire system of state authority at risk.

The second conclusion that can be drawn from the story briefly told here is that the peaceful, symbiotic coexistence of state and non-state authority so well exemplified by the Italian case over three postwar decades becomes unsustainable, and therefore unstable, once the market confers new wealth (and therefore power) on organised crime. And the Italian state by going along (like others) with the introduction of capital mobility and customer anonymity in the international financial structure had actually weakened its own authority. It had helped to create a transnational anarchical society of mafias that were all engaged in activities deemed by governments to be the 'wrong side of the law'.

In the past states had three options when confronted by such behaviour, whether organised or not. They could do nothing at all. This was rare but did happen, as with suicide in some secular states where the act is formally illegal but no penalties followed the taking of one's own life. At the other extreme, authority could use their coercive powers to suppress and punish any infraction of the law. Murder and treason were the two activities where states most commonly tried hard to enforce their laws. But in between these two extremes, there was always a third option. States could implicitly delegate some of their authority for maintaining some kind of social order to another organised source of authority, even if this meant turning a blind eye to transgressions of state laws by members or subjects of that counter-authority. Such arrangements worked (for a time at least) always provided both sides respected – and made their subjects respect – the implicit bargain regarding the division of responsibility. They became unstable however when the authority of either party was weakened, or when the non-state authority became so strong that it was thought to threaten the state. Some examples of times when states felt it necessary to suppress instead of tolerating non-state authorities would be the suppression of the Knights Templar by Philippe le Bel in France in 1307, the dissolution of Catholic monasteries by Henry VIII in England in the 1530s, or the witch-hunt against 'communists' in the United States in the 1950s.

The symbiotic coexistence ceases to be stable when either the established hierarchy of power in the state collapses – as in the former Soviet Union, or when the rival authority's power is perceived to threaten the state because it has acquired new foreign allies or new sources of wealth and influence. Then state policy is apt to change from peaceful coexistence to suppression. Trouble only starts, in short, (as with relations between states) when governments of states which have hitherto tolerated the coexistence of a rival non-state authority, perceive a significant shift in the balance of power threatening their own survival.

That was precisely what happened in the Italian case in the 1980s. By then, the market had given the mafias the chance to break out of the confines of the national market economy and society. And the state, paradoxically and perhaps shortsightedly, had gone along with the United States in allowing capital to move freely across borders and to find refuge in unregulated offshore bank and tax-havens. The result was that state authority was threatened – and not only in Italy. It was threatened not just by local organised crime but by a parallel anarchical society of rival authorities, each of them engaged in activities judged by state governments to be 'the wrong side of the law'.

The situation surely adds a new problematic to the ever-growing agenda of world politics. What the probable outcomes will be merits discussion by students of international relations. As they will be well aware, the chances of an international regime for the management or containment of transnational crime are likely to be poor. It would require far more cooperation and coordination between national police and enforcement agencies than either Interpol or high-level ministerial conferences have so far been able to achieve. To reduce or even limit the economic wealth and potential for political and social disruption of these transnational criminal groups to manageable levels would strike at the very heart of national sovereignty – the responsibility for maintaining law and order and administering criminal justice. It would require a worldwide police authority – and not just the proposed Europol – with extensive powers to arrest and prosecute the criminals anywhere in the world, including the United States. It would probably require giving governments the power to confiscate or sequester any properties or funds judged to have been acquired through illegal trading. It would also require an international court of criminal justice able to judge and punish. This is something that, so far, no government of a nation-state has ever contemplated.

If then suppression as an option is blocked by the refusal of state governments to give up their control of law enforcement, an alternative option would be to decriminalise the drug trade. This would deprive the mafias of the oligopoly rent they now enjoy as competition brought prices down. Some observers think this may happen, with or without some supervised licensing of outlets, as in the market for tobacco or alcohol (Ruggiew and South, 1995). Yet the criminal organisations might still survive, turning more to other clandestine and profitable trades. There would be social, political and economic risks and costs of allowing the transnational traffic in arms and immigrants to continue unchecked. The damage already done to the legitimacy and viability of an international society based on the authority of the territorial state as guarantor of order and the provider of welfare might still prove beyond repair.

The one option that this analysis suggests is *not* available is to reconstruct, on a transnational basis, the kind of symbiotic coexistence of state and mafia power that survived so long in Italy, in China, in Colombia and other places. If cooperation between the members of one anarchical society is difficult – as the vast literature on international organisation and regimes proclaims – any agreement on peaceful stable coexistence between *two* anarchical societies is doubly inconceivable and improbable.

The academic implications are profound. Both political science and especially international relations as its sub-discipline have both insisted on the state as the primary actor in world politics. Both have resolutely refused to accept this reality of market power and the consequent diffusion of real authority over economy and society. For that reason, neither can come up with explanatory theories capable of adapting to the emergence of transnational organised crime as a major threat – perhaps *the* major threat to the world system in the 1990s and beyond.

9 Insurance business: the risk managers

The business of insurance plays a growing and important part in the world market economy. Those who supply it are not seeking power over outcomes – but they exercise it none the less. And increasingly so. Yet it is hardly mentioned in texts on world politics; and in economics, the study of insurance is dominated by a few informed specialists, most of whom are ideologically committed to the value judgements of economic liberalism, putting the pursuit of free trade and untrammelled competition above all other possible policy objectives.[1]

How and why the insurers and risk managers exercise such power over outcomes, and with what consequences for the world market economy and for the allocation of values among social groups, national economies and business enterprises is a fundamental question for contemporary international political economy. For fifteen years I have waited, in vain, for someone to write a definitive analysis – not just a descriptive account – of this highly transnational business. From its beginning in the early 1970s, I have followed with interest the activities and publications of Orio Giarini's Geneva Association for the Study of Insurance Economics. Mostly it has been concerned with matters of technical and professional interest. Just occasionally papers have been published that address what you might call the political philosophy of insurance.[2]

One interesting study of insurance, by Virginia Haufler, was included in a collection of essays round the theme of international regimes

---

[1] A recent example is Carter and Dickinson (1992), written for the Trade Policy Research Centre in London with a neo-liberal approach. Its six-page list of references is useful but bears out my comment.

[2] An interesting example was Sir Herman Bondi's reflections on the irrationality of individual and national preferences in the management of risk (Bondi, 1988). Bondi, a distinguished scientist, was an advisor to British governments on science policy.

(Rittberger, 1993). It argued, correctly and in contrast to the state-centrism of most of the literature, that international regimes could also be created by private organisations. By way of example, Haufler pointed out that, until the 1930s, by tacit agreement the firms engaged in insurance had assumed that political risks, resulting from war or default on international debt, were uninsurable since they were unpredictable and there were no actuarial data to indicate probabilities. This changed in the Spanish Civil War, after which leading insurance firms agreed to exclude as uninsurable all risks resulting from enemy action on land, including air raids, but were prepared, at a price, to insure against war risks at sea. And then, after the near defaults on foreign debt in the 1980s, some insurers began to dabble in political risk analysis and – again, at a price – to offer cover against loss by foreign default (Haufler, 1994, 1995).

In this field, the only transnational organisation of any consequence is the Basle Union of Credit Insurers, of which more in a moment. Like a private cartel, the organisation's purpose is to avoid self-defeating cut-throat competition. In this aim it has only ever been partly success-ful. Haufler's essay digresses into other examples of non-governmental organisations exercising authority over outcomes which, as she says, may in some cases reinforce inter-state regimes while in others they conflict with them and in still others – as in insurance – they make their own contribution to the international economic order independently of states.

But it is still generally true that the most widely read academic journals in social science, whether in economics or politics, pay little or no attention to the political economy of the insurance business as it is conducted in the real world. This is surprising because structural forces in the market, in technology, in the authority of political regulators, in the nature and fortunes of the players, make this one of the most dynamic aspects of the world system. And as economic interdepen-dence grows and more and more people around the world become directly involved in the world market economy, so more and more lives and fortunes are affected by the ways in which the system manages risks, and by the ways in which the insurance business is conducted.

This lack, this neglect, is one reason for my attempting, as a part of this study of power in the global political economy, a brief and necessarily amateur outline of the business in its wider context. At the end of it, it may be possible to hazard some hypotheses about why the insurance business has suffered such academic neglect. But first, it will be necessary to explain just why insurance is such a crucial – indeed, indispensable – component of a developed market economy. We have to understand the division of functions between the players in the game and the divergence of the regulations under which they operate. We can then consider the powerful structural changes that in recent years have made it so much more competitive, so much more international and so much more politicised that by the 1990s 'free trade in financial services' became one of the hot issues of multilateral trade negotiations between governments. All that done, we can then return to the key questions. How much power does the insurance business exercise? Power over what and whom? And in the end, in whose favour does it operate, and at whose cost?

Insurance and the market economy

The moment a man or woman engages in an economic transaction with another, he or she incurs additional risk. All life involves risk; 'Nothing in this life is certain but death and taxes', as Mark Twain said. You may get ill, be injured, go deaf or blind, die prematurely. Your house may burn down, be blown down, flooded out. Your crops may fail, be ravaged by disease or pests. These are, so to speak, personal risks. And from the earliest phases of capitalist development, there have been people – actuaries – who were prepared to soften such blows of outrageous fortune by offering to pay compensation for losses due to personal risks. In short, they offered to convert your liability to risk into a liability to themselves to pay the cost of compensating you.

But the important point for political economy is that you add greatly to these personal, inescapable risks when you engage in a market economy. Willy-nilly, you add to them if you buy or sell, employ or become employed, if you save or invest. Then your personal risks are multiplied by the personal risks run by your partner in the economic transaction. If he or she cheats, disappears or becomes destitute and so is unable – or unwilling – to stand by the agreement underlying the proposed transaction, you too stand to suffer. Market economies, in short, multiply risks. And the more developed and complex and larger the market economy, and the larger the number of economic transactions, the larger the risks and the larger the number of people incurring them, whether directly or, very often indirectly and even unwittingly. Most of the depositors in BCCI had no idea of the risk the bank itself would close. Most of Maxwell's employees had no idea that he could or would rob them of their pensions.

It is equally true that risks are multiplied in any developed economy, whether it is market-based or state-planned. Take the old Soviet Union, for example. Many of the same enhanced risks ensued as industrialisation, the division of labour and the complexity of economic transactions replaced the semi-subsistence economy of a peasant agriculture. But in every case 'the State' took care of them, whether they arose from internal or external trade, from bad investment decisions, from environmental damage, from the consequences of power plays within the nomen-klatura. The responsibility lay with the state and the state was the universal insurer. The Soviet state, for example, operated a monopoly of commercial insurance, and was sharply criticised by foreign traders for insisting on a discriminatory practice whereby contracts for imports into the USSR were f.o.b. (free on board, i.e. insurable by the importer), while exports were always c.i.f. (freight and insurance costs prepaid by the exporter – the USSR). It was always the government that decided whose risks should be translated into costs, and it was the state that decided who should bear the costs. Mostly they were borne by the citizens, in taxes, in inflation, in shortages, in poor wages and poor public services, a neglected infrastructure and a polluted environment. Only when it came to the risk of nuclear attack by the United States were Soviet citizens comparatively well looked after by the State. It translated that particular risk into a massively onerous cost – the defence programme.

The essential difference was that the power to make decisions about risk was centralised in the socialist system, while in a market, or more accurately a mixed, economy, it is widely diffused and decentralised. In both the risk is 'translated' so to speak into a cost. In the socialist system the cost is imposed on the citizens as an administered price. In a capitalist system, it falls on the consumers of all goods and services in which insurance plays a part in the production and distribution process.[3] And even in market economies, the state has often taken responsibility for translating some risks into costs. One obvious risk is that of war. For example, just a week before war broke out in 1914, the British government took responsibility for merchant ships damaged or

---

[3] An obvious example is the cost to credit card holders of the insurance bought by the operators against the misuse by loss or theft of a credit card. Those who carefully look after their cards and never lose them help pay for this insurance if the cost is added to the annual fee. Or it is paid by those who fail to pay promptly and who are charged an extra high rate of interest.

sunk by enemy action. It did so because it realised that marine insurers would not cover ships against war risks, and sea-trade would otherwise come to a standstill once war was declared. No ship's master would dare leave port without insurance to hull and cargo. And in the Second World War, when air-raids started, the state again stepped in with the offer of (partial) compensation against war damage from falling bombs.

There are two other examples of state intervention in insurance. One has developed as industrialised states increasingly competed for export markets as sources of foreign exchange. The other has developed as all industrialised states perceived a common danger to the world economy from the risks of default on foreign debt by developing countries.

Growing competition for foreign exchange has involved the leading industrialised countries in curiously irrational subsidisation of insurance against the risks to exporters of foreign buyers (importers) failing to pay up when the goods were delivered to them. By one means or another, every one of the industrialised countries' governments have transferred to taxpayers some of the costs of subsidised export credit insurance. Britain had its Export Credit Guarantee Department – now privatised; France had Coface; Germany, Hermes; the United States had the ExIm Bank and OPIC; Canada, the Export Development Corporation. Through the Berne Union of Credit Insurers and the OECD, there have been a series of attempted agreements at standard rules to prevent competitive subsidisation. But they never worked for military sales, nor ships nor aircraft and every country always suspected the others of cheating.

More effective has been the international cooperation to reduce the risk – a risk to the whole system of which all became aware – of arrested foreign investment and economic development in response to the dangers of default on foreign debt. A World Bank scheme launched in 1988 during the 'lost decade' of development produced general agreement to set up the Multiyear Investment Guarantee Agency (MIGA). With capital subscribed by nineteen industrialised and over 100 developing countries, MIGA had a capital in 1994 of $1 billion, which enabled it to write contracts underwriting the investment risks of large projects which otherwise private investors might have hesitated to finance. While private 'political risk' insurance by Lloyds, the American Underwriters Association or the big banks is seldom written for more than two years at most, MIGA will underwrite projects for up to twenty years against the risks of expropriation, obstacles to currency transfers and political violence. By joining with other insurers, national and private, it increases the insurance available for foreign direct investment in indebted or unstable developing countries. Contracts have typically been written for large, costly projects involving foreign-owned firms in mining, power generation, chemical plants, communications systems, aquaculture. This is admirable in conception, but at the same time essentially discriminatory in favour first of large transnational enterprises, and second, their local partners and the host governments. It does not help investment in health, in education or social security; nor does it bring any benefit to small business or small farmers.

By contrast, even in peacetime, and for obvious state-preserving reasons, governments of most of the rich countries in Europe have also decided to take on the risks of sickness or unemployment by financing a welfare system. When they did so, they also decided the terms of access, the circumstances under which the premiums are paid, and by whom, and the qualifications necessary to benefit. Usually, some resource transfers, an element of progressive taxation, comes about through such state-run schemes. If, on the other hand, the main responsibility for insuring against the risks – of unemployment, old age, sickness or disability of some kind – is left by the state to the individual – as in the United States – then decisions are left to players in the market. This means that the potential buyers of insurance, and the sellers, together with any intermediaries, such as insurance brokers, or associations of special buyers such as clubs or professional bodies who negotiate on behalf of their members, between them take the decisions on access, price and availability of benefits that in other countries are assumed by the state.

Wherever the insurance business is left to the market, the result is usually that the rich, individually or collectively, can choose whether to translate, through insurance premiums, some elements of a risk into a cost. Insurance gives them that option. The poor, unable or unwilling, or both, to pay the premiums are left with the risk. I remember one summer canoeing down the river Lesse in Belgium and seeing up in the riverside trees the wreckage of holiday caravans – trailers to Americans. Hundreds had been swept away in flash floods. Few, I was told, had been insured. Their owners for the most part were small shopkeepers and factory workers. A caravan on a riverside camp-site was all they could afford for summer holidays. The additional cost of insuring against the risk of flood was beyond their means.

And in Africa, where AIDS threatens early death to mothers and fathers of young children, life insurance would seem a rational precaution for most Africans. But at the prevailing levels of rural poverty, most Africans do not have the option. Insurance, in short, is a financial service open, like the Ritz Hotel, to rich and poor alike, but whose customers in the main are (and have always been) those able to pay the costs and whose involvement in economic transactions – like international trade – gives them the means as well as the motive for doing so. The rich, it is sometimes said, are 'risk-averse'. What this means is that they, more than others, can afford to transform part of the risk into a cost.

Anatomy of the industry

I began by saying that insurance was indispensable to a developed market economy, and hence its significance for political economy. That perhaps deserves a word of explanation which will also clarify the different sectors of the business.

Early in the century, a young Chicago economist made an important contribution to liberal economic theory. His name was Frank Knight and the distinction he drew between *actuarial risk* and *business risk* incidentally still helps to explain the success of capitalist market economies (Knight, 1916). Actuarial risk, he observed, was statistically calculable. The number of 55-year-old men in America who would die in, say, 1925, was more or less predictable. The number of houses likely to be destroyed by fire in Chicago in August, could similarly be calculated statistically, at least within rough limits. Business risk was different. Success or failure was unpredictable. Yet, Knight observed, most entrepreneurs in a capitalist system were infused with hope and optimism. They believed that while others failed, they would succeed. It was this optimism which sustained the system. For some of them were proved wrong. Their businesses failed. They had miscalculated the incalculable chances of succeeding. They had carried the business risk, and they had lost.[4]

By the time Knight was writing, of course, the insurance business was well developed. It was involved in the management of actuarial risks – notably life insurance. And it was also involved to some extent in the management of some of the risks associated with business. This had

---

[4] The book was called *Risk, Uncertainty and Profit*. Perhaps because it portrays the capitalist entrepreneur more as dupe of the system than as exploiter of his employees' labour and surplus value, it has got little attention from Marxist historians and sociologists. And because it emphasises the irrational element in economic decision-making, it is not very popular in liberal circles either.

begun centuries before with the unavoidable risks to sea trade. Ships could be lost by shipwreck or piracy; cargoes could spoil or the buyers contracted to pay for them could fail to do so. One solution was to spread the risk by selling shares in the venture to several investors – the origin of joint-stock enterprises. Another was for those at risk to form a syndicate or cooperative. In matters of personal risks, they were called friendly societies or mutuals. In shipping, they were – and still are – called P and I clubs (Protection and Indemnity). Yet another was to find an investor who by taking on large numbers of ships and their cargoes could diversify the risk of any one failing. These were the insurers and it was the growth of merchandise trade by sea in the eighteenth century that led to the establishment at Lloyds Coffee House of a club of insurers prepared – at a price – to take on non-life risks that others shunned.

Knight's conceptual distinction between kinds of risk explains a major division in insurance business – that between Life and Non-life. Because the risks to the insurer in Life insurance were so much more predictable – because of actuarial data – this part of the insurance business was much more open to competition. Competition, however, failed to conform to basic economic theory in two important respects. First, the competition reduced market price below the costs of production. That is to say, total life insurance premiums usually fall below the cost of paying out on claims. But the insurance enterprise does not fail because the shortfall is normally more than made up from the income derived by the insurance enterprise from the investments it makes with funds from accumulated premiums.

Secondly, open competition in insurance is not exactly a level playing field in which success goes to the most efficient producer – at least, as 'efficiency' is usually understood. Customers in the market will tend to favour taking out policies with a large (and preferably old-established) enterprise in preference to a small, new one. The competitive advantage of the former has nothing much to do with efficient management or lower costs in providing the service. The customers simply believe – not always correctly – that it will be safer.

These two facts about life insurance explain why developing countries on gaining their independence often chose to regulate the national market by excluding competition from foreign insurers. They saw that the foreigners' comparative advantage was more perceived than real, especially if the government stood as guarantor for the national insurer. And it was also rational for the government of a poor country to put obstacles in the way of savings – in the form of insurance premiums collected from the customers – being converted out of the national currency and invested in the currency of a rich, developed country. Both arguments were used by, among others, Brazil and India. These were the two main governments which in the mid-1980s opposed the American proposal in the GATT's Uruguay Round of multilateral trade negotiations that liberalisation of trade in goods should be extended to services – notably insurance. But their opposition was in vain. Brazil was deeply in debt to foreign – mainly US – banks and badly needed from the Americans a Brady Plan renegotiation deal. India has long been a dependant of the World Bank. By the early 1990s, it had run into balance of payments problems and needed the blessing and support of the IMF – where, again, the US exercised the controlling veto power.

Life insurance is wide open to competition and is a comparatively straightforward sort of business. Banks are increasingly getting into life insurance, and direct selling by mail-order or telephone is taking the place of the door-to-door salesmen. Non-life insurance is now slightly bigger than life insurance and is more complex and less competitive. The claims tend to be larger and the risks less predictable. Some of the risks it covers derive from the unpredictable forces of nature – hurricanes, floods, earthquakes. Others arise from human error – air crashes and car accidents. Others from government regulation and the decisions of judges on legal liability for products, for professional errors and inadequate protection of consumers' or workers' safety. Yet others arise from technological change and scientific discoveries – as when the connection is established between ill-health and the use of asbestos in construction, or when the technology was developed for oil rigs to get oil from under the sea. Yet other risks arise from change in all sorts of markets – from commodities to exchange rates and interest rates. When non-life risks are fairly stable and more or less predictable, large transnational corporations have taken in recent decades to setting up their own 'in-house'; insurance companies. These are called 'captives', and they have been made welcome in places like Bermuda where regulation of how they operate is minimal – as are the taxes they pay and the information they disclose. A big oil company with a fleet of tankers, or a manufacturer with a very large fleet of company cars that have to be insured, can see the cash flow advantages of having the insurance premiums collected by its own captive enterprise, rather than paying it all over to an insurance company.

But when the non-life risks are large and unpredictable, the general commercial insurer will look for cover – just as bookmakers will 'lay off' large bets on an outsider. Hence the third, and increasingly important part of the insurance business – that of the large specialist re-insurance enterprises like Munich-Re or Swiss-Re, and of the major syndicates in the Lloyds market in London.

Recent structural changes have substantially increased the size of claims arising from some of these risks. One such change is financial – the escalating capital costs in production and in trade. For example, a big fire at any major airport will give rise to very much larger claims than the same fire would have done thirty or forty years ago. The increased size and cost of oil tankers means that the claims resulting from wreck and spillage will be many times greater than in the past. As the value and technical sophistication of corporate and private property has risen, so have the size of claims against the insurers. The comparison of figures on Lloyds overseas earnings in the 1960s and the 1990s is striking. Between 1965 and 1968, these rose from an estimated £14 million to a estimated £57 million. Two decades later, Lloyds business had expanded, premiums had risen and pre-tax profits in 1987 were around £500 million. Then profits turned to loss. By 1991, the estimated net losses amounted to $10 billion (£6.7 billion).[5] The sleeping partners of the underwriting syndicates – so-called Names – stood liable for unlimited claims on their personal fortunes. Many were bankrupt; not even a dispensation allowing them to borrow against future profits was enough to save them. The result was not only ruin for many Names. The UK balance of payments could no longer rely, as it did in the 1960s, on the City's 'invisible earnings'. And it seemed unlikely that the rather bizarre arrangement of financing the business by recruiting new Names would outlast the century. Already in 1994 there was a plan to transfer all business underwritten before 1986 to a new re-insurance company, NewCo, which would raise capital commercially.

Meanwhile, the escalation of the reinsurance market, and the risks inherent in it, have led to increasing concentrations of economic power. As with other kinds of international business, the business itself is not new – the first known case of a ship being reinsured was on a voyage from Genoa in Italy to Sluys in the Netherlands in 1370 – it is the size of it and its penetrating effects on everyday life and life-chances that is new.

---

[5] Figures for the 1960s come from the UK Balance of Payments White Paper, 1969, Annexe 5, as noted in my *Sterling and British Policy* (1971: 224). For the 1990s, figures were revealed by Lloyds in its annual report for 1994, reported in the financial press, 18 May 1994.

In the whole world, there are now rather fewer than 400 reinsurance firms. Their number is shrinking every year, as some firms give it up as too risky and others sell out or merge with others. Legal and General sold out some years ago. M and G, and Royal Insurance withdrew altogether from reinsurance. In 1994, there was a big merger of the US-based General Re (no. 4 in the Top Ten with 85 per cent of its business in the US market) and Cologne Re (no. 5, with 75 per cent of its business in Europe). Together they would be a major challenge to the top two firms in size – Munich Re and Swiss Re. The new firm, in which the US firm took the majority interest, would be based in neither the US nor Germany but in the Netherlands. *The Financial Times* commented that the merger 'signals further consolidation in an industry where the growing scale of risks faced by insurance buyers and insurance companies alike underlines the importance of size and strength . . . The position of small and medium-sized insurance companies has become less sustainable in recent years' (30 June 1994).

Significantly, it is the market, not government regulations, that decides how these big reinsurance risks will be managed. The big customers have a variety of options – many more than small customers. They also probably pay a discounted price, as in most businesses. The variations and permutations are highly technical and recondite. But roughly speaking, there is a choice between facultative cover (i.e. cover for specific risks as to a particular oil-rig, for example), and contract reinsurance (i.e. cover for a variety of risks) the extent of which is negotiated between insurer and reinsurer. Insurers are said normally to prefer 'facultative obligatory' contracts, in which they pass on only the most dangerous risks to the reinsurer. Obviously, obligatory contracts in which all the risks with a client are passed on tend to be cheaper.

They can also choose proportional or non-proportional reinsurance. The first fixes a percentage of the premiums to be passed on – the price to the insurer is usually about 16 per cent of the total premium received from the customer – to the reinsurer. The same percentage then applies to any claims made by the customer. Non-proportional reinsurance is based on a specially negotiated contract between insurer and reinsurer on which kind of claims will be paid by the latter, and on how much per claim or *in toto* he will pay. This is also called an 'excess of loss' contract, but again there are at least four major variants, like stop-loss contracts, excess of loss per risk and excess of loss per occurrence. The latter would have been a better arrangement for the reinsurers in catastrophes like the Hurricane Andrew in 1992 or the Los Angeles earthquake in 1993. Hurricane Andrew is said to have inflicted the biggest ever loss on the US insurance business and to have resulted in some of the damage-limitation responses subsequently seen in the global insurance business.

The other structural change in the business comes from government policies, mostly in the developed countries. The trend has everywhere been to assign greater legal liability for damage to persons, property or corporate businesses. Hospitals are held liable for mistaken diagnoses or bungled treatment. Universities are held liable for infringements of copyright. Lawyers and doctors for professional errors of judgement. Accountants for failure to disclose financial information. Enterprises are held liable to customers as well as employees. This trend was surely set first in the United States, where lawyers were allowed to retain as fees a percentage of damages awarded in the courts – and therefore had a strong incentive to go looking for profitable new business. The net effect, of course, is to raise the costs of goods and services to the average customer. An obvious example is the cost of insuring banks and others who issue credit cards against losses by theft or fraud. The cost is added to the interest charges or other fees charged to all the card users.

Another consequence is to give added authority to the insurers. As technological and financial change affects their business, they respond by putting a higher price on premiums for some risks over others, or by refusing to offer insurance cover on any terms whatsoever. This is often based on guesswork and prejudice more than actuarial experience. A well-known example is the refusal of life insurance to homosexual men, judged by the insurers as excessively at risk of becoming HIV positive and dying prematurely of AIDS. In effect, the insurers make a value judgement that alters options for potential customers: 'You must accept the risk of early death yourself because we have decided to refuse to cover it', they are saying.

They can, and indeed do, exercise the same kind of arbitrary authority over others when they refuse, for example, to sell insurance against theft to houseowners unwise – or unlucky – enough to live in burglary prone streets. Or, when they deny marine insurance to shipowners whose masters take the ship into a war-zone, as happened during the Iraq war. For if, as I have argued, authority in political economy is recognisable by the power to alter or modify the behaviour of others by using incentives and disincentives to affect the choice and range of options, there can be little doubt that as the world economy grows, the costs and risks of economic transactions escalate, allowing insurers and reinsurers to exercise increasing authority in and over the system.[6]

[6] In a short overview like this it has not been possible to cover all issues and aspects of insurance. For example, the 1990s were marked by the strong intervention of some governments, the US especially, to press for the liberalisation of trade in insurance services by other states. The relative success of the trend to liberalisation, in the Uruguay Round and in the European Union will probably tend to reinforce the power of the major insurance and reinsurance enterprises. There has also been a number of moves by banks to expand into the market for insurance, and of newcomers to engage in direct marketing to challenge established insurance firms. An increase in competitive pressures could lead paradoxically, to increased risk-taking by the risk managers (Mikdashi, 1992).

10 The Big Six accountants

The Big Six accountancy firms – Price Waterhouse, Peat Marwick McClintock, Coopers & Lybrand, Ernst and Young, Deloitte Touche Tohmatsu and Arthur Andersen – play an important and influential part in the world economy. How they came to do so, why they are all basically Anglo-American, what is the nature of their authority in the running of the world economy, and why states have allowed them such authority are all intriguing questions. They are also questions that need to be answered for any real understanding of the authority-market balance of power in the world system.

Few academics outside accountancy realise how big they are. Between them, they audit 96 of the top 100 British firms, and 494 of the *Fortune* 500. Their world-wide fee income, growing in some recent years by 25 per cent a year – totalled some $30 *billion* – about the same as Ireland's GDP. But it is not just as auditors that they are important. They have been instrumental in economic concentration as brokers in big merger and takeover deals involving international firms. As tax consultants, they have given these firms valuable advice on tax avoidance, thus limiting the authority of national governments to take a share of the wealth of big business. And they have become so much involved in corporate financing that they operate almost as banks, and certainly play a key part in the world's financial structure.

To explain how the Big Six got to play this important role in the world market economy, we have to go back 200 years to the importance of joint stock companies in the industrialisation of Europe – especially Britain – and America. Although the theory of the firm derived from the seminal work of Ronald Coase in the 1930s, which pointed to the cost advantages of internalising transactions (instead of conducting them through the market) as a reason for the existence of firms, historically speaking there was a much simpler reason why firms played so big a part in the emerging capitalist system. Though one man could start a business, he did not always have enough money of his own to make it grow and expand. Thanks to the legal protection of limited liability offered to the shareholders in joint stock companies, risk capital – other people's money – could be invested with reasonable safety in his firm. The shareholder's liability for loss was limited to the value of his investment. But in case it failed – as many did – through insolvency, someone independent, an auditor, had to be available to arbitrate and see fair play among the creditors, and between them and the shareholders. In England, by 1844, the law required shareholders to appoint such a person – usually one of the shareholders. He could also monitor the firm's accounts to see that the owners were not being defrauded and that it was being properly managed. By the end of the nineteenth century, the latter role of steward, or guardian of shareholder's interests, became dominant and professional accountants had taken that responsibility over from amateur shareholders.

Under this limited liability system, every public company was obliged by law to publish its annual accounts so that the shareholders were informed how their investment was being managed. They also had to have them professionally audited. Thus the auditor was responsible for assuring shareholders that the accounts gave a 'full and fair view' of the state of the business. Though this was thought necessary to prevent them being defrauded of their investment, the auditor was not responsible if, nevertheless, fraud did occur. And, in the British and American systems, what constituted a 'full and fair view' was (not entirely accidentally) left vague, undefined by set rules, and therefore subject to the 'professional' judgement of the accountant. In Europe, while the legal requirements on public companies for disclosure tended to be more precise, there were also many more private companies whose accounting obligations under the law were minimal. In Japan, too, the greater complexities of corporate organisation meant that the business of any firm was less open to public scrutiny than it would have been in the United States.

Until about thirty years ago, the role of accountants was defined by each national government and most operated almost entirely within the boundaries of national economies. What changed was the growth of international business and with it the provision of financial services, including accounting, to the operators in a world market. Like banks, accountancy firms – often partnerships rather than incorporated enterprises – followed their 'multinational' clients when they went abroad.[1] The domination of large US firms in international business, and the large number of old-established British multinationals gave an advantage to the large Anglo-American accountancy partnerships to whom many of them were already regular clients. That familiarity, combined with the domination of New York and London as financial centres, helped a process of concentration in which large partnerships swallowed small ones. When they did so, it was not necessarily because the larger firms had lower costs or gave more efficient service. As with insurance firms, size itself was a firm-specific asset in the marketplace. The larger the partnership, the bigger the comparative advantage in a market which behaved contrary to much standard economic theory. Its behaviour was rational only on the basis of perceived reputation rather than cost or efficiency.[2] The result of the mergers was that by the 1960s, there were just eight very large international accounting firms. More mergers reduced this to six. Any further concentration is considered less likely because it would cut too much into the profits to individual 'partners', while firms would gain no further economies of scale than they already have.

The other factor explaining the domination of the Big Six in international accounting is the steady growth of institutional investors – pension funds, unit trusts, investment enterprises – in the major stock exchanges. These investors are risk-averse and have shown a clear preference for the shares of those firms, including banks and other organisations, whose accounts were audited by the big firms.

This preference has been unaffected by a series of financial catastrophes and scandals in which one of the Big Six has played an important part. The collapse of the Pakistani-owned and managed Bank of Credit and Commerce International (BCCI) left thousands of depositors and shareholders ruined and angry. Some of them felt that while the blame was shared by central banks and financial regulators, it was the auditors – in that case Price Waterhouse – who should first have blown

---

[1] The point about partnerships is that the partners neither have to publish accounts nor disclose their profits. But they are personally liable to lawsuits. At one time recently, over 1,000 suits were pending against accountants in the US, with claims totalling $30 *billion*.

[2] There is a school of thought in economics that goes by the name of the Efficient Markets Hypothesis (EMH). The hypothesis is that if information is freely available, markets will function efficiently. But in business in the real world, important kinds of information are often not freely available, so the assumption that the market in accounting services is a free market, and therefore so efficient that it needs no regulation of any kind other than the competition of buyers and sellers is totally unrealistic.

the warning whistle. Then in 1995 it was Ernst and Young who were accountants to the ancient British bank of Barings, and who had said nothing in public – until it was too late – about the singular lack of supervision from London of the speculative trading in Japanese assets being carried on by a trader in Barings Singapore office. In both cases, the auditors' size and reputation provided a cloak for financial dealing which not only put the bank concerned at risk but put the whole international financial system under severe strain.

What is clear from the rapid growth of the Big Six is that none of them could have grown so large and profitable if they had remained as just accountants. Like manufacturing firms that produce a range of products, the big accountancy firms offer their clients a range of services wider and better resourced than those offered by smaller firms. Consultancy – and on public policies like privatisation or aid projects as well as for private business – has almost come to overshadow the accounting side of the business.

But why, the political economist will ask, did states allow such great authority and influence to be exercised within the limits of the law by such a small number of private firms? One answer lies in the preference of governments in the Anglo-Saxon tradition for indirect rule, leaving it, wherever possible, to the operators themselves to monitor and control themselves, whether they are doctors, lawyers, stockbrokers or insurers. Thus in both the US and Britain, professional associations of accountants – like those for the doctors and the lawyers – are often left to decide what is 'professional' and what is 'unprofessional' conduct. Not unnaturally, they have tended to give vague answers, maximising uncertainty:

> Professional accountants need uncertainty, lack of clarity, professional judgment and general mystification to maintain their distinction from ordinary people. But if it were generally realised that accounting principles have more to do with ritual and magic than with clarity or consistency, there would be a general loss of confidence in the accountancy profession and the financial statements that it produces.
> (Perks, 1993: 158)

Moreover, even in the United States where the statutory authority, the Financial Accounting Standards Board (FASB, known colloquially as Fazbee) is an independent body, its members are predominantly themselves accountants. FASB has seven members, acknowledged by and answerable to the Securities and Exchange Commission (SEC) but indirectly appointed by sixteen trustees of a financially independent, non-profit foundation. The whole set-up only dates from after the 1929 crash, before which, thanks to state chartering of corporations, financial reporting requirements were as loose as directors pleased. As part of Roosevelt's New Deal, the SEC was established so that in future investors could make more informed decisions. Unable to supervise every business directly, the SEC promptly passed on to the professional bodies the task of defining the principles of accounting. By 1973, after a series of changes, the FASB emerged. However, it seems that for fear of upsetting too many business applecarts at once, even the reformists on the Board tend to act rather slowly and cautiously. For example, in the 1990s, they wrestled with the problem of how to deal with firms that rewarded staff with discounted stock options. Should they be asked to declare their true (i.e. current market) value as costs, even though the option might not be exercised until much later when they were more valuable? In California especially, some of the high-tech firms for whom stock options were a cheap and easy way of rewarding (and hanging on to) key technologists, such a change would cut heavily into their declared profits and thus the value of their shares.

Another grey area of uncertainty, carefully left uncertain by the professional associations, concerns the dangers arising from conflicts of interest. When the big firms act for two or more competing multinationals, there can be a conflict of clients' interests. There is also a more general possible conflict inherent in the client–auditor relationship, in which the accountant is both policeman and defence counsel, so that partners can act both as financial brokers and consultants as well as auditors. The professional associations have also preferred a definition of professional responsibility that was narrower rather than wider. All their published statements of responsibility emphasise that the shareholder, rather than society at large, is the ultimate customer. Hardly surprising that *The Economist* once called the Big Six 'the foxes that guard the chicken coop'!

This point was given a rather extreme interpretation in a famous British case brought in 1984 that went right up to Britain's equivalent of the US Supreme Court. The Law Lords in the House of Lords then took a much more restricted view of the accountant's role than they had done twenty years before. Then, they had judged that the accountant had a duty to guard the investor against losses which might result from a negligently inadequate report on a firm's accounts. On the strength of that 1964 judgement (*Hedley Btrne vs Heller*), a corporate investor,

Caparo Industries, issued a writ against the auditor of a company in which it had invested. Instead of the substantial profit, based on stock valuations, predicted by the auditor, this company had made a loss (Perks, 1993: 53–4). But according to the judges in the 1984 case, the only purpose of an auditor's accounts was to provide shareholders as a body with the wherewithal to question the management, and if necessary use their voting rights against it. There was no responsibility to particular shareholders who suffered loss as a result of taking the reported accounts at face value. As Perks commented, 'It does seem that the law is excessively protective of auditors, and that in the public interest it ought to be possible to take action against them if they have been negligent in the performance of their duties' (Perks, 1993: 54).

One explanation for this protectiveness could have been the perceived danger, following American practice, of a flood of law suits against the accountancy firms. Already, about a tenth of the big firms' vast profits – running to hundreds of millions in Britain and billions of dollars in the US – is spent on legal fees and charges (*The Economist*, 17 October 1992). As with American (and increasingly also British) lawyers and doctors, the accountants have to take out insurance against the costs of suits brought against them. What it seems to add up to is a kind of symbiosis between all the professions – lawyers, accountants, bankers, insurers – in which all can lay off the risks *to themselves* of negligence or incompetence, while their clients have to take their chance. The insurers and lawyers make extra money, the accountants continue to expand their business – and all get a slice of the profits pie. The system seems to amount to a rather liberal legitimation by the accountants of whatever the management does or fails to do, giving it the freedom to move the goalposts as and when it suits them.

By way of showing how the Big Six (not to mention smaller accountants) are aided by the courts to legitimate change in corporate practices that often confer benefits on managers at the expense of salarymen, wage-earners and shareholders, consider the Tiphook case. This was a British-registered company engaged in the business of leasing containers and other handling equipment extensively used in transnational trade and transport. Much of Tiphook's business was in trade with America. In 1992, the management announced that thenceforward its accounts would be reported in US dollars, not pounds sterling and that its auditors would follow US instead of British accounting conventions. Although at first glance this seems an admirable move to greater transparency, since US rules are more demanding than British, there was more to it than that. The reason for the change, explained the chairman, was that the company's financial strategy had shifted from Britain to the US; more than half its capital was raised in the US, and its equity held in US depository receipts had likewise increased from 2 to over 50 per cent of the total assets. But the effect of the announcement on the stock market was to knock 10 per cent off the price of Tiphook shares. While management salaries were unaffected, the shareholders lost a tenth of the value of their investment without any change in the company's productivity or profitability. No one, apparently, questioned the decision (*Financial Times*, 1993).

In this whole picture, the accountants have tended to legitimate whatever the managers of multinationals like Tiphook might decide suited their interests. Tiphook was only unusual in that the management's decision led to stricter, not looser accounting practice. In other cases, when business goes transnational, it is more usual to TNCs to choose the most lax rules, the least demanding tax systems. Mostly they are secure in the knowledge that if governments were ever to agree on a harmonisation of accounting rules it would more likely be (as in environmental or competition matters) standardisation *down* to the least interventionist rather than standardisation *up* to the most interventionist.

Many of the changes noted so far were aided, inadvertently, by the inflation of the 1970s. This gave rise to what was called 'creative accounting' which meant, in effect, greater freedom to management to have the accounts presented in whatever way suited the purposes of the management. Obviously, as salaries and replacement costs rose, it made little sense to value existing stocks or property at the historic prices paid for them.[3] Their current, or market value, however, was much more open to subjective interpretation. Terry Smith, in a critical study of the profession in Britain listed no less than twelve different ways that accountants discovered in the 1980s to 'massage' a firm's reported profits, including putting some items 'off balance sheet', over- or undervaluing the assets of acquisitions, adding 'extraordinary' items etc. (Smith, 1992).

Market value accounting (MVA) can also add to systemic risks of

---

[3] Indeed, it was precisely the failure of many firms to adjust their accounts to inflation that resulted in asset-stripping takeovers, and new opportunities for brokers like Kohlberg, Kravis and Roberts. KKR made such vast profits out of arranging the finance for leveraged buy-outs of under-valued firms that in 1989 they displaced General Motors as the biggest clients of accountants Deloitte & Touche (Anders, 1992).

another kind. Banks, for instance, often hold government bonds and other official securities in their reserves. But if interest rates rise, the value of bonds tends to fall, putting bank solvency at the mercy of markets. In the US, the Fed has been more concerned for the safety of the banking system, and the market for government debt, while the Securities Exchange Commission has been more interested in an efficient financial market for corporate liabilities. Their divergent attitudes to MVA can be explained by their divergent concerns.

So we come to the nature of accountants' authority in the world market economy, the special role of the whole profession, and also of the Big Six in the global political economy. As to the profession, readers may be aware that social scientists, and especially sociologists, have in the past held some diametrically opposed opinions about the role of professional people in society – including doctors, lawyers, and teachers as well as engineers, architects and accountants who are sometimes classed as semi-professional because they are both more 'technical' and less independent. To simplify a long story, one school of thought has stressed the contribution of professional people to the stability of society and even to its respect for moral over purely material values; the other has stressed the partiality of the professions for the rich and the powerful in society, and therefore their system-sustaining character. The first school saw professionals as possessing not only special knowledge but also a primary orientation to community, or societal values and interests rather than to special individual interests. This school also saw the professionals as being responsive to a system of rewards (some honorific and some material) that were more symbols of their social status and achievement than outright payments for services rendered to clients. The demand for their services had greatly expanded with industrialisation and the rise of urban middle classes, but their detachment from the naked forces of the market gave them a privileged social status.[4] In short, they were a valuable counterweight both to the materialism of the market and the power of the state.

The other school of thought built on intellectual foundations laid by Max Weber. He saw growing bureaucracy and expanding professionalism as two sides of the same coin. The professional was caught up in the general process of rationalisation of society based on scientific advance.

[4] For a survey of sociological debates, see for example, Johnson (1972) which cites Talcott Parsons and Carr-Saunders, a distinguished British social scientist and Director of the London School of Economics during and after World War II, as belonging to the first school; C. Wright Mills and James Burnham as belonging to the more critical school.

C. Wright Mills, for example, saw the professions as succumbing to a 'managerial demiurge', becoming increasingly salaried rather than independent and using their special knowledge to sustain and legitimise a capitalist system. They were just one aspect, according to Burnham, of the managerial revolution. Johnson saw the first school as deriving its perceptions from the professions of medicine, law, social service of various kinds while the second school looked more at the role of engineers, architects, and accountants (Johnson, 1972: 14–18).

So, in the light of recent changes – notably of the internationalisation of production and of all sorts of financial services – which view is right when it comes to the role of accountants?[5] The answer depends on a more fundamental value judgement: security and stability, or economic growth and wealth creation? Is the security and stability of the market economy more, or less important than the capacity of firms to generate new wealth? If the future of the capitalist system, in the long term, can be assured only by maintaining confidence in its stability, then whatever sustains that stability is a public good. But if economic growth and wealth-creation have priority over other values, then so do the private interests of managers, and of shareholders. The objective of auditing and accounting is simply to protect these private interests. It is a private good, to be paid for out of corporate profits and tailored to suit corporate strategies. That was essentially the judgement of the House of Lords in the Caparo case.

Depending on the value judgement, the four key political economy questions are the usual ones. Who pays? Who benefits? Who carries the risks? Who gets the opportunities? At present the answer to the question, who pays? is that although governments and other public and non-profit organisations do increasingly employ accountants, the great growth in the profession, and especially the growth of the Big Six, owes most to its corporate patrons. And here it is the directors of the big firms that appoint the auditors, and arrange the payment of their fees, even though those fees come out of the corporate profits which might otherwise go to the shareholders. On the whole, therefore, although the work of the accountants does to some extent protect shareholders and creditors, it is the directors who benefit most. It is they who decide to

---

[5] It may be that no one view applies equally to all professions in all societies. A point about accountants made by one authority was that this was about the only profession whose growth and social status had not been accompanied by any independent research. Neither its members nor its professional associations had ever felt it necessary to reinforce its power with scientific inquiry.

what purpose the accounts shall be massaged, what message they shall convey to the markets and to society generally. And because profit in a capitalist system is accepted as a measure of efficiency, the accountant is bound to serve the interest of the firm rather than those of its employees, its consumers or suppliers, or those of society at large. The answer to the *cui bono*? question, who benefits?, therefore, is the accountants and their paymasters. And in the great majority of cases, their biggest paymasters are the large transnational corporations. The accountants are handsomely paid, and in return they legitimise a version of the truth that suits the paymaster.

As Perks concludes, this does not really mean that accountants are exercising independent authority. For the 'full and fair' picture of reality they present is, as he says, only powerful 'when allied with and supporting organizations that are already powerful, particularly major companies and central government'. The last point is important. For governments have sometimes been as guilty as firms in making sure that the accountants are economical with the truth. The United States government, for instance, in the 1980s saw to it that federal regulators used the tricks of the trade to hide an expected $5 billion loss to the agency that guaranteed the deposits with Savings and Loans. That saga ended with the US taxpayers being landed with up to $300 billion dollars to save the S&Ls, instead of the $5 billion that it would have cost if the problem had been revealed early on. 'Smoke and mirrors accounting', the press called it' (*Sañ José Mercury News*, 3 January 1994).

In Japan, when the bubble economy collapsed and as the full force of recession hit the economy in 1993, the government intervened with the banks to stop them writing down the value of their investments in company shares to the level set by the market. Fear of a run on the banks and a total collapse was the reason. Just as it had been when the US government in 1982 allowed US banks to count 'non-performing loans' to Mexico and other debtor countries as if they were still real assets, and not losses.

In Germany, profitable companies have long been allowed by the government to put aside hidden reserves that can be used in poor years to make the accounts look better than they are. The extent of this official protection came out when Daimler Benz, among other German multinationals wanted to have its shares traded in the US. That decision made the firm liable to US rules on disclosure, with the result that it had to declare a loss of $579 million for the first half-year, instead of the $102 million profit that its accountants could pronounce under German law.

Other countries, too, have ways of allowing management to hide the truth from public gaze. The extent of real losses from non-performing loans by banks, for example, only came out both in France and in Japan when 'major banks had to be rescued by the government.'

Nor are governments above using the services of accountants and statisticians to use smoke and mirrors to conceal their own shortcomings. The Federal Reserve in the 1970s invented the device of 'base drift' – effectively shifting the base to a new higher level – by means of which the real rise in the US money supply could be understated. Other governments have found similar dodges. And international organisations are even worse. The waste in the United Nations and the fraud in the European Union are familiar scandals. We may only conclude that the use of accountancy by these organisations, as by big corporations, tends to enhance their power, just as it is also a symptom of it. They could not employ accountants unless they had the resources to do so.

A good illustration of the point came out in Hearings by the Finance Committee of the US Senate in January 1989. American workers had been angered by the redundancies and plant closures that had often followed leveraged buy-outs brokered and financed by Kohlberg, Kravis and Roberts. The president of the AFL/CIO testified that his organisation's accountants had calculated that 90,000 jobs had consequently been lost to their members over the past decade. The allegation was contested by Deloitte, acting for KKR and quoted to the Senate committee by Senator Danforth (Rep. Missouri). The buy-outs, they contested, had actually expanded pay-rolls by 4.4 per cent a year, faster than payrolls had grown before the buy-outs. The Deloitte study was based on some guesstimates and projections and sometimes counted the jobs gained with acquisitions but not always the jobs lost when parts of a firm were sold off. Because of the ubiquitous counterfactual problem, there could be no objective truth; even splitting the difference between the two estimates would be a guess. But the significant result of the hearings was that KKR survived, and the US government did nothing even though a poll showed two out of three Americans thought the takeover wave of the 1980s was 'not a good thing', and though books like Max Holland's *When the Machine Stopped* and campaigns by the *Wall Street Journal* did tarnish the company's popular image and probably did some damage to its business. What finally destroyed KKR was not the government, nor public opinion, but the financial markets.

This power analysis is important when it comes to any discussion of reform, either of corporate or of official, accounting. That reform is overdue is agreed by many impartial observers, even by members of the profession (*The Economist*, October 17, 1995: 25). But how much is politically possible, given the vested interests involved? After the BCCI collapse, Britain's Cadbury Committee in 1992 said the government should at least change the law so that auditors, without breaching rules of confidentiality, could at least report reasonable suspicion of fraud to officials (Report, 1992). It did not, however, go so far as insisting that companies change their auditors every so often to avoid too cosy a relationship, though it did suggest that maybe different partners should be charged with the firm's annual audit. More radical was an earlier proposal for a State Auditing Board responsible for setting the rules (like the FASB) and for licensing accountants (Lyall and Perks, 1976: 34–6). Though raised in Parliament, that idea found little support, and even suggestions that accountants should be bound to report suspicions of fraud, or that fee income should not be arbitrarily fixed by the auditors have got nowhere.

It seems clear that in Britain, where whatever the party in power, City interests have always had a big influence on government policy, nothing is going to be radically changed. The United States, however, is somewhat more flexible and more inclined to favour openness in government and in business. The Tiphook and Daimler Benz cases show a trend in international business to accept the exigencies of American law and practice as the necessary condition for access to US financial and consumer markets. As in other matters, US structural power – the global reach of the federal government – is steadily increasing, and is the best hope for some limitation of the powers of the Big Six and others. Little is to be hoped or expected of the professional associations, nor of inter-governmental conventions. If the governments of states who are members of the European Union have found it hard to harmonise their company laws and tax systems, it is hardly likely that agreement could be reached among the leading industrialised states in the OECD, let alone that any significant progress can be made on a global scale through the United Nations.

11 Cartels and private protectionism

A striking feature of the knowledge structure of the international political economy today is the slight attention given by social scientists to private protectionism, as compared with public or state protectionism. By that term I mean the intervention of firms with the operation of the free market. Such intervention may be unilateral. This is commonly the case when a single firm – a TNC – has a corporate strategy that limits competition between its various affiliates in different countries. Each one is master in its own territory and is not allowed to poach – i.e. compete with – another affiliate of the same company. There is also an element of private protectionism when a firm has monopoly control over a technology, or a system of marketing, or a brand-name that keeps away competitors. Some private protectionism is legitimised by governments as with pharmaceutical patents, or public procurement policies that discriminate in favour of a particular protected firm to the exclusion of others.

But private protectionism is also often multilateral. It works through an association of firms agreeing among themselves to limit their production, fix their prices and collectively manage their respective market shares. Typically, such market-managing agreements are based on the principle 'dog does not eat dog' – that is, each associate is given a free hand by the others in the home market where the large company is large and rich enough to quell any serious competition and to set prices as it pleases. The export markets will be parcelled out, the Americans having Latin America, Germany having central Europe, Britain and France their former colonies and the Japanese the Asian markets. Or else there will be an agreement, product by product on the amounts to be sold or the prices to be charged. Cartel members also often operate a fighting fund, replenished when members are fined for underselling each other or for breaking other restrictive rules and doled out to those who claim to be victims of broken rules – effectively a private taxation system.

As a constraint on competition in the world market economy, such private protectionism may very well be every bit as significant in the international trading system as the tariffs, quotas, subsidies and sanctions imposed on trade by governments. The consequence for international political economy is also very clear. The institutional arrangements by which groups of firms, or even large firms acting by themselves, interfere with open competition constitute centres of power and sources of authority to which would-be buyers have no option but to bow.

Yet for the last twenty years, the literature on world trade – mostly written by economists – has studiously ignored such private protectionist practices. And the mainstream literature in international relations makes no mention of it (Holsti, 1967; Waltz, 1970). Even the international political economists who cover other politically significant aspects of the world economy do not seem to think it worth mentioning or analysing.

Naturally enough, the protectionist firms themselves, whether acting unilaterally or conniving together to maintain high prices or to restrict output, have kept quiet. It is only rational for them to prefer to keep their oligopolistic activities in the dark. Only in those cases – steel is the prime example in manufacturing, oil in commodity trade – where since the late 1960s governments, led in steel by the United States and in oil by Saudi Arabia, have become involved in legitimising market-sharing in international trade have the detailed arrangements been given publicity (Warnecke and Woolcock in Strange and Tooze, 1981; Mikdashi, 1986).

Otherwise, it is as if a curtain of silence had descended over the whole subject of cartels. The last major report by an international secretariat was published in 1977: the OECD's *Restrictive Business Practices of Multinational Enterprises*. Thereafter, most of the staff involved moved elsewhere and there was no follow-up. The same was true of the UNCTAD secretariat. A 1974 report, *Restrictive Business Practices; Studies on the United Kingdom of Great Britain and Northern Ireland, the United*

States of America and Japan had no sequel. The UN's Center for Transnational Corporations whose first report in 1978, *Transnational Corporations and World Development* had been rather critical of the multinationals, has become progressively milder in its commentaries.

Recent studies by academics – reflecting the state-centrism of most social science – have been myopically confined to those market-managing arrangements that involved governments, whether directly as in steel, textiles, oil, uranium, bauxite and tin, or indirectly as in gold and diamonds. For instance, the study by Mark Zacher and Jock Finlayson, *Managing International Markets: Developing Countries and the Commodity Trade Regimes* (1988) despite the title took an avowedly state-centric approach in line with the rest of the regime literature. It mentioned multinational corporations only as one of sources of influence on state policies. A more recent study, Deborah Spar's *The Cooperative Edge: The Internal Politics of International Cartels* sounds more promising but in fact curiously limits itself to just four case studies – gold, diamonds, uranium and silver. It concentrates entirely on the inter-state bargaining process behind the success or failure of each rather than on the role of producers and the market structures. Yet she admits that the most effective cartel of the four she studied, that in diamonds, almost entirely owed its success to the tight control over supplies exercised by one firm, Anglo-American, and the majority owners, the Oppenheimer family. The supporting role of the South African, Soviet and Israeli governments was just that – supportive.

Such myopia is all the more odd since one of the most often quoted passages of Adam Smith's *Wealth of Nations* refers to the endemic tendency of business people to combine together against the consumer. It is worth quoting once again because it reflects the common-sense experience of ordinary people the world over. No one who has gone to a furniture auction, for example, is unaware that s/he is likely to be frustrated by a prearranged ring of dealers determined to grab the best bargains for themselves even if this may sometimes mean running up the bids against the amateur buyers. (A 'combat fund' will compensate the member who has to do this; see below for an explanation of such common cartel practices). It is just one example of the phenomenon remarked by Adam Smith: 'People of the same trade seldom meet together, even for merriment and diversion, but the conversation ends in a conspiracy against the public, or in some contrivance to raise prices.'

Some empirical evidence

For example, nineteen firms manufacturing paper board in Europe were found by the EC's competition division to be operating a cartel disguised as a social club which met regularly in Swiss hotels. British and other producers of cement for concrete construction habitually met in a pub at Newbury to carve up the local market. Ship suppliers in the North Sea disguised their regular meetings as a coffee club (*Financial Times*, 17 August 1994). And so on. The watchdogs of the EC's competition directorate or of the Anti-Trust Division of the US Department of Justice consequently have had a hard job proving that stable market shares or matching prices are anything more than a coincidence.

Economic historians will be well aware that there is a strange contrast here between the dearth of research and its limitation to inter-state bargaining in the last quarter of the twentieth century, and the rather wider and more intense interest in cartels to be found in the 1930s and even the 1940s. An early text in international relations *Introduction to the History of International Relations* (Duroselle and Renouvin, 1947) made quite a point of the large role played by international cartel agreements in world politics before 1914. E. H. Carr's magisterial *Twenty Years Crisis* tells the interwar story by interweaving economic conditions and responses with more formally political ones. Two major postwar studies collected a great deal of empirical material on what had gone on in the 1930s (Stocking and Watkins, 1946; Hexner, 1945). There were also a number of more specialised studies at that time. Nothing comparable can be found after the mid-1970s, despite the years of stagflation and recession, followed by debt and deflation.

The one outstanding exception is a book that almost never was – Kurt Mirow's *A Ditadura dos Carteis* (1977, revised and translated into English and published as *Webs of Power; International Cartels and the World Economy* 1982). It had no sooner been published in Brazil than copies were seized and banned by the military government on the grounds that it discredited the country and its government by showing Brazil as the helpless victim of international cartels. Pirated copies quickly appeared and were soon sold. Meanwhile, the charge was so preposterous that civilian judges could not be found to try it and even the Supreme Military Tribunal eventually acquitted the author to the discomiture of the generals. But the net result of the ill-considered ban had put Mirow and his book in the limelight, leading eventually to an English translation.

Though much of the content – on the oil business, on steel and shipping, was fairly common knowledge, its disclosures regarding the electrical equipment were (so to speak) electrifying. They were the fruit of bitter personal experience. Mirow's family firm, founded by his great grandfather, started a new venture in the 1950s producing the kind of electrical equipment it had formerly imported from Germany. But its import-substituting prosperity came under attack from its big foreign competitors. It went bust and the family tried again in the 1970s. Kurt Mirow was convinced that Brown Boveri and other multinationals were practising predatory pricing, below cost. His case to the government failed for lack of evidence, but in 1972 brought a call out of the blue from an employee of the Brazilian subsidiary of a Belgian electrical equipment manufacturer. This man passed on inside information on the rules of a trade association innocuously registered as the Institute for the Study of Exports of Heavy Electrical Equipment (IBEMEP). Leaked documents showed its members as the major multinationals in the business, including Siemens and General Electric, Asea and AEG, and two local firms, one of which was soon taken over by Hitachi. Mirow then found out that IBEMEP was part of a larger world-wide association, the International Electrical Association (IEA) which also acted behind an innocuous front as a full-fledged cartel. IEA members accepted protection of each other's home markets, fixed prices, managed non-competitive bidding and financed a combat fund to beat and keep out competition. What had particularly upset the Brazilian military government was the suggestion that, for all their nationalistic bragging, they had actually connived at this foreign penetration of the economy and the attempted elimination of local enterprise by a well-organised but covert cartel of rich and powerful multinational firms. Only the generals' clumsy attempt at censorship, combined with Mirow's injured family pride and talent for investigation, had provided the coincidence of causes leading to a new study of international cartels at a time when most other writers appeared to have lost interest in the subject.

But why should this have been? Why is Mirow's book so exceptional? On the political right, the pervasive silence among liberal or neo-classical economists is striking. The subject of private protectionism seems tacitly taboo. A random survey of the economic literature on trade, whether theoretical or descriptive, yields sparse results. Paul Samuelson's popular text, for example does not get round to international trade until page 621, spends a great deal of time on theories of comparative advantage, even though these are now generally judged by management writers to be in need of radical revision. Just two pages are given to all kinds of restrictions on competition, with the dismissive comment that, for economists, it does not matter which devices are used to raise prices; whether they are private arrangements or those made by governments, it is all the same. Mergers, cartels or pool agreements, holding companies, trade associations, trusts or 'fair price' laws are all indiscriminately judged to be 'evil'. Yet on other matters, the role of government in relation to economy is a matter of great concern. Why not where public and private protection is concerned?

A more specialised and recent text, Nigel Grimwade's *International Trade, New Patterns of Trade, Production and Investment* (Grimwade, 1989) does not even index 'cartels', has one chapter on the rise of the multinational company and the expansion of intra-firm trade which says nothing about the extensive history, throughout the twentieth century, of inter-firm bargaining in manufacturing and services, all designed expressly to keep competitive newcomers out, to carve up the world market to the benefit of the producers and at the expense of consumers. Another book, John Jackson's *The World Trading System; Law and Policy of International Economic Relations* (Jackson, 1989) gives a very full account of the Bretton Woods institutions, the GATT and the evolution of US trade policy, ending with the comment that the 1988 Trade Act – the basis of Uruguay Round negotiations – lists restrictive business practices if practised in other states as one of the grounds on which the US government may invoke the punitive section 301 – but only if such practices restrict the sales of goods made by US firms in that country.

Theoretical texts in liberal economics naturally tend to predicate a world of perfect markets and rational (materialist) behaviour. Take Lipsey's *Introduction to positive economics* (1963) now in its 6th or 7th edition. Most theoretical propositions explained therein assume a national economy virtually untouched by global forces of structural change. Although Lipsey notes that oligopoly and the concentration of economic power is increasing, and with it predatory pricing and 'brand proliferation' by means of advertising, he sticks to the basic contention that costs and demand determine an equilibrium price and level of output. 'Rigorous' theory is justified:

> Foreign exchange markets, markets for raw materials, markets for many agricultural commodities, real estate, most futures markets, the market for gold and other precious metals and securities markets are but a few whose behaviour is comprehensible with, *but makes no sense without*, the basic model of perfect competition (possibly augmented

by one or two specific additional assumption to catch the key institutional details of each case.   (Lipsey, 1963; 306, my italics)

Such a judgement hardly squares with actual historical experience in any of the markets he mentions. But it accurately reflects a mind-set among many economists that bristles with distrust and suspicion at the very idea of political regulation of markets of any kind, but more particularly at such regulation at the hands of government.[1] In their book, state ownership always leads to inefficiency and waste; private enterprise is always to be preferred to public enterprise; and any limitation on the actions of firms is to be resisted. The profession's studied neglect of restrictive business practices is therefore understandable, if not defensible. The disinterest itself is ideologically biased; a classic case of 'theory' in social science always being – as Cox insists – 'for' someone.

It is less easy to understand the silence of the radical left on this subject, especially of those writers interested in international political economy, Robert Cox, for example, refers to the concept of the 'cartel-state'. But this has nothing much to do with market management. The term refers only to states in which a neo-corporatist bargain is forged between interested parties in society – business, labour, government – thus avoiding a greater evil – the fascist alternative of authoritarian repression (Cox, 1987: 195). Gill and Law refer only briefly to the bauxite agreement – one of the falsely optimistic commodity associations that fell apart – in the context of a discussion of North–South relations (Gill and Law, 1988: 293). Otherwise, they take the Leninist view that because of the essentially conflictual nature of national capitalist states, cartels have a built-in tendency to break down because of differential costs of production (Gill and Law, 1988: 58).

That judgement is not actually borne out by the historical record of the past century. Nor would the EC officials who are trying to make European firms behave in a more competitive manner and who have uncovered the paperboard cartel and many other instances of private protection agree. The fact is that there have been plenty of transnational cartel arrangements, and not only within Europe, that have persisted over recent years, as they have in the past. They have not always lasted. But the reasons for breakdown have not been, as Gill and Law suggested, differential production costs. In retrospect, the two most

---

[1] This is another clear example of the mental limitation by western political scientists that perceives 'politics' as consisting only of action by states. See above, chapter 3.

common causes of breakdown were wars – notably both world wars – and financial and economic crisis – as in 1929–31 – and the instability it brought to exchange rates, commodity prices, markets and governments.

The First World War brought to an end the oldest international manufacturing cartel of all – that among makers of steel rails which had first been organised in 1883. A more powerful and extensive steel cartel, first organised in 1926, collapsed in the free fall of all prices after 1929. It began to get together again by 1933, was joined by the British in 1935, but once again could not survive the outbreak of war in 1939. In both world wars, the Allied navies took over the management of sea-trade from the liner shipping conferences that, in all the seven seas, had regularly fixed prices and kept out competition. Only the Phoebus cartel maintaining the oligopolistic price of electric lamps managed to survive the interwar Depression, despite some members cheating by cutting prices to protect their market shares. But it too could not survive the war in 1939 (Mirow, 1982: 38–41).

To give the reader some idea of how – despite the silence of the academics – cartels really operate in the real world, and incidentally to suggest how the 'long peace' of the Cold War may actually have favoured their proliferation, let us take as an example a recently organised cartel set up in one of the oldest of international businesses – shipping. It is a business that well illustrates – today, no less than in the past – Adam Smith's dictum about agreements made at the expense of the consumer. It also demonstrated two other points I have repeatedly made – the impact on producers of market conditions, more especially when these tend to be cyclical; and, secondly, the impact on them and on outcomes generally, of changing technologies in the production of goods or (in this case) services.

In the 1970s, established shipping conferences, of which there were over 300, came under threat from two directions: the new technology of container shipping, and the world-wide fall in freight rates. The depressed market in shipping services lasted for the next two decades (Strange, 1976; Cragg, 1981). But by 1994, all the major shipping enterprises had converted to the use of containers. While their global trade association, the International Council of Containership Operators, popularly called The Box, was divided on the obvious long-term solution – an agreement to scrap the older part of the world merchant fleet – the big firms dominating the heavy-traffic transatlantic route had finally reached agreement. They would set up a super-cartel whose members would set uniform prices for different kinds of cargo, would agree to cuts in capacity by leaving empty an agreed percentage of container slots on each ship, and would enforce discipline on its members by fines and on their customers by the time-honoured practice of deferred rebates.[2]

The Transatlantic Trade Agreement (TTA) was first negotiated and signed in May, 1992 by the twelve big shipping enterprises in the Atlantic trade – Sea-Land (US), Atlantic Container (Sweden), Hapag-Lloyd (Germany), Moller-Maersk (Denmark), DSR-Senator (Germany), P&O and OOCL (UK) and Swiss, French, Korean, Dutch and Polish firms. Three more joined later and the terms of the deal were revealed in the trade press early in 1994. Rates were to vary according to the value of the cargo and to what the traffic could bear. They were to be moved up or down according to the state of the market, the degree of outside competition and other variables. The agreement also extended from transport by ship to transport by land since it also covered rates for land transport of the containers to and from the ports. Initially, because traffic eastward was only two-thirds of westbound traffic, the agreement was only one-way, east-to-west. But its members accounted for 70 per cent of the traffic and set up a secretariat and a policing Enforcement Authority to make sure its rules were kept. It had power to investigate alleged breaches, inspect accounts and records of members, their sub-contractors and associates, hear evidence and ultimately assess fines.

The secretariat ran the Capacity Management Program which could enforce empty cargo-space up to 25 per cent of any ship's capacity. Its power has extended to the smaller independent 'consolidators' who package small cargoes, two of whom have already been forced out of business.

And the regulators? Under Article 85 and pressure from the users, the European Commission did initiate an inquiry. But there is no overall EC law on shipping, and national laws have long tolerated the old conferences. And a 1986 decree only threatened action against cartels seeking to eliminate all effective competition. In the United States, the Federal Maritime Commission is the agency responsible for monitoring the TAA, but the 1984 Shipping Act indicated an exemption from anti-trust rules, and although it has been kept fully informed by the

[2] For this and other details on the TTA, I have drawn on an unpublished research paper, 'The Trans-Atlantic Agreement in plain words' by Manuel Terranova, a student at the Bologna Center, Johns Hopkins University in 1993.

cartel it was so far neither approved it nor declared it illegal. In effect, if the US government turns a blind eye on the TAA, it would be hard for the European Commission to act against it. Meanwhile, it is expected to be the model for other major trade routes.

Economic history, in short, shows clearly that the management of surplus capacity is and has always been an important and recurrent issue in political economy, and one to which states and firms have sought, and sometimes found, a variety of solutions.[3] In agriculture, the solutions, when they have been found, have been national, usually requiring the direct or indirect intervention of political authority over output, or over prices, or over both. The European Union's Common Agricultural Policy is a good example, but is mirrored by similar policies within Japan or the United States or any industrialised country – Sweden and Switzerland being extreme examples. In manufacturing, especially where barriers to entry have limited the number of competing enterprises, the solution has often been found in cartel arrangements between firms. Only when steelworkers or textile workers were threatened with sudden job losses, apparently as a result of market invasion by foreign producers, have governments become involved. Protectionist policies – like the American trigger price mechanism for steel in the 1970s, or the D'Avignon output cuts in the EC in the 1980s – have been used to supplement the efforts of firms to manage surplus capacity. Alan Milward has argued persuasively and on the basis of French protection for cereal producers in the 1880s that such intervention by the state can be seen as a 'set of stages in the widening participation of different groups in that body politic. In this sense', he goes on, 'the transition from mid nineteenth century liberalisation of trade was not a regressive atavistic response by conservative agrarian pressure groups but a progression in democratic political participation' (Milward, 1981).

Why then, have social scientists, with so few exceptions, not gone hunting for the transnational cartels of the 1980s and 1990s? Why have they not bothered to dig out the evidence that, in the most recent period of slowed growth in the developed industrial countries, cartels and restrictive agreements have once again been the preferred solution to

[3] Some of us have been alert to the political aspects of the problem for some time. In the 1970s, the slow growth of western economies gave rise to what was called the 'new protectionism'. Roger Tooze and I organised an inter-disciplinary, multi-professional discussion of the issues, few of which have changed substantially since. The results were published in a book, *The International Politics of Surplus Capacity: Competition for Market Shares in a World Recession* (Strange and Tooze, 1981). See also Strange (1979).

problems of surplus capacity? It would be odd indeed if, while public protectionism was being practised in some industries like steel or textiles, other industries also afflicted in the same way did not resort to self-help in the shape of private protectionism.

For lack of sufficient evidence, no definite answer is possible to that question. It remains a puzzle until the results of more investigative research can be assembled. Yet there are some plausible hypotheses for the silence of western social scientists and for the consequent dearth of data. One is that the major private-protectionist manufacturing cartels that were known to exist in the past – electrical products, chemicals, synthetic fibres, aluminium, for example – do still exist – but they have 'gone underground', so that they have become much less visible. Mirow says that no one knew where the headquarters office of the International Electrical Association had gone when it left London in 1973. Then a *Le Monde* reporter accidentally found its new office in Lausanne (Mirow, 1982: 245). There, under Swiss law, it was under no legal obligation to register, nor even to disclose its membership or make public the rules that bound them. The decision to leave London was most likely due to increased activity by the UK Monopolies Commission which had been given powers in the 1960s to investigate sectors suspected of price-fixing resale price maintenance or other restrictive practices.

A variant of this hypothesis is that formal agreements, written documents used to have to pass through the post so that they could be leaked to the media or the politicians. Now, not only are such formal agreements no longer the norm for transnational cartels. The new technologies of communication also contribute to a greater degree of secrecy for inter-firm messages. The acceleration in both vertical and horizontal concentration of economic power means fewer big firms competing in the world market. Everywhere except Japan and perhaps Germany, the 1980s were marked by a spate of mergers and acquisitions. Negotiating and financing them was one of the few ways big banks managed to survive the foreign debt crisis of the 1980s. The victims (as in Brazil) were usually smaller, middle-sized firms that had access to their home markets. Their absorption by international business meant that the gap between the dominant firms and their small competitors widened. There was less danger of unexpected challenges from them to the big players. And small groups made up of a few very large transnational firms, in which each is vulnerable to retaliation by the others, may feel no need of legal agreements. These in any case may be too inflexible to adapt to rapidly changing market conditions, or new products and processes. In some sectors – cars and chemicals, for instance – there has also been more vertical integration. Big firms either acquired or built close relations with both their suppliers and their distributors. This imitated the *keiretsu* relations common in Japan. And by internalising transactions in the value-adding chain, it also made the big TNCs more formidable, especially in their protected home markets.

A third hypothesis is also a variant on the theme *autres temps, autres moeurs*. A feature of the production structure in the world economy of the late twentieth century has been the accelerated rate of technological change, not only in what are thought of as the high-tech industries, but also in older ones like steel or textiles, or indeed agriculture and food-processing. In all the developed market economies, states have offered protection to the property rights of inventors and innovators by means of patent laws. And where other countries have claimed their rights to technology transfer, if necessary by pirating patented technology, the US and other developed country governments have put the protection of intellectual property rights on the international agenda. They have then put pressure on developing countries, bilaterally and multilaterally in the GATT, to conform. But while the outsider is prevented from using the patented technology, there is nothing to stop its 'owner' either from keeping it off the market altogether or from selling it to other selected big firms by means of licences, or from exchanging complementary licences with its fellow TNCs.

All this means that cross-licensing, tie-in sales agreements and other similar practices may make a collective agreement to form a cartel hardly necessary. As the management professors keep telling us, late capitalism is marked by a move from the identifiable discrete 'enterprise', company or firm to networks of firms linked together by various kinds of strategic alliances. Either these networks conceal a covert cartel, or they make it unnecessary.

There is a fourth and final hypothesis which is not incompatible with any of the other three. It is that the governments of states have given up the struggle, having found it increasingly difficult, if not impossible, to enforce the anti-trust and competition policies that are formally on the statute books. After all, a few isolated prosecutions and fines do not constitute a generally effective law.

In the lead in this respect is the United States. Although its apologists and intellectuals claim that it has the toughest anti-trust laws of any industrialised countries, the truth is rather different. In the first place, much depends on what priority is given to anti-trust suits by the White

House. Presidents Reagan and Bush were noted for having little interest in them. The big suit against IBM, which for years pre-empted most of the human and financial resources of the Department of Justice, was dropped in the 1980s; its place was not taken by any others and the funds allocated to the Department of Justice proved no match for the legal aid budgets of the big firms. The anti-trust division had neither the funds nor the staff to fight multiple court cases. The result was that it often had to be satisfied with a plea of *nolo contendere* – no contest. This meant that the offending firm admitted guilt, promised not to do it again and got off scot-free. The legal costs of such suits were much lower for the government than contested cases which required piles of evidence to be assembled and long legal battles over technicalities. The trouble was that there was no follow-up, no enforcement process to ensure that the promises given in such no-contest cases were kept (Mirow, 1982: 220–2). Mirow adds: 'The penalties applied to violations of US anti-trust laws are usually so petty that the crime pays off whether or not the criminal is caught . . . Only on the rarest occasions are executives convicted of felony violations and, although the law provides for prison terms, they are almost never imposed.'

In the European Community, the regulatory power seems stronger. The Rome Treaty in Articles 85 and 86 laid the basis for a common policy against inter-firm collusion and against the abuse by firms of a dominant position in any market. The latter principle was an implied presumption against big business that has never existed in America. It assumed, not without reason, that size was apt to give dominance and power, and power was apt to be abused. Abuse of market dominance was therefore proscribed. Translated into policy, this means that offenders can be fined up to 10 per cent of their world-wide turnover – much more than most US fines. There is also a separate directorate of the European Commission in charge of competition policy, and constitutional representation for consumer interests. Yet at the same time there has always been a fundamental ambivalence in EC policies toward manufacturing industry. On the one hand, the Commission is charged with protecting the European market and supporting European industry against American or Asian competition. On the other, it has this responsibility for investigating and bringing to justice firms operating in Europe that transgress its basic laws of open competition.

The most cursory survey of books on the European Community – European Union as the Maastricht Treaty says it should be called – shows that member states have paid far more attention to the supportive, protectionist role than to the policing, anti-cartel role. Ineluctably, there is an inherent conflict between enforcing fair competition and the industrial policies – in semiconductors, for example – in which instead of the national champion firms nurtured and built up by the member states in the 1960s and 1970s, the Commission is supposed to nurture and build up 'European champions'. As Tsoukalis observes, it took the Council of Ministers sixteen years, from 1973 to 1989, to take action on a Commission proposal to follow British and German leads against oligopolistic mergers. By the time it accepted the need for stronger competition laws, the number of mergers in European industry had risen from 115 in 1982/83 to 622 in 1989/90 – and that was based only on mergers involving the top 1000 firms. And even then, only three of the twelve member states had any agencies of government comparable to the US Anti-Trust Division, the British Monopolies Commission or the German Kartellamt. Without national enforcement, the Commission secretariat has been heavily handicapped. The law, moreover, was the result of compromise on the threshold, based on the combined turnover of the firms, beyond which a merger could be barred. And some uncertainty remained on the relative competence of national and EC administrations, and the exact criteria by which a merger might be barred or permitted. The extent of political discord on European industrial policy is reflected in the multiple ambiguities in the chapter in the Maastricht Treaty on industrial policy. It has been demonstrated, too, in the matter of European airfares, maintained by agreement among the airlines, often backed (and sometimes, as in France, openly subsidised, by governments). Again and again in the 1990s, the Commission has been obstructed in its declared intention of replacing the existing cartel agreements with open competition and so leading to lower airfares.

The conclusion seems clear that, while the rhetoric of free enterprise and open competition is necessary to the full integration of a world economy operating on a market principle, the rhetoric is often, in reality, empty of meaning. Both in the United States and in Europe, let alone Japan, the war against restrictive cartels is pretty much of a farce. In steel, in shipping, and probably in most chemicals, aluminium, electrical products, authority over the market is exercised by associations of firms organised in overt or covert cartels to rig prices in favour of the members – 'conspiracies against the public' in effect. And in political terms, since the regulators are blind, inert or impotent, such cartels constitute 'regimes within regimes'.

12 International organisations: the econocrats

One of the three hypothetical propositions in this book was that power had moved in recent times from the nation-states to international organisations. Some authority over some issues had shifted upward, as it were, from national capitals and their political institutions, to the scattered headquarters of international bureaucracies. International organisations – IGOs or intergovernmental organisations – are certainly more numerous and more visible than they were a generation or more ago. The annual meetings of the World Bank and the International Monetary Fund draw literally thousands of journalists every year. Their readers no longer have to be told what these bodies are; 'IMF' is already in the translingual, global vocabulary, along with STOP, Fax or Coca-Cola. But visibility and familiarity are not the same as authority. How much power do the worldly bureaucrats really exercise over outcomes in world economy and society?

And even if the evidence shows that they do have authority, there is a second and even more important question. On whose behalf is that authority used? For there are two alternative interpretations. One, dear to liberal internationalists and neo-functionalists in academic circles, is that this nascent authority is the embryo of supranational government, exercised in the interests of the world community. For all its frustrations and all its shortcomings, this shift from national to supranational authority is seen as the first glimmer of dawn after a long dark night. Recall, though, that the same liberal internationalists have been guilty of wishful thinking before. For example, many of them hailed the IMF's introduction of Special Drawing Rights in 1969 as the dawn of a shift from national money to an international currency. They failed to see that the United States had only agreed to SDRs because they saw them, on the contrary, as a helpful supplement, rather than as a substitute for the dollar (Strange, 1976: 350).

The other interpretation, more appealing to radical structuralists, post-modernists and other critics of modern capitalism, is that behind the veil of the international organisations we may perceive the hegemonic authority of the United States as the dominant economy, still, in the international political economy. Allied with the agencies of the US government, and reinforcing its authority, is the transnational business class whose interests the international organisations also exist to protect and defend. Within the soft velvet glove of the worldly bureaucrats, in this view, can be felt the iron fist of American power – power exercised on behalf of the ruling elites of transnational capital.

A first task therefore is to marshall the evidence sustaining each of these contested interpretations. Although there is material enough here for an entire book, a selective survey is also an indispensable part of this wider inquiry into the sources of power in and over world economy and society. The survey of evidence must of necessity be condensed and thus incomplete. But it should be enough at least to pose the in-whose-interest question, in the hope that subsequent research may pursue it further.

Note that this is a fundamentally different question than the regime one that has dominated the literature of international organisation – and the eponymous journal, *IO* – for almost a quarter of a century. The regime question has been about when, and how, governments could be got to cooperate; about what generated regimes, and what caused them to change. Only occasionally, and often only as an afterthought, did the *cui bono* question crop up. A notable exception was an edited volume in the late 1960s, *The Anatomy of Influence*, comparing the decisionmaking processes in a half-dozen UN specialised agencies (Cox and Jacobson, 1973). This did at least ask the question when and if these processes were influenced by 'private-regarding motives' – in less polite language, by the self-serving interests of international officials. Otherwise, it has generally been an implicit assumption of regime research that any increase in international organisation is a triumph of idealism over realism, that more is always better, and that cooperation is *ipso facto* better than conflict – no matter what the purpose of the cooperation, and whatever the outcome of that cooperation. And the unspoken assumption, of course, is that international officials are selfless dedicated missionaries with only the best interests of the world community at heart.

A separate section of the chapter will summarise the evidence regarding the authority of international bureaucracies based on the extreme case of the European Community (as it used to be, and perhaps should still be called). For it is generally acknowledged that this regional association of states – although it is not a union in the sense that the Union of South Africa, or even Switzerland which still modestly calls itself the Confédération Helvétique is a union – has nevertheless managed to go further than other international bodies in filching power from the member states. In the words of one (non-European) authority (Moravcsik, 1994: 29), it is 'the most successful example of institutionalised international policy co-ordination in the modern world'.[1]

The revived interest of US scholars in the progress of European integration in the decade since about 1986 has been a remarkable feature of academic discourse in the US. It can best be explained by their shared concerns with broader theories of international policy coordination. It is as if they said, 'If we can understand and explain how the Europeans managed it after we thought that the "building of Europe" had come to a standstill, then perhaps we can draw important general lessons about how to boost the influence and power of other international organisations.' In short, it was not so much a fraternal concern for the ideal of a federal Europe that drew scholars like Leon Lindberg, Robert Keohane, Stanley Hoffman, Andrew Moravcsik and others to a revived interest in EC affairs. It was the hope that from it, new insights into the wider prospects for multilateral inter-governmental organisations (IGOs) might be derived.

Yet it is not unfair to suggest that behind that hope lay the tacit assumption that IGOs – in the future as in the past – would never challenge and would generally serve the perceived national interest of the United States – whatever that might be. Since, however, the wider question of the authority of IGOs is also the main question at issue here, the evidence of specialists on European Community matters has to be studied to find their answers to two questions. One is whether the 'success' of the Brussels institutions is real; and if so, in what respects and over what politically important issues. The other is what were the main motivations behind the intergovernmental bargains that Moravcsik identifies as the stepping stones across the river to the promised land of irreversible political as well as economic integration. The second

---

[1] Acknowledging the early work of the neo-functionalists, Moravcsik usefully used the notion of sustaining bargains to explain how these set an agenda for a progressive shift in some policy areas from member states to EC institutions.

question is whether there may be the makings, the necessary and sufficient conditions, for similar bargains in other international organisations. But first let us address the question of the authority of IGOs in general.

The authority of international organisations

The question is simple enough. Among all the various activities of international organisations, which ones actually represent the independent exercise of authority by their officials? And which others represent the dependent exercise of authority resulting from an inter-state bargain of some sort involving the limited delegation of powers of execution to the organisation? The question rules out, by definition, a large part of the output of IOs, the things on which most officials spend most of their time and energy. These would include the preparation for meetings, regular and *ad hoc*, of representatives of member states, and all the administrative details that this entails. It includes the publication of annual reports and specially commissioned reports by staff or by outside consultants. These two functions alone probably consume the larger part of most organisations' budgets. A third important occupation of organisation officials is the collection of statistics. This has been a common preoccupation of participating governments since the early days of the League of Nations. It was one of the first concerns of the new-born United Nations in the late 1940s to give technical assistance to its less developed members – then mainly Latin American – in the compilation and publication of national income statistics. Similarly, a first charge on new members of the International Monetary Fund was so to organise their balance of payments statistics as to conform to the norms set by the founding members.

The reason for this concern with data is simple. Government cannot function without information. A first task undertaken by the Norman invaders of England in the eleventh century was the painstaking compilation of the Domesday Book – how many people, how many draught animals there were in each village, and how much cultivated land. Without the information, the tax-collectors could not so easily collect revenue for the new rulers. For the same revenue-collecting reasons, all states have collected information on exports and imports, and – back to biblical times and beyond – have conducted censuses of their people to assist them in fiscal and sometimes in military policymaking. But while information may be necessary for government, it is not a sufficient condition. You can have information without government, but government without information is apt to be too hit-and-miss to be effective.

For international organisations, the information has to be reduced to a comparable format. Economists have tended to look at all such standardisation of information as simply a collective good – something of benefit to all, and freely available to all. But while some standardisations are necessary for the better functioning of the market, others have a more directly political purpose, serving to further the interests and the ideology of dominant states. Political economists should be able to make the distinction between the two. For example, the standard ISBN classification system for books now used by libraries all over the world, serves the interests of scholars as well as publishers. The standardisation of pharmacological descriptions serves the interests of patients, doctors, pharmacists and the pharmaceutical firms.

One of the oldest-established systems of standardised information is the SITC – the Standard International Trade Classification. Its history goes back to 1853 when an international congress first tried to solve the problem of unifying the systems governments used to classify traded goods. Successive efforts to improve and update the system culminated in the Brussels Tariff Nomenclature (BTN) agreed in 1955 and was adopted by GATT. The Scandinavians objected that the changeover gave rise to 'insuperable obstacles to countries whose statistical resources are limited'. The UN responded by a hybrid system, SITC(R) and by the 1970s about 90 per cent of world trade was reported according to this system (Ray, 1976). The story is worth telling as an example of how technical questions in standardisation matters can be highly political. It is hardly necessary to add that once there is a common system by which trade liberalisation can be measured and compared, the international bureaucracies, in GATT and in the EU, have a powerful weapon to advance the cause of economic integration, of lowering barriers to trade and making protection less easily defended. The collection of standard data according to a common system, therefore, is not as politically anodyne an activity of international organisations as some people might think.

So beyond this apparently rather anodyne activity of collecting and standardising information, what else do international organisations do that could possibly justify a claim to the exercise of authority? Here, we must distinguish between functions and authority that are consciously delegated to the organisation by member states, and functions and authority that have been assumed by the officials, independently of the wishes or decisions of member states.

The most obvious area of dependent authority is found in the peacekeeping operations of the United Nations (PKO). This was the main purpose for which the United Nations was set up in the first place. Executive power in maintaining peace was delegated by agreement at San Francisco in 1945 to the five permanent members of the Security Council – the United States, the Soviet Union, China, Britain and France.

And what does the record show? That the concept of collective security enshrined in the UN Charter was flawed and impractical – and not only because of the Cold War and the stand-off between the superpowers. There were several reasons for this which can be briefly given because the literature on Peacekeeping Operations (PKOs) is extensive and the story is well-known to every student of international relations (Rosenau, 1993; Higgins, 1994; Bertrand, 1994). Firstly, because by general agreement it was barred from use in any internal conflicts; Article 2(7) protected all matters of domestic jurisdiction from UN intervention. Secondly, because the UN force supposedly held ready to act as international policeman on Security Council orders, never came into existence. Not only did the US and the USSR fail to agree on troop withdrawals from Europe and renunciation of atomic weapons. Where they did agree, it was on the *undesirability* of such a permanent ever-ready force. Both were adamant that the best the Security Council could hope for was voluntarily contributed *ad hoc*, national contingents under national military orders and discipline. No budgetary provision moreover could be agreed except on an *ad hoc* basis. On this too, all member governments were agreed. Everybody's business was nobody's business. And finally, there were the many cases – beginning with Palestine in the 1940s and ending with Iraq–Iran in the 1980s – where either or both superpowers preferred non-intervention to an involvement which might upset the delicate balance between them. Even in Yugoslavia in 1995, the reluctance of the United States to involve its troops on the ground owed more than a little to the opposition of the Russians.

All that changed with the end of the Cold War was that there was nothing to stop the United States making more use of the approval of the Security Council and of the UN's limited peacekeeping resources to pursue its own unilaterally-determined strategic objectives. To some observers, this seemed to give the appearance of an enhanced role for the UN. But it is a sham. As Maurice Bertrand, professor at the prestigious Graduate Institute for International Studies at Geneva has observed, the situation in which the US meets no effective opposition 'has permitted the United States to transform the UN according to its own views'. He goes on:

> It has been in a position to use the facilities offered by the 'collective security' system by activating some of its mechanisms and refusing to apply it fully. During the Gulf War, the provisions of Article 41 and 42 were applied but the Military Staff Committee (Article 47) played no role. Article 43 was not used to call upon member states to provide forces, and the intervention force – which was essentially American – remained under the sole authority of the United States. The permanent members of the Security Council all concurred with US proposals or decisions without objections. (Bertrand, 1994: 466)

The United Nations system has also been used as a channel – albeit a less important one than direct bilateral channels – for the distribution of official credit to member governments. To respond to the demands of developing countries that something be done to follow up on the promises of the Charter on economic and social development, the UN Development Programme and then the United Nations Conference on Trade and Development (UNCTAD) were set up. Once again, it is not necessary to repeat the conclusions of a large and generally critical literature on the grudgingly stingy flows of official aid to developing countries. More important than the trickle of money from UNDP and the special agencies such as, WHO, FAO, ILO or UNESCO to whom it passed on a large part of its funds were the regular meetings of donors known as Aid Consortia. In these, annual assessments were made in consultation with the developing country concerned – India was a prime example – of the minimal amount of foreign credit necessary for financial solvency in the coming year. Predictably, the donor – i.e. creditor – governments made their own decisions on how much they were prepared to put in to the collection box, and on how much of that would be channelled through international organisations.

The same principle has applied in the treatment of arrears of payments on foreign debt. In a system-sustaining organisation, it might be thought rational to have a standard treatment for governments in danger of defaulting on their payments of interest and capital to their creditors. Not at all. Already in the 1950s, the rational solution – from the point of view of the system – was rejected in favour of one which allowed creditors to discriminate in favour of some debtors and against others (Prout, 1976). This was a rational decision for the creditors. Their national interests naturally diverged according to their past history, geography and strategy. Thus, the United States gave preference in 1982, and again in 1994, to its near neighbour Mexico over its more distant though more solvent neighbour Brazil. Japan went to the aid of South Korea where many Japanese private investments were at risk – but not to the Philippines. Less effectively, the German government might have liked to go to the aid of Poland in 1982, but was politically inhibited from doing so. The net result of leaving each creditor to define the terms and modalities of debt relief was that authority was delegated on a case-by-case basis to international institutions other than the United Nations or the IMF or IBRD – the so-called Paris Club or official creditors and the London Club of private creditors.

There are other less politically important matters on which member states have delegated executive authority – or seemed to do so – to international institutions. Examples are to be found in all those areas where technological change requires not just standardisation or the coordination of practice, but a carefully negotiated agreement on the share-out of costs and benefits in order to achieve a common goal or to get the benefit of a collective good, but only on terms consistent with national interests. Two good examples are the negotiation of the MARPOL convention through the international Maritime Organisation, and the allocation of radio wavelengths through the WRAC conferences.

Delegated Powers

There is a conceptual difference between the use of international organisations as agents of national policies, as the means for carrying out or executing bargains reached by negotiation between national governments and the actual delegation of decision-making power to the officials of the international organisation. Such delegation is much more rare than the use of international organisations either as a convenient forum for multilateral discussion, or as an arena for political bargaining. Four major examples show that such delegation is conceded only when the system – some part of the structures of the world market economy – is perceived as being seriously at risk, and when the direct and indirect costs of delegated authority are relatively insignificant.

The first example would be the Structural Adjustment Loans (SALs), devised and administered by the World Bank and the IMF for those countries – mostly in Africa – so poor and so hard-up for foreign exchange that they are in danger of involuntary default on loans, most of which have been made to them by other governments. Such default would carry an implicit threat to the financial system, possibly bringing about a collapse of the fragile house-of-cards of credit and financial markets.[2] The danger lends urgency to the remedy; action cannot wait on long negotiation through the Paris or London Clubs. Hence the delegation to IMF and World Bank staffs. Whereas the IMF used to try hard to preserve the illusion that IMF conditionality was the same for all who drew on stand-by agreements, in these cases, when SALs are needed, such an illusion can no longer be sustained. It is left to the officials to get as much fiscal and economic reform out of the debtor government as possible while maintaining the appearance of an effort to keep up at least partial service of the past debts.

Note, however, that a double standard is at work here. Poor, indebted countries are told, firmly, that budget deficits are deplorable and government spending must be cut, including if necessary food and welfare subsidies to poor people. Yet the rich members whose votes dominate the Executive Board of the IMF also have budget deficits and are guilty of much greater public profligacy than poor ones. Servicing the public debt of the United States now absorbs about 5 per cent of the US national income. Japan, Italy, France, Britain and Germany are not far behind. Worst of all in the mid-1990s was Belgium. But because all these governments have little difficulty in raising money in international capital markets – even if at rather high cost – they are not subjected to IMF indirect rule. And when the United States was criticised by the IMF staff in the early 1990s for its failure to deal with the fiscal deficit, absolutely nothing effective was done – or could be done – to exercise discipline over the government in Washington.

Similar discretion is accorded international officials engaged in two other activities of the Bretton Woods institutions, specifically, the equity shareholders of the International Finance Corporation (IFC), and the project loans negotiated with developing country governments by the World Bank. The IFC was set up in 1960 as a subsidiary of the World Bank. It is directed to use its rather limited funds to encourage the participation of private capital in investments in developing countries. It can guarantee share issues, and it can itself participate in them, thus

[2] Except that a house of cards is a pyramid structure in which the base is larger than the apex. The global financial structure is in some sense the reverse: a pyramid of debt is insecurely balanced on a small apex of real assets. Awareness that the base may not be strong enough to carry the strains put on the volatile and mobile superstructure is one reason for concerted efforts to 'neutralise' as it were, the potential defaulters.

demonstrating the approval and confidence of a supposedly impartial public institution in the viability of the enterprise. Predictably, it has been more active in Latin America and Asia than in Africa where the lack of private investment is most marked.

World Bank loans have always been more discretionary than drawings on the IMF. Both institutions needed the confidence of member states and of financial markets to survive. The IMF's conservative reputation was guaranteed first by the limits on its lending set by members' quotas of contributions in local currency and gold (or dollars), and second by the shared vetos of the G7 governments over any increase in 'created' credit in the shape of Special Drawing Rights. Sustaining confidence in the World Bank's solvency was more difficult. It had contributions from member governments – but it was not to use those to lend. Instead, they were the collateral on which it borrowed as best it could in first, US, then later European, Japanese and other financial markets. To be able to do so, it had to present as conservative an image to the market as possible. Credit was to be given only for necessary spending in foreign exchange. It was to be dispensed only a bit at a time. Loans were guaranteed by all World Bank member states as well as by the Bank itself. And the loans were for specific purposes, not general budgetary support. Big, visible projects – such as the famous Aswan Dam project in the 1950s – were more likely to gain the confidence of conservative bankers and central bankers than credit for an agricultural cooperative. By the 1970s, this bias toward project finance and construction of one kind or another had begun to change. First under Macnamara, and inspired by the ideas of Paul Streeten on human needs, and Amartya Sen on entitlements, the Bank used its discretionary powers to do more for farmers and rural communities, even though this often meant indirect intervention in local politics.[3]

A final example of independent authority exercised by international officials is the delegation of responsibility to non-governmental organisations (NGOs) by subsidising them out of the institution's budget. This practice has grown quite fast in recent years as unforeseen crises created problems with which the international bureaucracies were ill-equipped to deal. A sudden flood of refugees from ethnic persecution, civil war or economic collapse, an escalating exodus of peasant or

[3] Robert Macnamara, Executive Director of the World Bank in the 1960s, was a former CEO of General Motors, and used his position to encourage the Brandt Commission in its North South Report to lend support to LDC demands for a new international economic order. Paul Streeten was a Hungarian-British economist at the World Bank. Amartya Sen is an economist with a social conscience who argues that economic development is pointless if it does not entitle poor people to the things that make a better material life.

nomad farmers from regions hit by drought and crop failures. An epidemic or disease, exacerbated by malnutrition or infected water supplies – these humanitarian crises could put the spotlight of world-wide television on an international organisation like the UNDP or the UN High Commission for Refugees. Private voluntary organisations (PVOs), long accorded quasi-official status in the United Nations Charter, had helped quadruple the number of recognised NGOs from 3,000 to over 13,000. Organisations such as the Save the Children Fund, Medécins sans Frontières or Christian Aid often had resident staff who were better trained and more familiar with the area or the problem than the desk-bound economists employed by the World Bank or the IMF. Their major constraint was nearly always financial. The symbiosis between them and the IGOs was obvious.

The conclusion must be that IOs, both in their dependent and independent exercise of authority, are essentially system-preserving. Their political activities have served to reinforce the authority of governments – fellow-members of the mutual-recognition club of member states. And in the world economy, they have served to extend and reinforce the legitimacy of market regimes both in the international financial system, in international trade and in international investment.

Europe – the extreme case?

While that conclusion may be true of the large multilateral organisations like the UN or the World Bank, it may not be so true of the European 'Union'. If the member states of the European Union or Community really have institutionalised policy coordination amongst themselves, this may mean that authority has significantly moved from national capitals to the central institutions of the EC. But has it? That is the question. Here we may ignore the Council of Ministers, as being clearly an inter-governmental body whose members are named by and respon-sible to national governments. It is only important insofar as it delegates authority to the Commission, to the Parliament or to the European Court, independent of national governments.

Let us start with the European Court of Justice. For, as two American scholars observed, 'No other international organization enjoys such reliably effective supremacy of its law over the laws of member governments, with a recognized Court of Justice to adjudicate disputes' (Keohane and Hoffman, 1991). Set up in the first place as a necessary arbiter when it came to interpretation of the 1958 Treaty of Rome, and its provisions for a common market, the Court worked in quiet obscurity in

Luxembourg for most of the 1960s and 1970s, enjoying, as Weiler says, the benign neglect of the media and the politicians (Weiler, 1994: 134). But whereas for most international judicial bodies, states are the subjects of international law, and international courts deal only with states and their rulings are applied by governments, this is not quite true for the ECJ. Other EC institutions, private enterprises and national governments may all be directly affected under the court's jurisdiction. Bit by bit, it has built up a body of European Community law on the basis of cases referred to it, according to the Rome Treaty, by national courts. National judicial institutions then voluntarily took responsibility for enforcing its decisions. Increasingly, their own judgements were made in the light of European Community law as determined by the Court. Although it is true that the European Court of Human Rights had breached the usual conventions by allowing individuals restricted access to it, no other international court had exercised such far-reaching authority over states as has the ECJ.

How this came about was partly due to exceptional political will among the original six member-states. But it was also due to a certain coincidence of interest between the ECJ and national courts and the lawyers who operated in them. The latter saw a new, wide-open and probably rewarding field for legal expertise. In this symbiotic relation with Luxembourg, national courts also found their importance enhanced rather than diminished. Because European Community law was in the making, there were large areas of uncertainty and this meant that here was a wide-open and probably a very rewarding field for legal expertise. Plaintiffs and defendants, meanwhile, especially if engaged in transnational business of any kind, badly needed clarification of rules and regulations which were often contradictory within member states or unclear from the text of intergovernmental treaties. Thus, the authority of the Court was sustained by a coincidental coalition of interests, public and private, national and transnational.

Weiler argues, however, that this slow transfer of judicial power may not be so easy in future. The passage of the Single European Act and later of the Maastricht Treaty, he thinks, may be putting too great a load of politically sensitive decision making on the Court. The political limelight thrust on it by the greater ambiguity of the Maastricht Treaty will make it harder to decide on purely legal principles whether the ECJ or national courts have competence to decide contested issues. Anyone familiar with the history of the Supreme Court decisions in the United States will appreciate the essentially political role which it played on such non-legal matters as racial discrimination, labour relations, religion or abortion. Because of the uncertainty created by conflicts of European national laws and because of the (often deliberate) ambiguity of inter-governmental agreements, a similar political role has been thrust upon the ECJ.

'Across a broad range', Weiler concludes, 'its decisions are likely to be subjected to a far greater measure of critical political, popular and academic scrutiny than in the past' (Weiler, 1994: 158). On the other hand, it is unlikely that the authority already gained will be lost. Court decisions may be questioned and debated, but the shift of authority away from national judiciaries looks irreversible. Weiler, in short, is warning of trouble ahead, of a possible slowdown, but not of any reversal of the trend.

Whether this trend in Europe is peculiar to the European Community or is a harbinger of a more general shift of authority to international judicial bodies is a much more open question. One big test in future will be how far the United States, Japan, and the European states will allow the new World Trade Organisation (WTO) to develop the rather weak dispute settlement procedures established under the GATT into something more like a judicial authority, respected by governments and by TNCs (see Curzon-Price, 1993). So long as GATT negotiations were about tariff levels, for which a simple formula could be used to gauge both comparability of trade concessions, disputes were relatively few. But once trade negotiations dealt in non-comparable non-tariff barriers, subsidies, and indirect protectionism of various kinds, disagreements multiplied. Were they to be settled in bilateral, eyeball-to-eyeball confrontations like the ones imposed by successive USTRs on the Japanese? Or were they to be referred to international arbitration? At the time of writing, it would be rash to predict which way trade relations between states will go. All that can be said with some confidence is that the firms that actually conduct most transnational trade would probably prefer, on balance, the latter solution, simply because a body of law based on established precedent is more transparent and less arbitrary and unpredictable than ad hoc bilateral horse-trading. Corporate strategists have always been happier with a stable political and legal environment in which they know where they stand. How far their preference can be made known to governments and made to influence them is a key question for the future.

So much for the authority of the ECJ. The authority of the European Commission is another but indirectly related matter. It arises specifically in the area of competition policy. As Tsoukalis explains, the internationalisation of production brought about a significant increase, from the mid-1980s on, in mergers and acquisitions by European firms. There were four times as many involving at least one of the top 1,000 firms in the EC with another in 1989/90 as there has been in 1983/4, and the increase was greater than mergers with outside enterprises (Tsoukalis, 1993: 103). Applauded for the promise of greater efficiency and competitiveness, such mergers could also be under suspicion of abuse of monopoly power in the market. Concentration of economic power had already led the British and German governments in the mid-1960s to pass laws governing the practice of mergers and acquisitions. By the 1970s, the European Court was giving judgement in a series of cases, beginning with the Continental Can judgement in 1973, on restrictive practices in the European Market.

By the late 1980s, the Court's judgements raised the possibility of some general EC rules governing cross-border mergers to replace the multiple and often contradictory laws and practice of national governments. The Commission responded with a directive (i.e. agreed regulation) which from 1990 on governed mergers involving firms with combined turnover of ECUs 5 billion or more. Although German resistance on behalf of national regulatory authority stopped the complete transfer of authority over mergers to the EC, some significant shift did take place. This was demonstrated in 1992 when the Commission ruled against a Franco-Italian takeover of the Canadian-owned aircraft firm, De Havilland, despite a good deal of criticism both within the Commission and outside it. Tsoukalis is in no doubt that 'power is being slowly transferred to the centre', even though many doubts remain about the content and scope of EC industrial and strategic trade policies (Tsoukalis, 1993: 113). On the other hand, this does not mean that the confederal (or proto-federal, according to taste) authority of the Commission could easily be exerted in positive, indicative planning or MITI-like intervention in the market economy. The authority, as before, is more easily exercised over what is forbidden, rather than over what is to be encouraged (Keohane and Hoffman, 1991: 11–12).

The truth of this is nowhere more apparent than in the innumerable petty regulations proposed by the European Commission regarding such political trivia as the wearing of seat-belts in cars, the standards of cleanliness in abattoirs, the trade description requirements for cosmetics, or the amount of paternity leave for new fathers. Under the presidency of Jacques Delors, there is no doubt that the Commission has proposed many more new directives for the consideration by the Ministerial Council. While some have been ignored, many have been accepted simply because there seemed no strong political reason to oppose them. Only too often, they were welcomed by national bureaucracies because they added to their power and responsibilities. They have not, it is fair to say, added to either the popularity of the Commission or the legitimacy of its authority in most of the member countries. It is not just that the benefits gained from the regulations seem small compared with the general aggravation imposed on those who have to comply. It is also that people are well aware that passing an approved EC directive into national law does not mean that national authorities are either able or willing to go to the trouble of seeing it enforced. Unenforceable law quickly becomes a bad joke. And ridicule is something no nascent federal authority can easily survive.

In the Europe-wide debates over the Maastricht Treaty, much was heard of the 'democratic deficit' which characterised the institutions of the European Community. Power was given to the Council of Ministers which sat in private and reached its decisions out of earshot of the press. Power was given to the Commissioners and their staffs who were appointed by governments on a kind of quota basis and were not held accountable to anyone except the President when they proved ineffectual, lazy or even less than impartial. More than two-thirds of the Commission's labour costs went on outside specialists engaged on short-term contracts. As much as 40 per cent of the Commission's annual budget was accounted for by fraud, most of it connected with the handouts under the Common Agricultural Policy (CAP).

Meanwhile, the European Parliament, although directly elected, lacks authority over both the Council, the Commission and the Court. Democratic processes have hitherto only functioned within national borders (Habermas, 1991).[4] It is generally regarded as a talking-shop for second-eleven teams of politicians who would mostly much rather have been elected to national parliaments. In most EC countries, most voters don't even bother to vote for their MEP; if they do, it is for local national motives – either to support or to challenge the party in power in the national capital. So although the Maastricht Treaty appeared to increase the powers of the European Parliament in relation especially to the Commission, political observers in Europe remain sceptical about the

---

[4] Quoted by Brigid Laffan in Bulmer and Scott (1994: 100). Laffan argues that EC institutions have shallow roots and that despite the regulatory politics that have been the core of European integration, the national state is still for Europeans the focus of their loyalty and allegiance.

practical effects. Certainly, more significant and legitimate as a demo-cratic institution than either the Council of Europe or the NATO Assembly, it has a long way to go before its proceedings are seen as more important to the Europeans than those of national parliaments.

On only two political issues can it be said that the EC's authority is sustained by more or less stable bargains between national govern-ments. One is trade negotiations with the United States, with Japan, Korea, Taiwan or other non-European governments or coalitions of governments. The other is monetary negotiations especially those relating to exchange rates. On neither can it be said that the EC has significantly extended its authority at the expense of national govern-ments over the past twenty or twenty-five years.

The Kennedy Round of multilateral trade negotiations begun in 1962 and continuing for the next six years was the first time that the member states appointed a single trade negotiator, Jean Rey, to act as their collective spokesman, notably with the United States. (Japan at the time was not a major trade rival). The subsequent story is long, technical and not very interesting (See for example, Curzon and Curzon, 1976; Winham, 1986; Destler, 1986). The relevant point about it in this context is that the solidarity of member governments behind their collective representative was rather greater in the 1960s than it was in the 1990s. Leon Brittan was then the EC Trade Commissioner charged with representing all twelve members in the negotiations with the United States towards the end of the Uruguay Round. Yet he found at the last moment that the French government would not go along with the deal he had hammered out with USTR Mickey Cantor. Though finally resolved by a further compromise at the eleventh hour, it looked more like two steps backward than one step forward for the integration of Europe as a single, united trading partner.

Money, however, not trade is a better test of how far there has been – or is likely to be – a real shift of authority from national capitals to Brussels. Despite what the economic theorists say about international trade and the comparative advantage of national economies, the basic fact remains that it is not governments that trade. It is enterprises. It is firms that decide to buy or to sell goods and services across national frontiers. Indeed, something near half international trade is accounted for by the transactions *within* firms, between their branches and affiliates located in different countries. What governments do, in the way of erecting barriers, quantitative or *ad valorem*, to these transactions is relatively marginal when managers of firms define global corporate strategies.[5] The test for the EC therefore is not how far trade relations are centralised through the Trade Commissioner. It is how far responsibility for monetary management is transferred from national Ministries of Finance and national central banks to a federal authority, either within the Commission or in a European Central Bank.

For more than a quarter of a century since 1971, the vision of European monetary convergence leading to a common currency has dazzled Europeans while the reality has, again and again, eluded them. Three times already, wishful thinking – the hope that a common, single currency – symbol of political union – could be added to a single common market that was more of a glorified free trade area than it was a real economic union, dominated European debates and resolutions. Back in the early 1970s, the Werner Plan was upset when the devaluation of the dollar had the markets pulling the strong and weak European currencies in opposite directions. The so-called Snake-in-the-Tunnel could not long survive such pressures. In the mid-1970s, inflation in the US and volatility in exchange markets led French and German leaders to resolve on the European Monetary System (EMS) in 1978. But the relatively easy ride it had – thanks mainly to the stability following Volcker's deflationary strategies in the US in the early 1980s – merely encouraged a second wave of wishful thinking about the possibility of having a European Monetary Union, with a single common currency and a federal central bank. Forgotten were the realignments imposed by market forces on the franc, the lira and other minor EC currencies. Forgotten was the failure to move from the first stage of the EMS – the exchange rate mechanism – to the second stage of fully fixed rates, a common pool of reserves for market intervention and agreed targets of monetary management.

Moreover, as Tsoukalis notes, the convergence of nominal interest rates in EC economies grouped around the D-mark – which ranged from 7 to 17 per cent in 1979, but only from 8–10 per cent by 1991 – reflected the *de facto* emergence of a D-mark zone in which the other countries always followed where the Bundesbank led (Tsoukalis, 1993: 200; also Marsh, 1992). Outside the D-mark zone, however, were five EC member states in which nominal interest rates had started the same period within three percentage points of each other. But by 1991, their rates had diverged ranging from about 22 per cent in Portugal to 10 per

[5] This was demonstrated in the 1930s. Economic historians concluded afterwards that protectionism in the Great Depression actually had relatively minor effects on either the flows or the contents of international trade. For details, see Strange (1986).

cent in the UK (Tsoukalis, 1993: 196, fig. 7.4). In short, the convergence of weaker currencies around the D-mark created an illusion of stability and policy coordination which in reality did not apply throughout the whole twelve member states.

This illusion, nurtured by the EC Commission under Delors, and sustained by the Franco-German agreement on the importance of monetary solidarity as the foundation of the Single European Market, was reflected in the provisions for European Monetary Union written into the 1992 Maastricht Treaty. Once again, as twice before in the 1970s, a timetable for progress by stages was laid down, assuming all the political obstacles could be overcome. But before the move from the ERM in Stage 1 to Stage 2 was due in 1994, the ERM itself had come apart with the market upset of September 1993 taking both the pound sterling and the Italian lira out of it. And by that time, it was by no means certain that the German government was quite as keen as it had once been in the aftermath of the fall of the Berlin Wall on exchanging the DM under Bundesbank control for an ECU under control of a European Monetary Institute. The optimism about monetary convergence that prevailed in the literature around 1992/3 had been based on the assumption that the first priority for every European government was to control inflation. (See for example the up-beat conclusion of Thygesen and Gros, 1992.) By 1993, rising unemployment and lagging investment in France and Germany raised a new and very awkward question: maybe these and not deflationary anti-inflation strategies were the political priority of the future?

When there is no such unanimity on goals, the shortcomings of member governments in relation to the indicators of convergence laid down in plans for EMU assume greater importance. Controlling money supply means putting a cap on government spending and fiscal deficits. Yet there was no sign that the Italian, Belgian or even German governments were able to do this, certainly not by 1999, when Stage 3 was supposed to start. A report from the European Investment Bank guessed that it would take Portugal at least twenty years to meet the financial liberalisation and deregulation requirements laid down for EMU. And it was one thing to announce the independence of a European central bank from political interference. Getting governments so to manage their public debts and deficit financing that they conformed to common rules was another. Tsoukalis (1991: 200) quotes the sceptical comment of Alexandre Lamfalussy, appointed head of the European Monetary Institute to prepare for EMU and formerly a distinguished Belgian banker: 'The combination of a small Community budget with a large, independently determined national budgets leads to the conclusion that, in the absence of fiscal coordination, the global fiscal policy of the EMU would be the accidental outcome of decisions taken by the Member States. *There would simply be no Community-wide macroeconomic fiscal policy* (my italics).

Tsoukalis' own comprehensive and informed analysis leads him to the conclusion that monetary union requires a much more developed European political system to be effectively managed (Tsoukalis, 1993: 226). Key member governments – notably of France and Germany – had wished the ends (or said they did) but were unable to wish the means. Nor were they able to convince the markets of the seriousness of their intentions. Transfer of authority from the member governments to federal institutions over this central responsibility of political authority in a market economy has not yet happened. Nor has the replacement of national defence forces by a European Army under control of a European Chief of Staff. At the time of writing, the shift to Brussels affects only the trivial pursuits of an international bureaucracy. It seems that European governments – though they are reluctant to say so – really prefer a vacuum of power over key matters of security, currency, law and order and foreign policy to a real transfer of power to supranational institutions.

And if this is the case with the extreme example of policy coordination – the European Community – it is likely to hold good for less ambitious international organisations. If the state has lost *significant* political authority in any direction, it is more likely to be downward or sideways than (so to speak) 'upwards' to supranational institutions.

Part III
Conclusions

13 Pinocchio's problem and other conclusions

Ever since the end of the Cold War, in many different places around the world, scholars have set up new centres for the study of something called 'global governance'. The words are supposed to convey some kind of alternative to the system of states, yet something subtly different from world government. The dictionary definitions of governance – 'a system of rules' – however, fails to make a clear distinction between governance and government. Perhaps deliberately, 'governance' sounds rather vague, while government is more precise and familiar. If there is a clear and essential difference between the two, it remains elusive.

What the sudden mushrooming of these new centres suggests, though, is that the search is on for better ways of managing society and economy than has so far been achieved through the unaided efforts of the individual nation-states. Foundations have readily provided the resources for research into 'global governance' – often without any clear idea of what it may mean. New journals and a great many conferences with similar titles have proliferated. At the same time, there has been a parallel revival of interest among policymakers as well as academics in the possibilities for reform of existing international organisations from the United Nations to the World Bank and the International Monetary Fund.

Few would disagree, I think, that the results of this spate of intellectual activity have been extremely meagre. There has been a great deal of political rhetoric. There have been large and growing piles of solemn reports recommending how existing organisations could be reformed and made to work more efficiently, less wastefully and with a more inspired vision of a better future for world society and the world economy. But nothing much has changed. Nor is it likely to. Realists in and out of government, the universities and the media are confirmed in their scepticism about the readiness of states to concede real authority and independent legitimacy to inter-governmental committees and assemblies. They remain cynical about the potential contribution of international organisations to the human condition. Liberal internationalists, meanwhile, still cherish their inextinguishable optimism by pinning their hopes on the appeal of reason. Rational choice, supported by the appropriate game theories, is used to explain increased contact between state bureaucracies. It can also explain the obstructive intervention of those same bureaucracies when their exclusive powers and privileges are in jeopardy. Empirical evidence suggests that the points of resistance to inter-governmental conferences and secretariats taking over the three most significant areas of policy from the state remain what they have always been. One is the right to use armed force, or not to use it. The second is the right to tax and to borrow. The third is the power to determine what is lawful and what is criminal. Since governments of states are the constituents of inter-governmental organisations, the meagreness of results from research into global governance and institutional reforms is not to be wondered at. Starting from a state-centric assumption, it cannot surmount the obstructions raised by states against radical institutional reform.

That is why this book has started with quite different questions, seeking an escape from the state-centrism of almost all contemporary social science.[1] The first, basic question was 'Who, or what, is responsible for change?' The second was 'Who, or what, exercises authority – the power to alter outcomes and redefine options for others – in the world economy or world society?' I cannot possibly claim to have found the full answer to either question. But my argument has sketched an alternative approach or line of inquiry in international political economy. But perhaps the empirical examples in the last few chapters have offered a signpost, tentatively pointed in a new and different direction. The final questions it points to are these. Firstly, what different outcomes are to be expected from the changed mix of state and non-state authority that can be observed in world economy and society, taking 'outcomes' to encompass the consequences for the world system as a whole and for generations, social groups and market sectors as well as for inter-national relations? And secondly, is the totality of authority

[1] I would except from this criticism the geographers and the historians, more particularly the economic historians and the business historians, and some (but not all) sociologists and anthropologists.

over market and society, over the long term, good enough, in the sense of promising a sufficiency of political, economic and social order for the market-based economic system to survive and prosper, and in assuring its citizens what they consider a sufficiency of rights and liberties from the arbitrary intrusion of authority? To that question I can only give a personal and subjective answer, with which others may disagree. But first it may help to recapitulate the steps taken in earlier chapters, and the broad conclusions emerging from this approach.[2]

To the first question concerning sources of change, conventional international relations theories give very unsatisfactory answers. The self-styled 'structural realists' perceive change only in terms of the relations between states. Thus there can be in the international system a bipolar balance or a multipolar balance between the most powerful states. Or, conceivably, there may be a more unbalanced imperial or hegemonic structure of state power, either at a global level or regionally, in which case, the structure of the world system might be one of three or more *blocs* each dominated by a regional hegemon.

This is really one-eyed social science. We have a world market economy in which most of the people who live in the state system earn their living in that market economy and so acquire the wherewithal to pay their taxes to state governments. Yet the market is overlooked. Change in that market is taken for granted. We also live in a world in which the most striking aspect of change, of which everyone is sharply aware, is technological. The world of work and play has gone from horses to cars, aircraft and spacecraft, from pen-and-ink to computers and mobile phones, from assembly lines of people to assembly lines of robots – and all in a century. Yet an important branch of social science seems blind to this kind of change.

A better short answer, therefore, to the question, 'Who, or what is responsible for change?' is three-fold – technology, markets and politics. But politics must include (as explained in chapter 2) much more than governments and politicians. These are important because choices in technology and change in markets can be affected by the decisions and non-decisions of governments. But politics also includes the actions and

---

[2] Obviously, the argument here builds to some extent on the approach to IPE developed in *States and Markets* (1988). But, as a number of students and other readers have pointed out, there were internal contradictions in that book reflected in the title. While implicitly criticising the state-centrism of most of the IPE literature, I too fell into the trap of concentrating – perhaps not exclusively but certainly over-much – on the authority of states over markets. That was an error which the present book, by taking a broader view of authority and power, and wider conception of politics is trying, however tentatively, to make good.

decisions of all those who seek the support of other wills to gain their objectives. Not least it must include the actions and decisions taken by corporate strategists as they respond to change in the market and change in technologies affecting the fortunes and life-chances of the firm and its prospects for survival against competition. Their political decisions will shape the course and development of production of goods and services and thus of international trade and transnational investment. The wealth and ultimately the power, and the relative vulnerability, of states will be affected.

The point has been well taken by two British financial journalists, Matthew Horsman and Andrew Marshall, who remarked, 'Like the nation-state, the TNC has become a variegated form with multiple loyalties and duties' (Horsman and Marshall, 1994). Quoting the doyen of business management, Peter Drucker, on the *political* nature of corporate policymaking and diplomacy and the power of firms to change society and politics as much as business, they furthermore observed: 'The head of a large transnational is a modern Prince, a strategist who must negotiate his way through a hostile world . . . Most companies', they added correctly, 'have seen an enlargement of their political functions with units devoted to "public affairs" and "embass-ies" in Brussels and Washington. The aims of the TNC are not purely profit-related; they include much longer-term considerations including corporate survival' (Horsman and Marshall, 1994: 213).

Such perceptions are consistent with the notion that change can be explained by the two-way interaction of the three variables already mentioned – technology, markets and politics. Each one affects, and is affected by the other two but in different degrees. To leave any one of the three out of account is to suffer from serious intellectual myopia.

The truth of that remark is sustained by most of the empirical sketches found in previous chapters. One of the current and prospective issues for states concerns competition policy. All the secretariats of interna-tional economic organisations now recognise that while some common international framework of rules and dispute settlement is desirable for international trade, a necessary – or at least a logical – complement would be a set of much more consistent international rules on competi-tion. If a monopoly, or a small oligopoly of large enterprises is allowed in one national economy, while another makes rules against such economic concentration, then the market, and trade in the market, is distorted by the difference. So, if we take the cartel between container ship operators briefly described in chapter 11, we see, firstly, that the technological change from the old methods of handling general cargoes to container handling first undermined the old system of shipping conferences to which the developing countries in UNCTAD had objected so strongly in the 1970s. Then we see that the container operators, faced with the same market conditions of uncertain demand, over-supply and surplus carrying capacity that had generated the conference system, promptly engaged in politics to set up another system of market management. The open question remaining was whether national governments would regulate or tolerate the system.

Or we can take the highly dynamic case of telecoms, sketched in chapter 7. In this, far more than in shipping, the who-gets-what has been revolutionised by the accelerating rate of change in technology. The market in the provision of communication services, once predominantly national, becomes global – but on the initiative of the US government forcing US-based TCOs to seek market shares abroad to recoup the capital costs of the new technology. Other states which formerly had controlled and managed their national markets now found their PTTs challenged by the combination of new technology and foreign competitors. State policies changed in response. But, 'structural realists' please note, not as a result of a shift in the power balance between states. Only the triangular model of market, technology, politics is able to explain changes which (as shown in chapter 12) are found both in international organisation, in domestic policies for national economies, and in the competition between firms in the market.

Another feature which the triangular model also accommodates is the fact that there are striking variations across sectors in the nature and kind of authority and how much it, or they, intervene with the play of market forces. Compared with differences between national laws and institutions affecting the economy, the differences are apt to be much greater between sectors of the world market economy. Some are highly competitive, while others are highly oligopolistic and dominated by a few very large enterprises. Some, like textiles or shoes, are relatively open to newcomers, and are apt to be rather competitive. Others, like cars, aircraft or newspapers, have high barriers to entry which may be technological as in patentable pharmaceuticals, or financial as in airlines.

If we are concerned about change, and the sources of change, it is surely clear that the laws, institutions and policies that characterise and prevail within national economies change rather slowly. (That is essentially true of financial laws, institutions and policies – as seen in

Germany or Japan, for example.) By comparison, the pace of change in technology, and the pace at which capital as well as knowledge has become mobile have been much more dynamic. But they have affected sectors of the world market in different ways and to different degrees, and therefore with differential social and political consequences.

It follows that much of the work in comparative politics that is essentially state-based is misplaced. If the host-state is not always the most important independent variable, it makes no sense to compare the policies of two host-states *in general*. The analytical tool is too blunt an instrument. That is why some of the best work in international political economy – paradoxically enough – has come out of the regimes literature. Although starting from the nature of the inter-governmental system of rules and agreements, such work when it deals with sectors like cars, textiles, air transport, oil or banking cannot by its nature ignore the role of firms, nor the technological and market variables affecting them, and their consequent impact and influence on state policies.

What inter-sectoral comparisons bring out is that, within national economies, there are some sectors which are very state-dependent; that is, they are greatly constrained by the intervention of state authority with the market. Agriculture is an obvious example, at least in all the industrialised countries. There are others which are relatively state-independent; that is, the authority of government is less important than other kinds of authority – perhaps banks, perhaps professions, perhaps mafias. What is evident, too, is that the number of sectors has grown enormously in which the competition used to be between national firms (locally-based enterprises), and is now between transnational firms competing against one another for market shares in a number of national markets. Examples of sectors where competition until quite recently used to be mostly national but is now mostly global include beer, fresh flowers, fish, architectural designing, car-hire and many specialised financial services.

The third question posed earlier was about the changes in outcomes that might be expected as a result of the diffusion of authority over markets and society. The question concerns those issues with particular political, economic or – not least for the political economist – social significance, both for the international political economy as a system and for different social groups in it, rather more than for countries and nations. While there could be disagreement on which issues and outcomes are really significant and which are not, let us at least take the three major issues which might be expected to occur on most lists. One would be the security issue: how much order, how much protection from violence, does the changed mix of authorities provide? The second would be about jobs, incomes, employment; how much wealth, and what chances of employment, does the changed mix of authorities provide? And the third would be about the management of money as the very foundation of any market economy; how well do the authorities manage money and maintain confidence in its value as the basis for trade and investment? On which of these issues has change in the mix of authorities most affected outcomes?

One way to suggest the answer on each of these major issues would be to start from the three hypotheses proposed earlier in the book. Recall that these were: (1) that power had shifted upward from weak states to stronger ones with global or regional reach beyond their frontiers; (2) that power had shifted sideways from states to markets and thus to non-state authorities deriving power from their market shares; and (3) that some power had, so to speak, 'evaporated', in that no one was exercising it.

On the major issue of security and protection from violence, the combination of the first and second hypotheses suggests that the overall outcome may have been a loss of security. The increased asymmetry of power between major and minor states when added to the end of the superpower balance in the Cold War means that there has been a growth of what Alain Minc has called *zones grises* – grey areas, in which either because of local or civil war or a breakdown of state authority, the risks to life and property have substantially risen. At the same time, the enlarged influence of markets in arms has provided the means of violent threats to personal safety and the security of property. Minc's argument in *Le Nouveau Moyen Age* is that these areas without legitimate, acknowledged authority, in which the law of the jungle rules, are growing, especially in Africa and in the former Soviet Union. Authority is divided between the formal institutions of the state and local potentates, chiefs or gang leaders; between vassal and suzerain, the responsibility for keeping order is as unclear as it was in the middle ages. 'La victoire de la marche va de pair avec l'ascension des zones grises. Aussi longtemps que l'économie capitaliste se limitait à des pays, pour la plupart démocratiques, accoutumés à l'Etat moderne, le liberalisme fonctionnait autour de deux poles, le marché et la régle de droit, la seconde encadrant le premier' (Minc, 1993: 72). The retreat of the state, as argued above in chapter 5, is bound to be accompanied by a decline in the rule of law, and an increased risk of violent conflict, but more within the territorial borders of states than across them.

On the second major issue concerning the creation of wealth and the prospects for employment, the changes hypothesised here give a mixed answer. The greater power of markets has been instrumental in creating millions of new jobs in Asian and Latin American countries. But there has also been some loss of jobs and job prospects in manufacturing in the industrialised countries, only partly offset by the growth of part-time work and jobs in the service industries. As in the earlier European and American transitions to industrial production, change driven by markets brings costs as well as benefits, pain as well as profit. In the past, the authority and resources of the state were available to find ways – agricultural protection and subsidy or welfare transfers and public services – to relieve the pain and to ease the transition within the national economy. Now that the world market economy has outgrown the authority of the state, national governments evidently lack both the power and the will to make good the deficiencies of inequality and instability that have always gone with growth and change in market economies. No political authority has appeared that is both able and willing to prime the pump of a world economy that slips into recession.

Economic history has demonstrated, again and again, that every market economy has needed at times to be judiciously steered between the whirlpool of inflation and the hard rock of depression and deflation. The pains of adjustment will be less if the world market economy manages to avoid both Scylla and Charybdis. Steady growth sustained by a steady but not excessive creation of credit will give time for old workers to retire or find new jobs, and for people in the presently rich countries to adjust their expectations for the future and to contemplate the probability of a standstill or even a fall in their levels of consumption. From a world system perspective, neither change is necessarily catastrophic, or even destructive. Human life is and always has been uncertain; the lives of whole social groups, no less than those of individual men, women and children, are liable to ups and downs. Time is the essential element allowing people to adjust, mentally, emotionally and materially to either the ups or the downs.

Is it enough?

It is on this crucial question of financial management that the political economist is likely to differ most fundamentally from the ultramontane liberal economist for whom almost everything, even the issue of money and the provision of security against violence, can be left to the market. And it is to this question therefore that serious academic and political discussion should begin to turn in the next decade and beyond. Many authors in the 1990s have referred to the new world *disorder*, failing to see the new world order heralded by President Bush soon after the collapse of the Soviet Union and its empire (Horsman and Matthews, 1994; Minc, 1993). But the crucial question now is how much disorder can the world market economy tolerate before it starts to unravel, wind down, fall apart? With the hope of encouraging further discussion and debate on this rather important point, and on the basis of some of the material relating to state and non-state authority contained in earlier chapters, I propose a mildly optimistic answer, modified with one truly major *caveat* concerning the management of money and finance.

Economic history would seem to show that while insecurity and political disorder can be very uncomfortable for many people (and indeed lethal for some), it has to be very bad indeed before all economic life comes to a complete halt. The evidence from earlier troubled times – such as the eleventh century AD in Europe, or the Thirty Years War in the seventeenth century, and certainly from the Napoleonic Wars – is that no matter what the risks and uncertainties of daily life, people go on trying to earn a living, and to improve it by 'trucking and bartering' (in the old phrase) with each other to get more of what they want. That was part of the message of Brecht's *Mother Courage*; the old pedlar with her cart survives.

With a world economy, in which there are ever more of Minc's *zones grises*, there will also be areas of countries and of towns where nothing – neither property nor life – is very safe, but where many people nevertheless manage to eat, sleep and keep warm. Such areas will, in future as in many times in the past, be avoided by careful investors; trade with them, lacking export credit insurance, will languish. Like no-go areas in big unruly cities like Los Angeles or Belfast, or like strife-torn countries like Rwanda or Sri Lanka, they will be largely left alone, cut off from international trade, investment and corporate planning. The exceptional links that remain in tact will be with entrepreneurs tempted by the prospect of high profits to go with the high risks. Once again economic history suggests that there have almost always been a few tycoons rich and daring enough to take a chance.

The collective management of foreign debt over the past 50 years is instructive here. Without a formal regime, without forward planning or

191

any coherently worked out strategy, the creditors – governments, banks and international organisations – have nevertheless found ways of protecting the system from the consequences of war, civil conflict, bad and corrupt local government and incompetent economic management. The small and unimportant defaulters are either ignored or subjected to a kind of indirect colonial administration. The large and more important ones – Mexico or Iraq in the mid-1990s are good examples – are either rescued or given just enough time and enough room for manoeuvre to avoid outright default. The case of South Africa before 1992, or of Rhodesia in the 1960s, suggests that there is more rhetoric and symbolism in 'pariah' status than unbearable punishment.

All this would seem to suggest that like a human body whose limbs have had to be amputated, the world economy can still continue to find ways to function in a less than complete or ideal fashion. It remains true that the treatment accorded to different debtor countries can vary widely. One is treated as an unfortunate casualty to be given first-aid and sympathy. Others are treated as unwelcome sources of contagion, with whom close contact is to be avoided until the fever has passed or a new doctor is in charge. There is no international regime, no accepted code of rules to decide which it is to be. The authority of governments tends to over-rule the caution of markets. The fate of Mexico is decided in Washington more than Wall Street. And the International Monetary Fund is obliged to follow the American lead, despite the misgivings of Germany or Japan.

The management of foreign debt, incidentally, is a good example of the structural power of powerful states exercised indirectly through the bureaucracies of international organisations. It was the stronger states, with most global reach, which both directed and constricted the response of the international bureaucracies to the debtors. Although there were occasions when the delegation of authority to an international institution, as to any other body, seemed to give it some independent power of its own, that was usually more an illusion than reality. As Marie-Claude Smouts has commented, this is where regime theorists mislead. They cloak an American ideology inasmuch as they legitimise *A la carte* cooperation between states (Smouts, 1987: 158).[3] There is cooperation in the issue-areas and with the countries of

[3] 'The victory of the market is accompanied by the rise of "grey areas". As long as the capitalist economy was contained within countries – most of the modern and democratic – liberalism functioned between two poles, the market and the rule of law, in which the latter encompassed the former' (my translation).

America's choosing; the choice of areas and of partners is a political choice and at the same time a demonstration of the authority exercised indirectly as well as directly by the United States over the world economy and society.

If the world economy can probably survive no-go areas in which political insecurity results in great economic uncertainty, can it also survive the rapid relocation of manufacturing industry away from the countries that used to be described as 'developed'? This shift, already under way but by no means finished, is a consequence not of state authority but of the power of markets and of corporate strategies responding to markets. It is already causing economic pain, in America, in Europe and not least in Japan; and there is often strong political opposition to any kind of liberalisation of trade or immigration rules that is thought to make the pain worse.

Again, history is a good guide. This is not the first time that economic change has brought a redistribution of income in society. And on other occasions – with the shift from wealth and employment derived from agriculture to wealth and employment derived from manufacturing, there was political protest and fierce resistance. That can be expected again. But as before, the Luddites, the Chartists and all the other losers from change and redistribution will not succeed in reversing the trend. State policies may help to assuage or slow down the adjustment. They will not stop the need for it. And the economic system, as before, will probably benefit. More new producers of wealth means more new consumers. The additional demand will stimulate further investment and more employment, though not always in the same places or for the same people as in the past.

One incidental consequence of such global shifts will certainly be to increase the separation of firms from the governments of their home bases. American, British, even Japanese firms, finding new markets where demand is growing, will also find they need to pay more heed to the wishes of whatever central or local, state or non-state authority governs these new markets. They will sometimes tend to be less compliant to their former masters.

These dilemmas for firms, and the political stresses for governments, resulting from the relocation of manufacturing industry, will be more or less sharp depending on how well or badly the global system of money and credit is managed. Here, much more than in the trading system, is the weak spot of the market economy under pressures of political and economic change. There is no world central bank to exercise the judicious control over the creation of credit and the expansion of the money supply that historical experience has shown needs to be exercised. There is no world central bank with powers to control and regulate a banking system that operates transnationally in internationally integrated financial markets. There is no world central bank to enforce common standards on insider dealing and other practices or to check the abuse of the system by mafias engaged in organised crime. Such powers have seldom if ever been statutory, based on laws. They have been based on the central bank's role as lender of last resort to the other banks. It had to have the resources to act as rescuer when banks got into trouble as a result of bad luck or bad management, or a combination of the two. The knowledge that it had the discretion either to use those resources or to withhold them was the source of its authority over the banks and the conduct of their business. It was an authority exercised by a system of recognisable signals, even though sometimes these were hardly more than nods and winks.

It follows that one of the most important questions for international political economists today is how to recreate that kind of authority for the integrated world financial system and thus for the good of the world economy. Is the International Monetary Fund a possible candidate for the job? If not, where else can we look? Kindleberger's famous analysis of the world economy in the depression of the 1930s correctly diagnosed the cause of the long slump of the 1930s as the absence of a hegemonic authority able to act the part of a world central bank. Britain, he said, was no longer able to act the part, and the United States was unaware of the need to and unwilling therefore to try. Political economists ever since that diagnosis have assumed that hegemonic authority was desirable for the stability of the world economy and in times of crisis probably necessary to it. Hegemonic stability theory consequently has come to dominate the literature and to be accepted as axiomatic, even though disagreement continued over the limits of hegemonic responsibility and the means by which it could or should be exercised.

What seems to have been generally overlooked is that the only two instances of hegemonic intervention in the world economy were both political accidents, coincidences of economic dangers and political responses that may never be repeated. The first was the exercise of hegemonic power by Britain in the nineteenth century and before the First World War; and the second was the exercise of hegemonic power by the United States in the two decades after the Second World War. The political accident in the first case was that British domestic and foreign policy was, alone among the European great powers, under the strong influence of the financial interests in the City of London. It could almost be said that the financial interests of City bankers dictated British policy even when this was at the indirect expense of British agriculture or British manufacturing industry. That was the conclusion of the study of British imperialism by Cain and Hopkins (Cain and Hopkins, 1993). Their conclusions accord with earlier work by other economic historians (Ingham, 1986; Feis, 1931). Feis, for example, showed how Britain was peculiar among the great powers of the nineteenth century in that the government did not habitually make use of the financial institutions as a tool of foreign policy. The coincidence that partly explained British exceptionalism was that Britain, as active trader and first-comer in industrialisation was wealthy. Its protestant culture favoured saving over ostentatious spending. The capital accumulated was there to lend. The political interest in both the formal empire and the economic interest in the United States and other countries like Argentina or Egypt coincided with the interests of the City as financier to both.

The stabilising hegemonic intervention of the United States after the Second World War was another accident that is also unlikely to be repeated. There was a rare coincidence in those postwar years of the political interests of the US government and the economic interests of US industry. Having just fought a war to stop Europe falling under German domination, the United States government was not likely to let it fall under the domination of the Soviet Union. At the same time, the memory of 13 million Americans out of work in 1940 was still fresh, and the risks to American business of a postwar recession were being openly discussed. Reviving and at the same time opening the European economy to American enterprise was the solution in the American economic interest, just as offering military guarantees against further Soviet expansion westwards was the solution to American geopolitical interests. A rare window of opportunity occurred in which the coincidence of national and systemic welfare could be translated into hegemonic intervention.

To hope for another such happy coincidence in the 1970s or the 1990s – or indeed at any other time in the foreseeable future – would be over-optimistic. The reversion of US policy to a more self-serving, unilateralist use of hegemonic structural power – what is euphemistically now referred to as 'strategic trade policy' is, in the longer perspective of international financial history, only to be expected.

That is why the second Mexican debt crises of 1994/5 is so significant.

It suggests that the IMF cannot easily be built up as a substitute for a world central bank and lender of last resort. In the first Mexican debt crisis which broke in 1982, the creditors were foreign banks, European as well as American. The US government offered a rescue package but also used it to coerce the banks to join with it in giving Mexico new credit and extended time to reschedule its debts. In the second Mexican debt crisis in 1995, the creditors were bondholders and firms, mostly US firms. The US government, having recently concluded the NAFTA with Mexico, had a particular interest in the second rescue but this time needed support not from imperilled banks but from other governments.

Yet it was only with some difficulty that the US persuaded the IMF to help finance it. While the threat the first time had been to the whole international banking system, the threat the second time was much more to US interests. And just as the United States had been visibly indifferent to the plight of German banks that had lent to Poland in 1982, so the German government in 1995 openly expressed its reluctance in going along with a second Mexican rescue involving the IMF.

What this story suggests is that, while the secretariat of the IMF may have been happy to expand its role as a nascent world central bank, the IMF's executive directors who are appointed by national governments, were unlikely to agree to this even though they might cooperate in *ad hoc* fashion in a crisis. Meanwhile, the ability of the United States to act as leader, and international lender of last resort, is already less than it was in 1982. More than a decade of promises to correct the US budget deficit has gone by without any sign of the promises being kept. The protests voiced by foreign statesmen at Group of Seven meetings have been less effective than the decisions of the foreign exchange markets, devaluing the dollar. For the dollar to recover all its lost ground, the markets will need more than promises from the US government.

The increased power of the markets, which has been a consistent theme of this book, is important mainly because it is apparent in the international financial system, and some reasonable stability in the financial system is essential for the viability of the whole world market economy. If the power of financial markets is not balanced by any countervailing power such as used to be exercised by national central banks, this change in the mix of authority really is – or could be – a serious matter. The other consequences in the area of security or of economic adjustment are – in systemic terms – painful for some but tolerable for the system.

The only other important consequences of the retreat of the state and the diffusion of state authority sketched in earlier chapters relates to legitimacy and democracy. These matters have been much discussed by political scientists in the last few years. The tone of most of these discussions has been optimistic to the point of complacence. The Cold War over, democracy replaces one-party police states, conferring new legitimacy on the governments of ex-socialist countries. In South Africa and in Latin America, too, political liberalism has gone hand in hand with economic liberalisation.

But the stories told here suggest that the complacence may easily be overdone. The end of history, in Fukuyama's sense, may not be yet. The net result of the diffusion of authority upwards and sideways from the state to other states and to non-state authorities adds up to a democratic deficit much wider than that talked about in the European Union. The concentration of power in what Perry Anderson called the absolutist state was the means by which a politically controlled framework of rules was put round the emerging capitalist or market economy. But these absolutist states were soon seen – as in the English Civil war, the French revolution and the subsequent liberal revolutions in other European countries – to lack legitimacy. The framework for the market economy could only be legitimised by making it accountable to national demo-cratic institutions of government. These institutions insisted on a standard of public service and a measure of redistribution income within the state.

But if those institutions are now suffering the kind of diffusion of authority I have described, not much remains of the accountability of market forces to political constraints. If the asymmetry of state authority means that the voters in most countries are denied the option of Keynesian counter-cyclical demand management to create jobs for example, and if they sense that any government they elect is at the mercy either of decisions taken by the United States (or in Europe, the Federal Republic of Germany) then the casting of a vote from time to time becomes a merely symbolic act. Democracy is as apt to decline as a result of boredom and frustration as of the violent overthrow of constitutional government.

Moreover, none of the non-state authorities to whom authority has shifted, is democratically governed. Firms – the new players in transna-tional economic diplomacy – are hierarchies, not democracies. The multiple accountability of CEOs to shareholders, banks, employees, suppliers and distributors, not to mention strategic allies, means that like renaissance Princes, they can usually divide and rule. No single elected institution holds them accountable. The cartels and oligopolists that practise private protectionism and manage markets for their own comfort and convenience are even less accountable. Neither are the insurance businesses or the big-time accountancy partnerships. And the mafias least of all.

What is lacking in the system of global governance – if it can be called a system at all – and which in the past was the means of making the liberal state democratically accountable, is an opposition. To make authority acceptable, effective and respected, there has to be some combination of forces to check the arbitrary or self-serving use of power and to see that it is used at least in part for the common good. It may not necessarily be – as in parliamentary systems like the British or the German – a 'loyal opposition' whose wish to displace the government of the day makes it sensitive to public opinion and dissent. The checks may also be built in constitutionally as in the United States, where the power of the executive is balanced by those of the legislature and the judiciary. This is what Daniel Deudney has called 'negarchy' – the power to negate, limit or constrain arbitrary authority (Deudney, 1995).

This is a useful concept and perhaps at least as relevant to the present predicament of world economy and society as that of a loyal opposition. For without world elections, there can be no set of alternative authorities ready to take over the direction of the system in the way an opposition takes over from a government. Negarchy, on the other hand, is only another word for a balance of power. If that old concept so familiar to students of international relations were to be adapted to the diffusion of authority described in this book, it might generate some new ideas about world order.

A second question for research and debate therefore would seem to be concerned with the potential sources of negarchic power. Some have seen some embryonic signs in the transnational movements supporting non-governmental organisations like Amnesty International or Friends of the Earth. I myself have suggested that when it comes to the unilateralist use of American power, especially in matters of trade, a coalition of European and Japanese governments might be effective – although at the time of writing there does not seem much sign of this materialising (Strange, 1995).

And the last issue to emerge from this analysis of the dispersion of authority in world economy and society is one for each of us as individuals. I once called it Pinocchio's problem. The strings that held each of us to the nation-state seemed to me rather like the strings that were attached to Pinocchio, making him the puppet of forces he could neither control nor influence. His problem, at the end of the story, was no longer that when he told lies his nose grew longer. He had already learnt that lies were wrong. His problem when he finally turned, magically, from a wooden puppet into a real boy was that he had no strings to guide him. He had to make up his own mind what to do and whose authority to respect and whose to challenge and resist.

If indeed we have now, not a system of global governance by any stretch of the imagination, but rather a ramshackle assembly of conflicting sources of authority, we too have Pinocchio's problem. Where do allegiance, loyalty, identity lie? Not always, obviously in the same direction. Sometimes with the government of a state. But other times, with a firm, or with a social movement operating across territorial frontiers. Sometimes with a family or a generation; sometimes with fellow-members of an occupation or a profession. With the end of the Cold War, and with the triumph of the market economy, there is a new absence of absolutes. In a world of multiple, diffused authority, each of us shares Pinocchio's problem; our individual consciences are our only guide.

References

Albert, Michael and Hahnel, Robin 1991, *The Political Economy of Participatory Economics*. Princeton: Princeton University Press.

Albert, Michel 1993, *Capitalism against Capitalism*. London: Whurr.

Almquist, P. and Bacon, E. 1992, 'Arms Export in a Post-Soviet Market', Arms Control Today, July.

Anders, George 1992, *Merchants of Debt: KKR and the Mortgaging of American Business*. London: Cape.

Arendt, Hannah 1985, *The Human Condition*. Chicago: Chicago University Press.

Ariff, Mohamed and Hill, Hal 1995, *Export-Oriented Industrialisation: the ASEAN Experience*. Sydney: Allen and Unwin.

Arlacchi, P. 1992a, *Men of Dishonour: Inside the Sicilian Mafia*. Trans. New York: Morrow.

1992b, *Mafia Business: The Mafia Ethic and the Spirit of Capitalism*. Trans. London: Versa.

Arlacchi, P. and Paoli, L. 1995, 'Dall' eversione alla coesistenza, Rapporto sulle attuali strategis della grande criminalitá', *Micromega*, forthcoming.

Art, Robert and Waltz, Kenneth (eds.) 1971, *The Use of Force: International Politics and Foreign Policy*. Boston: Little, Brown & Co.

Assemblée Nationale, Commission d'enquête 1993, *Rapport . . . sur les moyens de lutter contre le tentative de pénétration de la mafia en France*. Paris, 23 January, 53.

Association Internationale pour l'Etude de l'Economie de l'Assurance. 1994, *The Geneva papers on risk and insurance: a quarterly journal on risk, uncertainty and insurance economics*. Vol. 13. No. 49. July, 1988. Geneva: Association Internationale pour l'Etude de l'Economie de l'Assurance.

Augelli, Enrico and Murphy, Craig 1988, *America's Quest for Supremacy and the Third World*. London: Pinter.

Baechler, J. 1975, *Revolutions*. Trans. Oxford: Blackwell.

Berle, Adolf and Means, Gardiner 1932, *The Modern Corporation and Private Property*. New York: Macmillan.

Braudel, Fernand 1974, *Capitalism and Material Life*. London: Fontana.

Bull, Hedley 1977, *The Anarchical Society: A Study of Order in World Politics*. London: Macmillan.

Bulmer, Simon and Scott, Andrew (eds.) 1994, *Economic and Political Integration in Europe: Internal Dynamics and Global Context*. Oxford: Blackwell.

Burnham, James 1942, *The Managerial Revolution*. London: Putnam.

Buzan, Barry, 1983, *People, States and Fear*. Brighton: Wheatsheaf.

Cain, P. J. and Hopkins, A. G. 1993, Vol. 1 *British Imperialism: Innovation and Expansion 1688–1914* and Vol. 2. *British Imperialism: Crisis and Deconstruction 1914–1990*. London, Longman.

Calleo, D. 1982, *The Imperious Economy*. Cambridge MA: Howard University Press.

Camilleri, Joseph and Falk, Jim (eds.) 1992, *The End of Sovereignty? The Politics of a Shrinking and Fragmenting World*. Brookfield VT: Elgar.

Caporaso, James 1989, *The Elusive State: International and Comparative Perspectives*. London: Sage Publications.

Carr, E. H. 1939, *The Twenty Years Crisis*. London: Macmillan.

Carr-Saunders, A. M. 1933, *The Professions*. Oxford: The Clarendon Press.

Carter, Robert and Dickinson, Gerard (eds.) 1991, *Obstacles to the Liberalisation of Trade in Insurance*. London: Harvester.

Cerny, Philip 1989, *The Changing Architecture of Politics: Structure, Agency, and the Future of the State*. London: Sage.

Chase-Dunn, Christopher, K. 1989, *Global Formation: Structures of the World Economy*. Oxford: Basil Blackwell.

Chesneaux, J. 1965, *Les sociétés secrètes en Chine, XIX–XX sièces*. Paris: Juillard.

Cline, William 1987, *Mobilizing Bank Lending to the Debtor Countries*. Washington, DC: Institute for International Economics.

Codding, G. 1952, *The International Telecommunications Union: An Experiment in International Cooperation*. Leyden, Kluwer.

Commissione Italian Parliament 1993, *Relazione sui rapporti tra mafia e politica*, 6 April, Rome.

Comor, E. A. (ed.) 1994, *The Global Political Economy of Communication: Hegemony, Telecommunications and the Information Economy* London: Macmillan.

Corbridge, Stuart, Martin Ron and Thrift, Nigel (eds.) 1994, *Money, Power and Space*. Oxford: Blackwell.

Cox, Robert 1987, *Production, Power and World Order*. New York: Columbia University Press.

Cox, Robert and Jacobson, Harold et al. 1974, *The Anatomy of Influence: Decision Making in International Organisations*. New Haven: Yale University Press.

Cressy, D. 1969, *Theft of the Nation*. New York: Harper and Row.

Cronin, Bruce and Lepgold, Joseph 1995, 'A New Mediaevalism? Conflicting International Authority and Competing Loyalties in the 21st Century', Paper for Harvard conference 'The Changing Nature of Sovereignty', Cambridge, Harvard.

Crouch, Colin and Streeck, Wolfgang (eds.) 1996), *Modern Capitalism vs. Modern Capitalisms: The Future of Capitalist Diversity*. Oxford: Oxford University

Press.

Curzon, Gerard and Curzon, Victoria 1976). 'The Management of Trade Relations in the GATT' in A. Shonfield (ed., *International Economic relations of the Western World, 1959–71*, Vol. 1, Oxford: Oxford University Press.

Dahl, Robert 1961, *Who Governs?: Democracy and Power in an American City*. New Haven, Conn: Yale University.

Dam, Kenneth 1970, *The GATT: Law and International Economic Organisation*. Chicago: University of Chicago Press.

De Jouvenal, Bertrand 1957, *Sovereignty: An Inquiry into the Political Good*. Chicago: University of Chicago Press.

Destler, I. M. 1986, *American Trade Politics: System Under Stress*. Washington DC: Institute for International Economics, New York: Twentieth Century Fund.

Dicken, Peter 1992, *Global Shift: The Internationalisation of Economic Activity*. London: Paul Chapman.

Diebold, William Jr. 1981, 'American Views and Choices', in Susan Strange and Roger Tooze (eds) *The International Politics of Supreme Capacity*. London: Allen and Unwin.

Dowd, Douglas 1993, *Of, By and For Which People? U.S. Capitalist Development since 1776*. New York: Sharpe.

Drucker, Peter 1989, *The New Realities: In Government and Politics, in Economy and Business, in Society and in World View*. New York: Harper Row.

Dunning, John 1988, *Explaining International Production*. London: Harper and Collins.

Dunning, J. H. 1993, *The Globalization of Business: The Challenge of the 1990s*. London: Routledge.

Duroselle, Jean-Baptiste and Renouvin, Pierre 1968, *Introduction to the History of International Relations*. London: Pall Mall Press.

Dyson Kenneth and Humphries, Peter (eds.) 1990, *The Political Economy of Communications – International and European Dimensions*. London: Routledge.

Easton, David 1953, *The Political System: An Inquiry into the State of Political Science*. New York: Alfred A. Knopf.

The Economist 1995, 'Too Close to the Managers', 17 October.

Encarnation, Dennis 1992, *Rivals Beyond Trade: America versus Japan in Global Competition*. Ithaca: Cornell University Press.

Evans, Peter, Jacobson, Harold and Putnam, Robert (eds.) 1993, *Double-Edged Diplomacy: International Bargaining and Domestic Politics*. Berkeley: University of California Press.

FATF, Financial Action Task Force Working Group 1990, *Report*. Paris, 7 Feb.

Feis, Herbert 1931, *Europe the World's Banker 1870–1914*. New Haven: Yale University Press.

Ferguson, M. (ed.) 1986, *New Communication Technologies and the Public Interest – Comparative Perspectives on Policy and Research*. London: Sage Publications.

Ferguson, Yale and Mansbach, Richard 1994, *Polities: Authority, Identities and Change*. Raleigh: University of South Carolina Press.

Financial Times 1993, 'Accounting Changes Obliterate Tiphook's Profits', 15 July.

Finlay, M. 1987, *Powermatics – A Discursive Critique of New Communications Technology*. London: Routledge.

Finlayson, Jock and Zacher, Mark 1988, *Managing International Markets: Developing Countries and the Commodity Regime*. New York: University of Columbia Press.

Frey, Bruno 1984, *International Political Economics*. Oxford: Blackwell.

Frieden, Jeffry 1987, *Banking on the World: The Politics of American International Finance*. New York: Harper & Row.

Funabashi, Y. 1989, *Managing the Dollar from the Plaza to the Louvre*. Washington DC: Institute for International Economics.

Galbraith, J. K. 1975, *Money: Whence it Came, Where it Went*. London: Deutsch.

Gaylord, M. 1990, 'The Chinese Laundry: International Drug Trafficking and Hong Kong's Banking Industry', *Contemporary Crises*, 14, 23–7.

Gill, Stephen and Law, David 1988, *The Global Political Economy: Perspectives, Problems, and Policies*. New York: Harvester.

Gilpin, Robert 1968, *France in the Age of the Scientific State*. Princeton NJ: Princeton University Press.

Gilpin, Robert 1975, *US Power and the Multinational Corporation: the Political Economy of Foreign Direct Investment*. New York: Basic Books.

Grieco, J. 1990, *Cooperation Among Nations: Europe, America and Non-Tariff Barriers to Trade*. Ithaca: Cornell University Press.

Grimwade, Nigel 1989, *International Trade: New Patterns of Trade, Production and Investment*. London: Routledge.

Gros, Daniel and Thygesen, Niels 1992, *European Monetary Integration: from the European Monetary System to Monetary Union*. Harlow: Longman.

Guzzini, S. 1995, '"The Long Night of the First Republic": Years of Clientilistic Explosion in Italy', *Review of International Political Economy*, vol. 2, Winter, 27–61.

Hall, John. (ed.) 1986, *States in History*. Oxford: Blackwell.

Hart, Jeffrey 1992, *Rival Capitalists: International Competitiveness in the United States, Japan, and Western Europe*. Ithaca: Cornell University Press.

Haufler, Virginia (forthcoming, *Dangerous Commerce: Risk, Protection and Regimes*.

Herbert, Stephen 1979, *The Multinational Company: A Radical Approach*. Cambridge: Cambridge University Press.

Hexner, Ervin and Walters, Adelaide 1946, *International Cartels*. London: Pitman.

Hills, J. 1994, 'Dependency Theory and its Relevance Today: International Institutions in Telecommunications and Structural Power', *Review of International Studies*, 20.

HMSO 1992, *Report on the Committee on Financial Aspects of Corporate Governance*.

Hoffmann, Stanley 1968, *Gulliver's Troubles, or the Setting of American Foreign Policy* New York: McGraw.

Holland, Max 1989, *When the Machine Stopped: A Cautionary Tale from the*

Industrial America. Boston: Harvard Business School Press.

Holsti, K. J. 1967, *International Politics: A Framework for Analysis*. Englewood Cliffs NJ: Prentice Hall International.

Horsman, Matthew and Marshall, Andrew 1994, *After the Nation-State: Citizens, Tribalism and the New World Disorder*. London: Harper Collins.

Hrbek, Rudolf and Weyand, Sabine 1994, *Betrifft: Europa der Regionen*. Berlin: C. H. Beck.

Hu, Yao-So. 1995, 'The Nationality of the Firm', unpublished paper, University of Warwick.

Ingham, Geoffrey 1984, *Capitalism Divided? The City and Industry in British Social Development*. Basingstoke: Macmillan.

International Telecommunications Union 1968, *1865–1965: A Hundred Years of International Cooperation*. Geneva.

International Telecommunications Union 1994, *Final Report – World Telecommunications Development Conference*. Geneva: International Telecommunications Union.

Jackson, John 1989, *The World Trading System: Law and Policy of International Economic Relations*. Cambridge MA: MIT Press.

Jacobson, H. 1993, 'ITU: A Pot-Pourri of Bureaucrats and Industrialists', in Cox and Jacobson (eds.), *The Anatomy of Influence: Decision-making in International Organisation*. Yale: Mansell.

Japanese Embassy in Rome 1993).

Jervis, Robert 1976, *Perception and Misperception in International Politics*. Princeton: Princeton University Press.

Johns, Richard Anthony 1983, *Tax Havens and Offshore Finance: A Study of Transnational Economic Development*. London: Frances Pinter.

Johnson, Terence 1972, *Professions and Power*. London: Macmillan.

Julius, DeAnne 1990, *Global Companies and Public Policy: the Growing Challenge of Foreign Direct Investment*. London: Pinter Publishers.

Julius, De Anne with Brown, Richard 1993, *Is Manufacturing still Special in the New World Order?* New York: Oxford University Press for American Express.

Keohane, Robert 1984, *After Hegemony: Cooperation and Discord in the World Political Economy*. Princeton NJ: Princeton University Press.

Keohane, Robert and Goldstein, Judith (eds.) 1993, *Ideas in Foreign Policy: Beliefs, Institutions and Political Change*. Ithaca Cornell University Press.

Keohane, Robert and Hoffman, Stanley 1991, *The New European Community: Decision Making and Institutional Change*. Boulder CO: Westview Press.

Kindleberger, Charles 1970, *Power and Money: The Economics of International Politics and the Politics of International Economics*. New York: Basic Books.

Kindleberger, Charles 1983, 'On the Rise and Decline of Nations', *International Studies Quarterly* 27: 5–10.

1984, *A Financial History of Western Europe*. London: Allen and Unwin.

Knight, Frank 1921, *Risk, Uncertainty and Profit*. Boston: Houghton Mifflin.

Knorr, Klaus 1973, *Power and Wealth – The Political Economy of International Power*.

London: Basic Books.

Kobrin, Stephen 1995, 'Beyond Symmetry: State Sovereignty in a Networked Global Economy', unpublished paper, Wharton School, Philadelphia.

Krasner, Stephen 1994, 'Abiding Discord in International Political Economy', *Review of International Political Economy*, 1/1.

Krueger, Anne (ed.) 1988, *Development with Trade: LDCs and the International Economy*. San Francisco: International Center for Economic Growth.

Lasswell, Harold and Leites, Nathan et al 1949, *Language of Politics: Studies in Quantitative Semantics*. New York: G. W. Stewart.

Lau Fong, Mak 1981, *The Sociology of Secret Societies: A Study of Chinese Secret Societies in Singapore and Peninsular Malaysia*. Oxford: Oxford University Press.

Lawton, T. 1995, 'Technology and the New Diplomacy: The Creation and Control of EC Industrial Policy with Special Reference to Semiconductors' PhD thesis, European University Institute.

Leontief, Wassily, Carter, Ann and Perti, Peter 1977, *The Future of the World Economy: A United States Study*. New York: Oxford University Press.

Lernoux, P. 1984, *In Banks We Trust*. Garden City NY: Arrow.

Lipsey, Richard 1963, *An Introduction to Positive Economics*. London: Weidenfeld & Nicolson.

Lipton, Merle 1985, *Capital and Apartheid*. London, Gower.

Lloyd's Register of Shipping 1994, *Annual Report*. London: Lloyd's Register of Shipping.

Lukes, Steven (ed.) 1986, *Power*. New York: New York University Press.

Lyall, D. and Perks, R. 1976, 'Create a State Auditing Board?' *Accountancy*, June.

Mann, Michael 1986, *The Sources of Social Power Volume 1: A History of Power from the Beginning to A.D. 1760*. Cambridge: Cambridge University Press.

Mansell, R. 1994, *The New Telecommunications – A Political Economy of Network Evolution*. London: Sage Publications.

Marsh, David 1992, *The Bundesbank: The Bank That Rules Europe*. London: Heinemann.

Mason, Mark and Encarnation, Dennis (eds.) 1994, *Does ownership matter? Japanese Multinationals in Europe*. Oxford: The Clarendon Press.

Mikdashi, Zuhayr 1992, *Financial Strategies and Public Policies: Banking, Insurance and Industry*. London: Macmillan.

Mills, C. W. 1959, *The Sociological Imagination*. New York: Grove Press.

Milner, Helen 1988, *Resisting Protectionism: Global Industries and the Politics of International Trade*. Princeton: Princeton University Press.

Minc, Alain 1993, *Le Nouveau Moyen Age*. Paris: Gaillimard.

Ministero dell'Interno 1994, *Rapporto annuale sul fenomeno della criminalità organizzate per il 1993*. Rome: Camera dei Deputati, doc. XXXVIII–bis, no. 1, 17–19.

Mirow, Kurt and Maurer, Harry 1982, *Webs of Power: International Cartels and the World Economy*. Boston: Houghton Mifflin.

Moffitt, M. 1984, *The World's Money: International Banking from Bretton Woods to the Brink of Insolvency*. London: Joseph.

Morgenthau, Hans J. 1954, *Politics among Nations*. New York: Alfred A. Knopf.

Murphy, C. 1994, *International Organisation and Industrial Change: Global Governance since 1850*. Cambridge: Polity Press.

Murray, Robin 1975, *Multinational Companies and Nation States*. London: Spokesman.

Mytelka, Lynn Kieger (ed.) 1990, *Strategic Partnerships and the World Economy: States, Firms, and International Competition*. London: Pinter.

Natalicchi, G. 1995, 'Telecommunications Policy of the European Community', unpublished PhD thesis, City University, New York.

National Police Agency 1989.

Nye, Joseph 1990, *Bound to Lead: The Changing Nature of American Power*. New York: Basic Books.

Office of Technology Assessment, US Congress 1993, *Multinationals and the National Interest*. Washington DC: US Government Printing Office.

Olson, Mancur 1982, *Rise and Decline of Nations*. London: Yale University Press.

Oman, Charles, Chesnais, François, Pelzman, Joseph and Rama, Ruth 1989, *New Forms of Investment in Developing Country Industries: Mining, Petrochemicals, Automobiles, Textiles, Food*. Paris: Organisation for Economic Co-operation and Development.

Organisation for Economic Co-operation and Development 1977, *Restrictive Business Practices of Multinational Enterprises*. Paris: OECD.

Paoli, L. 1993, 'Criminalita organizzata e finanza internazionale', *Rassegna Italiana di Sociologia*, 34, no. 3, 391–423.

Perks, R. W. 1993, *Accounting and Society*. London: Chapman and Hall.

Picciotto, Sol 1992, *International Business Taxation: A Study in the Internationalisation of Business Regulation*. London: Weidenfeld and Nicolson.

Pinder, John 1991, *European Community: The Building of a Union*. Oxford: Oxford University Press.

Polanyi, Karl 1944, *The Great Transformation*. New York: Octagon Books.

Porter, Michael 1990, *The Competitive Advantage of Nations*. New York: Free Press.

Prebisch, Raul 1950, *The Economic Development of Latin America and its Principal Problems*. New York: United Nations.

Prestowitz, Clyde 1988, *Trading Places: How We Allowed Japan to take the Lead*. New York: Basic Books.

Putnam, Robert, 1988, 'Diplomacy and Domestic Politics: The Logic of 2-Level Games', *International Organization* 42: 427–60.

Reich, Robert 1983, 'Beyond free trade', *Foreign Affairs*, 16: 773–804.

Rizopoulus, N. 1990, *Sea-Changes: American Foreign Policy in a World Transformed*. New York: Council on Foreign Relations.

Robock, Stefan, H. and Simmons, Kenneth (eds.) 1989, *International Business and Multinational Enterprises*. Homewood I: R. D. Irwin.

Rothschild, Emma 1995, 'What is Security?', *The Quest for World Order*, special issue of *Daedalus*, Summer 1995. Boston, American Academy of Arts and Sciences.

Rosecrance, R. 1985, *Rise of Trading State: Commerce and Conquest in the Modern World*. New York: Basic Books.

Rosenau, James 1990, *Turbulence in World Politics*. Princeton: Princeton University Press.

Rittberger, Volcker (ed.) 1994, *International Regimes*. Oxford, Oxford University Press.

Ruggie, John Gerald (ed.) 1993, *Multilateralism Matters: The Theory and Praxis of an Institutional Form*. New York: Columbia University Press.

Ruggiew, V. and South, N. 1995, *Euro-Drugs: Use, Markets and Trafficking in Europe*. London: UCL Press.

Sakamoto, Yoshikazu (ed.) 1994, *Global Transformation: Challenges to the State System*. Tokyo: United Nations University.

Sally, Razeen 1992, 'Multinational Enterprises, Political Economy and Institutional Theory: Domestic Embeddedness in the Context of Internationalisation? PhD thesis, University of London.

Sampson, Anthony 1987, *Black and Gold: Tycoons, Revolutionaries and Apartheid*. London: Hodder and Stoughton.

Sampson, Anthony 1995, *Company Man*. London: Hodder and Stoughton.

Samuelson, Paul 1961, *Economics: An Introductory Analysis*. New York: McGraw-Hill.

Savary, Julien 1984, *The French Multinationals*. London: Pinter.

Schmidt, Vivien 1995, 'The New World Order Incorporated: The Rise of Business and the Decline of the Nation-State' in *What future for the State?* special issue of *Daedalus*, Spring, 1995. Boston, American Academy of Arts and Sciences.

Schmitt, Hans 1972, 'The National Boundary in Politics and Economics', in R. Merritt (ed., *Communication in International Politics*. London: University of Illinois Press.

Sen, Amartya, 1982, *Choice, Welfare and Measurement*. Oxford, Blackwell.

Sen, Amartya 1984, *Resources, Value and Development*. Oxford: Blackwell.

Serio, J. 1992, 'Shunning Tradition: Ethnic Organised Crime in the Former Soviet Union', *Criminal Justice International*, Nov.–Dec.

Servan-Schrieber, Jean-Jacques 1967, *Le Defi Americain* (The American Challenge). Paris: Denoel.

Shonfield, Andrew 1969, *Modern Capitalism: The Changing Balance of Public and Private Power*. London: Oxford University Press.

Simon, Herbert 1982, *Models of Bounded Rationality*. Cambridge MA: MIT Press.

Sklair, Leslie 1991, *Sociology of the Global System*. New York: Harvester Wheatsheaf.

Smith, Adam 1776, republished 1976, *An Inquiry into Nature and Causes of the Wealth of Nations* London: Strahan and Cadell.

Smith, Terry 1992, *Accounting for Growth: Stripping the Camouflage from Company Accounts*. London: Century Business.

Soros, George 1987, *The Alchemy of Finance*. New York: Wiley.

Spar, Deborah 1994, *The Cooperative Edge: The Internal Politics of International*

Cartels. Ithaca: Cornell University Press.

Sterling, C. 1994, *Thieves' World: The Threat of the New Global Network of Organised Crime*. New York: Simon and Schuster.

Stocking, George and Watkins, Myron 1964, *Cartels in Action*.

Stopford, John and Strange, Susan 1991, *Rival States, Rival Firms Competition for World Market Shares*. Cambridge: Cambridge University Press.

Strange, Susan 1971, *Sterling and British Policy: A Political Study of an International Currency in Decline*. Oxford: Oxford University Press.

1986, *Casino Capitalism*. Oxford: Blackwell.

1988, *States and Markets* London: Pinter.

1994, 'Wake up, Krasner, the world *has* changed', *Review of International Political Economy*, 1/2.

1995, 'The Defective State', *Daedalus*, 124/2, Cambridge MA: American Academy of Arts and Sciences.

1995, 'European Business in Japan', *Journal of Common Market Studies*, 33/1.

Strange, Susan and Tooze, Roger 1981, *The International Politics of Surplus Capacity: Competition for Market Shares in the World Recession*. London: Allen & Unwin.

Teubner, Gunther 1993, *Law as an Autopoetic System*. Oxford: Blackwell.

Time 1993, 'Triads Go Global', 1 February, 39–47.

Time 1994, 'Formula for Terror', 24 August, 46–55.

Tyson, Laura D'Andrea 1992, *Who's Bashing Whom?: Trade Conflict in High-Technology Industries*. Washington, DC: Institute for International Economics.

Tsoukalis, Loukas 1993, *The New European Economy: The Politics and Economics of Integration*. Oxford: Oxford University Press.

United Nations 1978, *Transnational Corporations in World Development: A Reexamination*. New York: United Nations, Economic and Social Council.

United Nations 1988, *Transnational Corporations in World Development: Trends and Prospects*. New York: United Nations Centre on Transnational Corporations.

United Nations 1992, *World Investment Report: Transnational Corporations as Engines of Growth*. New York: United Nations. Centre on Transnational Corporations.

United Nations 1993, International Narcotics Control Board. *Report for 1992*. Vienna: UN Publications.

Van Walsum-Stachowicz, Judith Margaretha 1994, 'Corporate Diplomacy and European Community Information Technology Policies: The Influence of Multinationals and Interest Groups 1980–1993', thesis, LSE.

Vatter, H. 1985, *The U.S. Economy in World War Two*. New York: Columbia University Press.

Vernon, Raymond 1966, 'International Investment and International Trade in the Product Cycle', *Quarterly Journal of Economics*, 80: 190–207.

Veseth, Michael 1990, *Mountains of Debt – Crisis and Chane in Renessaince Florence, Victorian Britain and Post-war America*. Oxford: Oxford University Press.

Wachtel, Howard 1986, *The Money Mandarins: The Making of a New Supranational Economic Order*. New York: Pantheon Books.

Walter, I. 1989, *Secret Money: The Shadowy World of Tax Evasion, Capital Flight and Fraud*. Rev. edn. London: Unwin Hyman.

Waltz, Kenneth 1979, *Theory of International Politics* Reading MA: Addison-Wesley.

Watson, Adam 1992, *The Evolution of International Society*. London, Routledge.

Weber, Max 1978, *Economy and Society: An Outline of Interpretive Sociology*. Berkley: University of California.

Weiler, Joseph 1994, 'Journey to an Unknown Destination: A Retrospective and Prospective of the European Court of Justice in the Arena of Political Integration', in Bulmer, S. and Scott, A. (eds, *Economic and Political Integration in Europe: Internal Dynamics and Global Context*. Oxford: Blackwell.

Wight, Martin 1946, *Power Politics*. London: RIIA.

Winham, Gilbert 1986, *International Trade and the Tokyo Round Negotiation*. Princeton: Princeton University Press.

Ziegler, J. 1990, *La Suisse lave plus blanc*. Paris: Editions du Seuil.

Zysman, John and Laura Tyson 1983, *American Industry in International Competition: Government Policies and Corporate Strategies*. Ithaca: Cornell University Press.

United States Senate 1983, *Crime and Secrecy: The Use of Off-Shore Banks and Companies*. Hearings, 98th Congree, first session.

United States Senate 1992, *Current Trends in Money Laundering*, Hearings, 101st Congress, 2nd session.

Index

accountancy firms, 51, 93, 98, 99, 133
  Big Six, 135, 137, 138–40, 142, 143, 146
  and conflicts of interest, 139
  'creative accounting' by, 141
  and financial scandals, 137–8, 145
  history of, 135–6
  and the law, 140–1
  mergers of, 137
  reform of, 146
  role of, 136–7, 143–5
  self-regulation, 138–9
  services offered by, 135, 138
actors, 38–9, 68–70
Africa, 57, 71, 127–8, 168, 170
agriculture, 48–9, 156, 158, 188
aid *see* foreign aid
alcohol trade, 113, 114, 121
Amnesty International, 95
anti-trust rules, 155, 158–9
Arendt, H., 36
arms trade, 114, 118, 121
art market, 97
Asia, 51, 57, 58, 59, 95, 103,
  170, 190
  mafias and, 113
  state in, 6, 74
  and world markets, 6–7, 78
associations *see* institutions; international
  organisations; non-governmental
  organisations (NGOs)
athletics, 96
auditing, 135, 136, 140, 143, 146 *see also*
  accountancy firms
authority, 4, 12, 25, 37, 84, 86, 92, 99, 111,
  133–4, 184–5, 187
  absence of, 46
  diffusion of, 197, 199
  functions of, 42

  of international organisations, 161–2,
  164–71
  in international society, 13–14, 42,
  118–21
  loss of, 5, 189–90
  multiple, 38, 40
  political, 35, 38
  state and market, 44–5 *see also*
  non-state authority; states

Baechler, J., 111
Bank of Credit and Commerce
  International (BCCI), 118, 124, 137,
  146
banks, ix, x, 11, 12, 27, 28, 29, 51, 52, 53,
  64, 77, 99, 118, 119, 126, 130, 133,
  137, 138, 142, 157, 188, 194, 195, 196
bargains, 99, 152, 176
Barings bank, ix, 138
baseball, 96
Basle Union of Credit Insurers, 123
BAT (British American Tobacco), 48–9
Belgium, 169
Bertrand, M., 166–7
Bosnia, 27, 72
bounded rationality, 20–1
Brandt Reports, 58
Braudel, F., 45
Brazil, xiv, 55, 59, 78, 81, 130, 150–1, 157
Britain, 3, 21, 22, 23, 61, 62, 126, 136,
  137, 139–40, 146, 150, 169, 194–5
bureaucracies *see* international
  organisations

California, 63, 139
capabilities, 19, 22, 23, 25
Caparo Industries, 140, 143
capital, 9, 10, 47, 62

Horsman, M., 85–6, 186
Hymer, S. 11

IBM, xiii, 75, 159
immigrants, illegal, 114, 121
import-substitution, 74, 75
independence, political, 5–6
India, 22, 49, 51, 52, 55, 59, 75, 130
individuals, 4–5, 34, 35, 44, 70–2, 100
industrial relations *see* labour relations
industrialisation, 57–9, 193
inflation, 12, 61, 73–4, 76, 141, 190
information, ix, x, 51, 53, 102, 164–5
infrastructure, 79–80
institutions, 42, 91 *see also* international
    organisations
insurance business, xi, 51, 52, 93, 98, 140
    academic neglect of, 122–3
    authority in, 133–4
    commercial, 128–9, 131–4
    competition in, 129–30
    costs of, 131, 133, 134
    firms in, 131
    and the market economy, 124–8
    non-life, 130–1
    structural changes in, 131–3 *see also* life
        insurance; re-insurance
intellectual property rights, 97–8, 158
Intelsat, 107–8
'interdependence', xiii
inter-governmental organisations (IGOs)
    see international organisations
International Finance Corporation (IFC),
    169–70
international law, 45, 67, 118–21, 172–3
International Maritime Organisation, 168
International Monetary Fund (IMF), 74,
    93, 161, 164, 169, 170, 192, 194, 196
international organisations, xiii, xiv, 42,
    93–4, 161
    and accountancy, 145
    authority of, 161–2, 164–71
    and delegated powers, 168–71
    and developing countries, 167–8
    and foreign debt management, 192
    functions of, 164–6
    information role of, 164–5
    reform of, 183–4
    and telecommunications, 106–7 *see also*
        non-governmental organisations
        (NGOs)
international political economy, ix, x,
    18–19, 99
    authority in, 13–14, 91–2
    and 'bounded rationality', 20

change in, xii, xv, 11, 92
functions of authority in, 42–3
and insurance business, 122–3
mix of values in, 34–5
money and credit in, 10–11
multiple agendas of, 39–40
outcomes in, 27–30
political authority in, 37
and political science, 32
power in, 24–5
and sectoral study of markets, 41–2
states and markets in, 34, 37
theories of, 4 *see also* politics; world
    economy
international relations, 12, 31, 37
failures of, xv–xvi, 4, 10, 32
and legal basis of states, 118–21
and power, 19, 24–5
and private protectionism, 148, 149,
    150
state-centrism of, x, 32, 39, 84, 121, 149,
    184, 185
state theories in, 66–73 *see also*
    international political economy
International Telecommunications Union
    (ITU), 107 investment, 7, 9, 43, 47,
    129
    institutional, 137
Italy, 3, 92, 93, 111, 112, 114, 115–16,
    119,120, 121, 169

Jackson, J., 152
Japan, xv, 6, 8, 9, 22, 23, 24, 25, 33, 52,
    55, 59, 83, 105, 158, 168, 169, 193
    companies in, 136, 144
    mafias in, 112
    national identity in, 70–1, 72
    offshore trading companies, 48
    and outcomes, 28, 29
    protectionism in, 81
    state in, 74, 75
    TNCs in, 50–1, 57
    trade with U.S., 78
JESSI, 56, 81
Johnson, T., 143
joint ventures, 47, 59
Jouvenel, B. de, 35–6
justice, 34, 38

Keohane, R., 20, 22, 23, 24, 69, 163, 171,
    174
Keynes, J. M., 30, 76
Kindleberger, C., 21, 22, 46, 194
Knight, F., 128–9
Knorr, K., 18

CAMBRIDGE STUDIES IN INTERNATIONAL RELATIONS